MW00603598

Habits
of a
Peace
Maker

OTHER BOOKS BY STEVEN T. COLLIS

NONFICTION

*Deep Conviction: True Stories of Ordinary Americans
Fighting for the Freedom to Live Their Beliefs*

*The Immortals: The World War II Story of Five Fearless Heroes,
the Sinking of the Dorchester, and an Awe-Inspiring Rescue*

HISTORICAL FICTION

Praying with the Enemy

10

Habits to Change Our Potentially Toxic
Conversations into Healthy Dialogues

Habits
of a
Peace
Maker

STEVEN T. COLLIS

SHADOW
MOUNTAIN
PUBLISHING

Image credit: page 65, AllSides Media Bias Chart™ is © 2023 by AllSides.com. Used with permission.

© 2024 Steven T. Collis

All rights reserved. No part of this book may be reproduced in any form or by any means without permission in writing from the publisher, Shadow Mountain Publishing®, at permissions@shadowmountain.com. The views expressed herein are the responsibility of the author and do not necessarily represent the position of Shadow Mountain Publishing.

Visit us at shadowmountain.com

Library of Congress Cataloging-in-Publication Data

Names: Collis, Steven T., 1978– author.
Title: Habits of a peacemaker : 10 habits to change our potentially toxic conversations into healthy dialogues / Steven T. Collis.
Description: [Salt Lake City] : Shadow Mountain Publishing, [2024] | Includes bibliographical references and index. | Summary: "Steven T. Collis, one of the world's leading experts on civil discourse, reveals ten practical habits that can help you navigate the potential minefields of hard topics and leave you and those you converse with feeling thoughtful and productive"—Provided by publisher.
Identifiers: LCCN 2024009978 (print) | LCCN 2024009979 (ebook) | ISBN 9781639932979 (hardback) | ISBN 9781649332974 (ebook)
Subjects: LCSH: Interpersonal communication. | Conflict management. | BISAC: SELF-HELP / Communication & Social Skills | BUSINESS & ECONOMICS / Leadership | LCGFT: Self-help publications.
Classification: LCC BF637.C45 C6354 2024 (print) | LCC BF637.C45 (ebook) | DDC 303.6/9—dc23/eng/20240318
LC record available at https://lccn.loc.gov/2024009978
LC ebook record available at https://lccn.loc.gov/2024009979

Printed in the United States of America
Lake Book Manufacturing, LLC, Melrose Park, IL

10 9 8 7 6 5 4 3 2 1

For Jon. See you on the other side.

CONTENTS

INTRODUCTION

When most people hear what I do for a living, they think I'm insane. As a law professor at a leading law school who specializes in the First Amendment, I get paid to discuss, full-time, the most pressing and divisive issues in our society: abortion, LGBTQ+ rights, racism, religious liberty, freedom of speech, academic freedom, the role of the media in our society, and constitutional law. I travel all over discussing those matters, from Rome, to London, to Canada, to Eastern Europe and South America, to every corner of the United States. I speak with media, academics, diplomats from around the world, foreign and domestic judges, high schoolers, religious leaders, college and graduate students, devout churchgoers, devoted atheists and agnostics, members of the LGBTQ+ community, those who believe in traditional notions of sexuality, and people across the ideological spectrum. But here's what will surprise most readers: as of yet, neither I nor the people I speak with have experienced a negative outcome in our conversations. We have not been shouted down or cancelled. No one has pivoted on anyone in a rage. Our conversations have not devolved into shouting matches or accusations. In truth, they have always been productive. I often come away with a sense of mutual respect, having learned something new; and, hopefully, my interlocutors have felt the same. Together, almost always, we have inched a bit closer to finding solutions to some of society's most pressing problems.

This book is born of those experiences—moments when people who are so very different from one another find a way to reach across the chasm and enjoy a time of productive peace in each other's presence. I want others to have those moments, and to have them often. Among us are those who have learned the practical skills to do this. Peacemakers. This book aims to pass their habits on to you.

At the outset, I want to be clear: I do not purport to offer solutions to the world's complex problems. I don't have all the answers. I hope you will come to see that you don't either. The issues humanity faces are complicated. They require multiple minds working together to discover and craft sophisticated solutions. That is why we need each other. We need to talk to one another in conversations that allow the free flow of ideas and the building of steps to a new and brighter world. As Judge Learned Hand once said in a judicial opinion, our system "presupposes that right conclusions are more likely to be gathered out of a multitude of tongues, than through any kind of authoritative selection. To many this is, and always will be, folly; but we have staked upon it our all."*

Most of us realize that the core of the world's political discourse is rotting. We all see the sickness. We would also like to be part of the solution, not just in society, but in our homes and with our acquaintances. Our problem is that we don't know what to do. Hopefully, understanding and implementing these habits will help.

In many respects, the entire system in the peaceful countries of the world is dependent on the belief that we can do what I am discussing here. In the United States, eighty years ago, the Supreme Court captured why. It did something quite remarkable. Some people today won't believe the story. In a series of cases in the early 1940s, during World War II, groups of Jehovah's Witnesses challenged whether public schools could force their children to pledge allegiance to the flag of the United States. According to their religious beliefs, they could pledge allegiance only to God, not to anything or anyone else. They asked the Supreme Court of the United States to rule that, under the Free Speech Clause

---

* Yes, that was his real name. Actually, his full name was Billings Learned Hand. His cousin was named August Noble Hand. Draw your own conclusions.

of the Constitution, they were free to choose not to say the Pledge of Allegiance.**

They lost every case.

Then, between 1942 and 1943, three justices on the court retired. The president appointed their replacements, and the Senate confirmed them. Some of the remaining justices changed their minds. With those changes, the court recalled each of the Jehovah's Witness Pledge cases and reversed them all. Think about that. Were this to happen today, it's not hard to imagine the media circus that would follow, with any number of pundits and X junkies sounding off on the justices and the legitimacy of their decisions. Instead, it all happened relatively quietly, with a few newspapers commenting on it and little fanfare.

After that remarkable reversal, the court issued what is perhaps the most seismic decision it has ever written. The opinion is important for many reasons, but two aspects of it relate to the point of this book and the project of peacemaking overall. First, two of the justices changed their minds. That will be important later in the book. Second, Justice Robert H. Jackson's reasoning represented an important shift in our thinking about living alongside and talking with people who think very differently from us. After detailing humanity's long history of trying to stifle differences of opinion and force unity of thought on all people, Justice Jackson declared:

> Ultimate futility of such attempts . . . is the lesson
> of every such effort from the Roman drive to stamp
> out Christianity as a disturber of its pagan unity, the
> Inquisition, as a means to religious and dynastic unity,
> the Siberian exiles as a means to Russian unity, down
> to the fast failing efforts of our present totalitarian
> enemies.*** Those who begin coercive elimination of

** Notably, the Pledge of Allegiance did not include the words "under God" at the time. The phrase was not added until 1954.

*** He was referring to the Nazis, then-imperial Japan, and then-fascist Italy.

dissent soon find themselves exterminating dissenters. Compulsory unification of opinion achieves only the unanimity of the graveyard.

It seems trite but necessary to say that the First Amendment to our Constitution was designed to avoid these ends by avoiding these beginnings. . . .

. . . We apply the limitations of the Constitution with no fear that freedom to be intellectually and spiritually diverse or even contrary will disintegrate the social organization. . . . But freedom to differ is not limited to things that do not matter much. That would be a mere shadow of freedom. The test of its substance is the right to differ as to things that touch the heart of the existing order.[1]

Looking at our society today, with so much of our dialogue descending into polarized arguments, we may be tempted to think the Supreme Court was wrong. Perhaps we cannot have intellectual and spiritual diversity without the social order disintegrating. Maybe the internet and all its half-truths and echo chambers and distorting algorithms have proven the Supreme Court naive.

I don't believe that. I think the Supreme Court's reasoning in that case was correct then and remains so today. We can have dialogue over difficult issues. We can discuss hard topics. We can find powerful solutions to the seemingly insolvable problems that persist in our society. We can turn our conversations with our family members from fights to fruitful exchanges that enlighten our minds and inch toward answers to hard problems. I hope this book can play a part in helping you reach that goal.

A few important notes before we begin. In contrast to the writing I do for academics, I do not mean for this to be a scholarly treatise on the First Amendment, Socratic dialogue, the nature of human thought, the Enlightenment and its positives and shortcomings, the many ways human beings develop knowledge, moral psychology, the philosophy of law, or any number of other esoteric academic subjects. We will touch on those topics, like a stone skipping across water, but do not fear that we will sink into them. I mean this book to be a practical guide, one that will help you talk about the hardest of subjects in a way that will leave you and those you converse with feeling thoughtful and productive, not combative and angry. For sure, we will explore some of the latest academic theories, as well as those which have stood the test of time. We will sightsee together the thinking of those few academics and their acolytes who refuse to engage in peacemaking. You will come to understand why they think the way they do and when to realize you are dealing with someone with whom civil discourse is impossible, at least with certain topics.

But my more important hope is that you will walk away with practical skills. By and large, the subjects that "touch the heart of the existing order" are the ones we talk about the least, or the least productively. We yell at one another. We gaslight. We twist one another's words and meanings. We embrace facts that support our conclusions and ignore those that don't. We accuse one another of being fascists or communists or racists or bigots or fools or ignorant or lazy or selfish or shortsighted. Or we sit in silence, afraid to discuss anything of substance.

At some point or another, we will all recognize that those methods of discourse may be great at generating dopamine for us and money for social media and cable television companies, but they are futile—futile in persuading others to believe as we do and in solving the world's very real problems. Once we recognize that pointlessness, hopefully well before we are too old to do anything about it, we will want to find a better way.

This book is not meant to be of service to only one group or only one part of the political spectrum. To put it another way, I don't care about your politics. Nor do I care about how you feel about any given issue in our society. The chapters that follow do not justify either the political right or the political left, and to the extent they condemn anyone, they condemn us all. They call out our basic shortcomings, no matter our political preferences, and provide tools to rise above them. I intend it for people of good faith everywhere who are tired of discord and would rather engage in productive discourse that can help provide effective solutions to real problems.

I also do not mean for this book to take away from the solid efforts of those who are working for structural changes to solve the problems in our discourses. The efforts of folks like Jonathan Haidt and Greg Lukianoff to push for limits on social media use and viewpoint diversity in our knowledge-making institutions are important. But too many of us have grown up in a world where we have forgotten, never learned, or were not even exposed to the skills needed to talk about hard topics in a productive way. Many of us want to be able to do it. Some may be motivated by their religion and its teachings to be a peacemaker, some out of a desire for more fruitful discussions about politics, others for nothing more than a hope for peace in their homes. Whatever your motivations, for those yearning to learn how to do that, this book is for you.

Unsurprisingly, peacemakers employ many of the habits that make them effective long before they are in actual conversations. The habits lie as much in how they approach each day as in how they handle specific conversations. We will explore both, of course, but preparation for talking about hard topics is as important as the methods used in the exchanges.

So think of this book as about *becoming*. I hope this intrigues you in the name of making the world a better place, but even if it doesn't, selfish considerations may pique your interest. Research consistently shows that those who are peacemakers, who have mastered a certain level of what researchers call "agreeableness," consistently see better outcomes in nearly every area of life: career, family, friends, and performance in every organizational setting.[2] In short, if you don't want to learn these lessons to keep democracy afloat or to better yourself, you could do it just to thrive in your life. Either way, we all benefit.

I have organized the book in a way that makes sense to me, but you should not feel the need to read it strictly from front to back. Each chapter provides useful guidance on how to achieve moments of peaceful, productive dialogue with the people in your life. While later chapters will refer to previous ones, that should not stop you from jumping ahead if a particular topic catches your interest. The cost to you from reading out of order will be minimal.

For some of the principles in this book, vast bodies of literature and scholarship already exist. For those interested in digging deeper, I have included endnotes to the sources. My hope is that if you find a particular practical tip useful, you will feel inclined to dive deeper into the literature exploring it.

Throughout the book, I share thoughts and anecdotes from a variety of folks. They are peacemakers in their own ways and provided me with invaluable insights into their habits and ways of thinking. You should not assume that because I have included someone in this book, I agree with them on every issue. In fact, the opposite is true. A number of the people I mention or highlight I have profound disagreements with on issues that strike at the heart of what it means to be human: morality, politics, religion, even the nature of reality itself. Regardless of how they feel about any of those topics, if they are peacemakers, we can learn from them. We must.

I encourage you to add your own methods for becoming a peacemaker to the list of habits you can adopt. For example, readers will come from a variety of religious traditions that provide additional wisdom and insight. I cannot realistically cover the teachings of every faith tradition on earth. I have identified common tools peacemakers across faith traditions (including atheists and agnostics) employ to engage in constructive dialogue. Add to them the teachings of your own tradition, and you will be that much more enriched.

In sum, this book does not claim to offer answers to society's great questions; it tries instead to pass on some of the greatest gifts I have ever received: the tools to find those answers ourselves, in delightful dialogue with the people in our lives.

HABIT ONE
INTELLECTUAL HUMILITY
AND REFRAMING

Most of us need to recognize that, most of the time, we don't know what we're talking about. That may seem offensive, but the sooner we recognize it, the sooner we can open our minds to peacemaking and close the door on the kind of contentious behavior that damages relationships. We can also save ourselves—and society—a lot of pain, because dealing with something we think we understand but really don't often makes the situation worse than it was at the outset.

Consider this example from my personal life. When I was nine years old, I lived in a small home in New Mexico. Most of the family shared just one bathroom. At the time, small boys like me in that town thought it was cool to spike up our hair. I went into the bathroom one morning, spewed a generous portion of mousse into my hand, and massaged it all into my hair. A few minutes later, my look was spiked, and I was feeling good. When I walked out of the bathroom, I bumped into my mom in the hallway.

"What's that smell?" she said, sniffing the air.

I proudly pointed to my head and said, "It's the mousse."

Her eyes widened. She gasped. She spun me around and pushed me back into the bathroom. Before I could even process what was happening, she thrust my head into the sink and started washing my hair out.

"What!?!" I yelled through the gurgling water.

It turns out that what I thought was mousse was actually Nair—my mom's hair-removal product.

Within days, large patches of my hair had fallen out. For the rest of the summer, anyone who saw me thought I had some horrible illness.

We get in trouble in life when we're dealing with something we think we understand but don't. That's true for young boys who confuse Nair for styling mousse, it's true for policymakers trying to create laws or make big decisions, and it's true for each of us in our personal discourse. If we want to engage in productive, healthy conversations with those close to us, the first step is for everyone involved to recognize how little they often know about many topics. From that starting point, we can all approach our interactions with others with a better perspective.

Conversations are more likely to deteriorate when participants are acting with too little information. If you want to guarantee a fight between two people, throw out a controversial subject about which neither of them knows much, then stand back and watch them take positions and try to justify those positions. The goal of this chapter is two-fold: (1) to help you recognize the lack of knowledge in yourself and others (but mostly yourself); and (2) to provide you with a method for turning that recognition into a tool for constructive conversation.

"A LITTLE LEARNING IS A DANG'ROUS THING; DRINK DEEP OR TASTE NOT"

During law school, I often studied until the evening, when I would break and head home for dinner with my wife and two little boys. Each night, as I left the law school, I walked through a large wooden door. Etched in stone in the frieze above it were these words from the eighteenth-century English author Alexander Pope: "A little learning is a dang'rous thing; drink deep or taste not."[1] Day after day, week after week, month after month, I walked under those words. I have never forgotten them.

The older I get, the more I appreciate the wisdom the words reflect. Too often, we act with very little information, sometimes to devastating results. For example, during the 1300s, when the Black Death was ravaging much of Europe, on its way to killing nearly twenty-five million people, scholars tried to identify the source of the illness. If they could identify the cause, they could find a cure. A group of academics at the University of Paris in 1348 noticed three recent phenomena: Saturn, Jupiter, and Mars had all lined up under the sign of Aquarius; the air at times seemed polluted; and there had been earthquakes. These scholars had identified three factual events and then declared that each of them must have been part of the cause for the plague. Obviously, they were wrong.[2] The real cause was a mutated form of *yersinia pestis* bacterium. The scholars had acquired a little learning and stopped searching for answers. They declared the causes, and people acted accordingly. The result was mass graves for half the population of Europe. Only later, when others kept searching for answers, did they realize that quarantining infected people and improving sanitation and personal hygiene would stop the disease's spread.[3] That is but one example; the annals of history are filled with similar devastating tales of what happens when humanity acts without enough information.

But policymaking is not the only realm where too little information can be devastating. It affects our personal lives as well. We have all been there:

During a family visit, Uncle James walks into the room. His niece, Gabby, is working on a school project related to discrepancies in pay between men and women.

"What are you working on?" James says.

"The gender pay gap," Gabby says. "Women need to be treated equally in the workplace."

"There is no gender pay gap," James says. "That's just fake news. I've been working at my job for ten years, and the women make just as much as I do."

"Just because it's not happening at your job doesn't mean it's not happening other places," Gabby says. "Employers don't value women as much as they do men."

"That's nonsense," James says. "People get paid based on their value, so if women are getting paid less, then they aren't as valuable."

You can take it from there.

Neither Gabby nor James are experts on employee pay, employer-employee relations, labor negotiations and collective bargaining agreements, statistics, data collection, specific employer practices, the causes of wage decisions at a particular employer, bias for or against people based on sex, or any number of other points of information they might need to solve this specific problem they are discussing.

Put yourself in one of their shoes, or pretend you are sitting on the couch next to Gabby, and she and James turn to you for your opinion. How could you help turn this situation into one that doesn't ruin the entire family visit? The initial answer begins with you.

It doesn't matter what your relationship is to James and Gabby, and, in fact, in some instances, thinking that your position in the family has bearing on what you should do could actually be a negative, something we'll discuss a bit later when we explore avoiding arguing from a position of authority.

RECOGNIZE HOW MUCH THERE IS TO KNOW

Any time a controversial subject lands in front of us, we face the temptation to want to launch immediately into our opinions about it. To combat that lure, the first thing we should do is recognize how little we know. In the back of our minds, Alexander Pope should be whispering, *"A little learning is a dang'rous thing."*

We should also take confidence that modern research has proven Alexander Pope correct. In their article "Overconfidence among Beginners: Is a Little Learning a Dangerous Thing?" social psychologists Carmen Sanchez and David Dunning confirmed that once people learn a small amount about a subject, they surge to a "'beginner's bubble' of overconfidence."[4] What is interesting about Sanchez's and Dunning's research is that they showed that many people start out with a level of humility and caution. But then, quickly after they learn a small amount about a subject, they begin to feel they are experts.

The antidote to feeling you know so much that you can confidently argue for hours about it is to recognize *how much more* you can learn on any given topic. To put this in perspective, I will make a confession of sorts. I get paid full time to study, write, and teach about only one subject, the First Amendment of the United States Constitution. That amendment includes five (arguably six) clauses: the Free Exercise Clause, the Establishment Clause, the Speech Clause, the Press Clause, and the Assembly and Petition Clause. I'm a professor, so my job is to spend my days learning all that I can about those clauses and passing that knowledge on to my students and other academics. That goal consumes almost all my working hours. It is what I have been doing now for nearly a decade.

Despite all that, I would guess I know just a fraction of what I would like to know—what I could know—about the First Amendment. And that doesn't take into account what I'm not aware of. On the shelves in my office are literally hundreds of books on those clauses, more than I will ever have time to read. There are hundreds more I could order but have not. On top of that, in online databases, academic journals contain thousands of articles related to the First Amendment, from scholars all over the world in nearly every discipline out there: economics, health care, social media, artificial intelligence, constitutional interpretation, democracy, education, antidiscrimination laws, academic freedom, Indigenous peoples, colonialism, moral psychology, cognitive behavioral therapy, philosophies of law, how humanity constructs knowledge, and on and on. The empirical questions related to the clauses of the First Amendment are practically endless, as are the historical questions. The same is true for comparative legal analyses, where scholars look to see how other nations and cultures are protecting the same freedoms, to the extent they are at all.

I wish I could study all of it, take it all in. But even if my brain could hold all that information, I would never have the time to do it. As Chief Justice William Rehnquist reminded us, "For all of life's disparities in talent and wealth, each of us is given exactly the same amount of time in each hour, and in each day, and in each year. It is a limited amount, and it is impossible for anyone to be so rich in 'time' that he can enjoy every single one of the things which time may buy."[5] I simply do not have the time to consume all the knowledge I would like to about the First Amendment.

You may ask why I buy and keep so many books if I know I will never have time to read them all. Part of it, I will confess, is silly. I like books as decorations. And I like looking erudite for my students when they stroll into my office. It's a professor thing and reflects my own aesthetics and insecurities. Part of it is functional: I do order every book with the intent to read it; I also do peruse at least part of every book as part of my research, even if I don't have time to read every page.

But there is a far greater purpose behind it, one I stumbled into by accident. Keeping those books on my shelves reminds me of how little I know. I am forced to recognize that even in the one subject matter I am paid to study and explore full time, my brain contains only a sliver of what is out there. I don't consider this a negative. It has become a valuable asset to me. The statistician Nassim Nicholas Taleb calls all those unread books of mine an "antilibrary." The antilibrary, he argues, combats our natural human tendency to overestimate what we know.[6] My collection of unread books, combined with my awareness of the vast expanse of scholarly articles I will never have time to read, helps me combat something scholars refer to as the Dunning-Kruger Effect.

First discovered by social psychologists David Dunning and Justin Kruger, it is the tendency of people who have low ability or knowledge in a specific area to overestimate their ability or knowledge.[7] In the context of civil conversation, the Dunning-Kruger Effect plays a nasty role. For most of us, the intensity of our opinions corresponds with how little we know. In other words, when we know almost nothing about a subject, we tend to have strong opinions about it. Later, as we come to realize how ignorant we are, our opinions soften. Finally, only after we have achieved a high level of expertise will we allow our positions to become once again more forceful.[8] But by then, we will understand the subject well enough to discuss it productively. For subjects in which we will never become experts, it is a great achievement just to overcome the Dunning-Kruger Effect by reaching a point where our intellectual humility forces us to acknowledge that we don't have all the answers.

If I know that I understand only a fraction of what I would like to understand about the one topic I am paid to study full time, how much less, then, do I know about areas in which I am not a subject-matter expert? That list of topics is nearly endless: foreign policy, politics, economics, immigration policy, environmental science, health care, public schools, tax policy, and student debt, to name a few.

Each of us needs to recognize that we know almost nothing about any of these topics, even if we are an expert on one or two. Like a little boy playing with his mother's Nair, we like to think we know what we are dealing with, but in reality, we are only aware of just enough facts to let us fight with our friends, family, and bots on social media.

In their book *The Knowledge Illusion*, cognitive scientists Steven Sloman and Philip Fernbach provide important insights into just how little we individually know. Their primary point is that humanity as a collective has achieved a staggering amount of knowledge, in everything from artistry to quantum physics. Collectively, we are brilliant. As individuals, however, our knowledge is often miniscule and pathetic. Most of us, they write, don't even understand "simple everyday objects" like the hairpin, "the various materials it is made of, where each material comes from, how each material is used to manufacture hairpins, where hairpins are sold, and who buys them."[9]

None of us should find this insulting. It is simply reality. Look around you right now and consider the objects you see, including this book. How did they get made, specifically? What engineering was involved? What laws and regulations? Who invented them and how many iterations did it take to get the objects to where they are today? What machines? What computers and programming languages were involved? What chemistry? What elements from the periodic table were used, and where were they procured? How do the atoms and molecules in each of those elements affect how the objects were created? Does the atmospheric pressure around you affect any of the objects? I could go on forever. When we engage in this exercise, we come to realize that our own knowledge is so small as to be statistically close to zero percent of all the knowledge available. And that is just for where we are right now.

So let's face reality together: if the zombie apocalypse happens to-morrow and disrupts all of the world's supply chains and products we rely on and get so easily from the store, most of us are going to be dead after a short time. It won't be because of the zombies—it will be because we don't know how to grow food, access clean drinking water, or create any of the many things we rely on for modern life.

Even in our interpersonal relationships, lack of knowledge can be a powerful source for discord. Consider how we judge other people regarding how they raise their kids. Many of us have had or will have the opportunity to witness someone else struggling with a small child. Perhaps a little boy is out of control, twirling in circles in the middle of a nice restaurant. His parents, nearby, are watching him with a sliver of a nervous smile on their faces. Many of us would judge them in that situation. But before rushing to judgment, we should consider how much information we have. Perhaps the mother and father are the parents of four other, older kids, all of whom know how to behave well in public. They may have read every book on parenting and that, combined with their years of experience raising their other kids, makes them quite possibly the best parents in the world. This particular child, however, may be on the low end of the executive functioning spectrum,[10] which means most normal parenting techniques don't always work, and his capacity for self-control is near zero at this particular time. The family had been driving in the car for twelve hours that day to attend the funeral of the father's brother, who died unexpectedly. Even if they wanted to, the parents couldn't take the child outside because they need to be there for the rest of the family. They know that if they intervene with his running in circles, the outcome will be worse, not better. I could go on. The point is that, even when we tend to judge others, we are often doing so with just a fraction—often less than one percent—of the available information. Recognizing our lack of knowledge can keep us from judging, which can prevent discord.

All of this should humble us, but it can also be a powerful vehicle for being peacemakers, because intellectual humility is the first step toward framing conversations in a way that results in positive dialogue.[11]

HOW TO REFRAME YOUR CONVERSATIONS

Adopting intellectual humility can help us form the habit of framing conversations in a way that helps everyone involved discover new truths. Such conversations are delightful. Unlike adversarial conversations in which each party might feel inclined to lob accusations, well-framed conversations help the world progress.

Whenever two or more people are discussing a given issue, how the topic is framed is perhaps the most important step in the process. Framing occurs at the beginning of every conversation, whether we like it or not. For example, when a reporter asks a question of their guest, they are framing the conversation in a specific way that will inevitably lead to a different discussion than if they had framed it another way. Where we see this most starkly is with lawyers engaged in litigation. Lawyers are trained to frame arguments in a way that makes outsiders view their case and client in the best light.

Consider a simple dispute: an employee receives an offer of employment for a new job out of state. He puts his old employer on notice. He puts his house on the market. It goes under contract. Then, the new employer learns something about him in their background check that troubles them and they pull his offer. He now has no job, his house is under contract, he will be forced to move his entire family while having no job, and he may suffer considerable financial and emotional damage from the whole ordeal. He feels the job offer was premature and the company never should have offered it if they were still doing a background check. The employer feels the former prospective employee should have told them much sooner about the potential issue in his background. Had he done this, they never would have made the offer.

If a case like this were to go to court, the two lawyers would frame it very differently. The lawyer for the former prospective employee would stand up in court and say something like: "This case is about the harm that comes from broken promises." The attorney for the employer would rise and say: "This case is about lying and hiding crucial information."

You can see how each approach would change the course of the conversation. Because this is a legal dispute, both frames are adversarial in nature. They involve one side making an argument the other side must refute, which then leads the first side to refute the refutation. And so on. That is how law works in the United States. It is a system that developed over a long period that found an adversarial approach the most likely to yield the truth in a court of law.[12]

It may be tempting to think that if an adversarial system works to reveal the truth in legal proceedings, we should adopt it in our private lives as well. We should keep that temptation in check. In a court of law, strict rules force a certain level of emotional control and civility in the courtroom. Contrary to the nonsense often shown on television, most courtrooms are orderly and proceed according to firm procedures. Quality lawyers do not shout over one another, make bombastic accusations, lie, present false evidence, or engage in over-the-top rhetorical arguments (except in just one part of the process where certain arguments are allowed). They are required to present evidence in an orderly way, subject to specific rules that guide the proceedings. These rules—rules of evidence, rules of civil procedure, and rules of appellate procedure—are well known by counsel on each side and are nonnegotiable. For example, in almost all instances, parties are not allowed to surprise one another with evidence; they must disclose what they know so the other side has a reasonable amount of time to respond or find counterevidence.[13] Rules like this are why an adversarial system can yield the truth in a court of law without devolving into social-media-level fighting.

We don't enjoy rules in our daily lives that keep our argumentative relatives in check. That means that adversarial framing is most likely to result in conflict. People are put on the defensive. They must immediately develop arguments and make assertions. Conversations devolve not into a discovery of new truths but into everyone involved trying to defend whatever position the conversation's initial framing provided them.

Thankfully, there are other ways to frame conversations. Additionally, the ability to recognize when someone else has framed the conversation in a way that will or will not lead to productive discourse is crucial. If you bring up a topic, you can frame it immediately in a way that will lead to a proper exploration of it. If someone else brings up the topic in a way that will inevitably lead to fighting, you can move to reframe the issue. Perhaps it goes without saying, but it is crucial to keep your voice calm and moderate when framing, never accusatory or argumentative.

One of the best methods for framing is to show that all participants are trying to solve a problem and that most of them likely do not have all the information they need to do so. This move changes the goal of the conversation for each participant. It is no longer about each person trying to persuade the others, the way lawyers do, but it is about everyone involved working together to find a shared solution while recognizing they probably don't have nearly as much knowledge as they thought they did.

Note that to pull this off successfully, you do not need to know everything about a given topic. All you need to know is enough about the subject to frame or reframe the problem in a way that will be productive. Two examples will show how you can do this. One is our hypothetical between Uncle James and his niece, Gabby. The other is from a real-world situation.

In our hypothetical about the gender pay gap, James and Gabby turn to you and ask your opinion. They have already begun the conversation in a way that will lead to endless fighting, gaslighting, strong opinions, and zero productive discourse. Now the spotlight is on you. The family's entire weekend rests on your shoulders. Thousands of possible sentences could flow from your mouth. Both Gabby and James want you to support what they have said. Hopefully, you will have the intellectual humility to recognize how little you know. Rather than give Gabby or James what they want, your goal is to reframe the conversation. So, you could say something like the following:

> This seems like a complex topic, so I need to know more information. I think we'd all agree that if there is an employer intentionally paying men more than women for the exact same work, that's a problem, but I don't

have enough information yet. I would also want to get the cause right. If we get the cause of the problem wrong, we'll spend all day arguing about it and never actually find a solution.

A lot probably depends on where you're getting your statistics, Gabby, and what jobs you're talking about, because the gap is probably different in different industries. What industry are you looking at? What employer are you analyzing?

That might sound way too stilted for a family conversation in the living room, but you get the idea. Think about how that response would change the tenor of the conversation. You have begun by acknowledging your own lack of knowledge. Hopefully your response will trigger some of the same acknowledgment in James and Gabby. Asking specific questions about the sources of Gabby's information is a good way to get both James and Gabby thinking about where to look for data and how to interpret it. You also frame the conversation in a way that shows that the three of you are not enemies. You all want to solve the problem, if it exists, but you need to understand how severe it is and its exact nature. From that launching point, the three of you can then start talking specifics to understand the true problem, or, more likely, realize you might not have enough information to solve it yet, which will hopefully encourage you to do some digging together for answers. What could have become a fight instead turns into a treasure hunt.

This is precisely what happened in the real world when a real gender pay gap issue arose within a hospital system. Several years ago, the administrators of a large hospital network were grappling with a major problem: A 33 percent gap between the pay of men and women in the network's hospitals. The network's administrators, assuming what many people assume, began by operating under the premise that the gap was a result of intentional discrimination or implicit bias. They hosted every training they could think of to weed those out, but the problem persisted.

To get to the root of the problem, they finally decided to hire an outside consulting firm to dig into the numbers. The consulting team got to work. Their first step was to reframe the conversation by finding the true cause of the problem, rather than relying on assumptions. So rather than state opinions, as we might do in our conversations, they asked questions. Specifically, they asked for every bit of data the hospital system could provide them. One of the first details the team recognized was that the 33 percent figure was accurate but represented average pay *across the system*. In other words, it was comparing the salaries of doctors with nurses, and nurses with administrative staff, and so on. It was not comparing men and women in the same positions.

The team recalculated the numbers after ensuring they were comparing men and women in the same jobs in the hospital system. The 33 percent gap closed to 8.9 percent. Still a problem, but a very different one from where they started. Suddenly, the COO of the system, a woman, felt emboldened. The original number was so high, she had felt she could never find a solution. The lower number seemed manageable, and she wanted to continue the search for its cause so she could potentially solve the problem.

Further analysis revealed that overtime pay was causing the discrepancy. The hospital system allowed its nurses to earn overtime by working twelve-hour shifts, beginning each day at 7 a.m. The first shift would work until 7 p.m., then the next shift would arrive and work until 7 a.m. That was how the system had always operated. But, for some reason, men in the hospital system were generally working more of these overtime hours than women. The team then asked the next obvious question: *Why?* Was it intentional bias—men receiving more offers to work more hours than women? Did it have nothing to do with bias—men simply wanting to work more hours? Was there something structural in the system that was preventing women from getting more hours? The consultants maintained their intellectual humility and kept digging. Eventually, they found the cause in the start time of the shifts.

On average, the female nurses needed childcare support more than the male nurses did, but it was extremely hard for them to find childcare at 7 a.m. Instead, they were working 9 a.m. to 7 p.m. shifts and forgoing the overtime pay offered for starting at 7 a.m.

The team found that many of the female employees who were working these shifts *wanted* the extra hours. A typical response from them was, "'It's really hard to find childcare in the morning, but if I can get my kids to school and come to work, it's easier to find in the evenings. And so . . . if you shift the schedule back, we [could] work as many hours [as our male counterparts].'"[14] The hospital system made a simple change. It adjusted its schedule so that the shifts began at 10 a.m. The discrepancy in pay between men and women largely vanished.

I do not share this story to suggest that all discrepancies in pay between men and women are the result of scheduling issues. In some instances, it may well be because of explicit bias. In others, it may be because of some other cause none of us is considering.* The point is that the consulting team acknowledged from the start that they did not have all the information needed to understand the situation. They asked

---

* If you are interested in how this particular anecdote might play into broader political debates about the gender pay gap, consider this: on some level, it undermines the claims of some on the political left that all gender pay discrepancies can be explained by lasting prejudice against women. It bolsters the position of those on the political right who claim that society has progressed beyond blatant discrimination against women.

On the other hand, many on the political left would say that there are systems in place that affect various cultural minorities differently, and those systems often result in disparate outcomes that make it harder for those minorities to succeed. They argue that we should be looking for these systemic problems and trying to fix them. They would say this anecdote supports their view by offering evidence of a systemic problem—finding adequate childcare is an obstacle faced more often by women. Are there other areas where systems that seem to be neutral are in fact causing harm in ways we just haven't considered? If we could explore those types of questions honestly, without devolving into accusations and partisan politics, we may find all sorts of improvements we can make in our society that almost all of us can support.

for more information and then reframed the conversation in a way that led to productive dialogue and the asking of more important questions that eventually resulted in a solution. The C-suite of this hospital system had twisted themselves into knots to solve what seemed like a major problem in their system. They had tried solution after solution after solution, all because they had assumed they knew the cause of the problem. Reframing the problem and the conversation yielded the fruitful outcome.

We can do the same in any conversation of which we are part. The first step is to recognize how much we don't know. The second step is to frame the conversation so that everyone involved starts from that same place and then works together to solve a common problem. This is not the only technique to engage in civil discourse, but it is an important first step.

WHAT IF YOU ACTUALLY ARE
THE REAL EXPERT IN THE ROOM?

Quick pro tip before we begin: If you're confident you are the expert in the room regarding more than one or two topics at most, please go back and read the last section again. Remember, just feeling like you know more than the person you're talking with does not make you an expert. And even if you are an expert on a broad subject, you will not be an expert regarding someone else's experiences.

That said, let's continue. As we now know, most of us are at least somewhat uninformed about most things. But each of us is an expert in at least one or two very specific topics. I mentioned I know only a fraction of what I could know about the First Amendment, but that fraction is still a great deal of information more than others who are not experts in my field. And it includes lots of discrete topics about which I am an expert. Likewise, the parents who spend every waking hour thinking about and agonizing over their children know far more about those children than anyone else in the room. We are all experts about our own experiences. We all have a few topics like that. The challenge is that not everyone will want to acknowledge our expertise.

A few years ago, I published a book about a controversial topic in the United States: religious freedom. You know exactly what happened. Within days, people arrived on my social media feed with the intent to attack. One person hurled a series of insults at me, random political figures, and the notion of religious freedom generally. He had absolutely no clue what religious freedom really is and had not read my book, but consistent with the Dunning-Kruger Effect, he had strong opinions about it.

The good news is that this is not a reason to fret. The principles of intellectual humility and reframing still apply. Being the expert just means you have that many more tools for doing the reframing. But you must resist the urge to showboat or to be the know-it-all in the room. No one likes that. The best way to respond is to first hold your fire. You don't need to jump in immediately to put everyone in their place.

Wait until the right opening, which is usually when argument has stopped and people have looked to you for your opinion.

When the window opens, you can say, "I've thought about this a lot. The problem those of us in the field are trying to solve is . . ." That is your opportunity to frame the conversation. Lay the problem on the table in all its complexity. In doing so, put forth the best arguments from both sides in the conversation. Doing so will signal that you truly are an expert on the topic, but it will also send a signal to the other participants that the topic may be far more complex than they realized. Of course, the possibility always exists that you'll be dealing with someone who is not interested in civil discourse and who will not acknowledge the complexity of the problem or your expertise. We will discuss personalities like that in a later chapter. But in many instances, once you have used your expertise to frame the conversation, the others in the conversation will open their minds to asking you questions. Or, they may even provide you some insights you had never considered before. Either way, you will be one step closer to a productive and enjoyable conversation, not a shouting match.

You should avoid the temptation to shout your credentials from the rooftop, especially out of the gate. Someone else in the room may provide them for you, which can be helpful, but contending that a group should listen to you merely because of your position of authority is rarely useful. Once the opportunity arises and people are willing to listen to you, it's far better to signal your expertise through framing and providing evidence and reason that will resonate with anyone.

One of my favorite movies of all time is *Groundhog Day*. I won't defend that statement here. It's okay if you didn't like it. One scene makes it easier to understand the flaws with arguing from a place of authority. The main character, Phil Connors, played by Bill Murray, is trapped in an endless loop, forced to live the same day over and over again. Eventually, he decides to better himself and to serve others. As part of that, he begins taking piano lessons. Each new repeat day, he tells the teacher it is his first lesson, even as his skills continue to improve from novice to intermediate to expert.

At one point, after he has been taking lessons for a lengthy period, his piano teacher tells him, "Not bad, Mr. Connors. You say this is your first lesson?"

Phil responds, "Yes, but my father was a piano mover, so . . . "

The moment is hilarious for obvious reasons: having a piano mover for a father does not give anyone expertise in playing the piano. But he throws the line out there as if the opposite were clearly true.

We do the same all the time in conversations, and generally, other people don't appreciate it. There can be times when a person's own authority can trump every other consideration. Perhaps they have first-hand knowledge of an event, or they are the subject of conversation. I'm not talking about those instances. I'm talking about when the conversation is focused on a topic that concerns everyone in the room, and we attempt to end it by bragging about our own genius or training.

Either we are relying on a false position of authority that gives us no expertise on the topic whatsoever, much like Phil Connors's fake piano-moving father, or we come across as an arrogant jerk who is more interested in touting our credentials than sharing any useful information. Simply having credentials does not make us persuasive, so we will want to get into the habit of persuading people with reason, logic, evidence, humor, and the shared goal of finding solutions, not our personal authority.

Doing so will bring us closer to being true peacemakers, especially in those few areas where we truly know more than others around us.

HABIT ONE: WHAT WE'VE LEARNED ABOUT INTELLECTUAL HUMILITY AND REFRAMING

In this chapter, we learned that peacemakers practice intellectual humility and reframing. This means:

THEY RECOGNIZE HOW LITTLE THEY KNOW.

Any time they discuss a subject, they should remind themselves how little they know and how much they still can learn about it.

THEY REFRAME CONVERSATIONS TO MAKE THEM PRODUCTIVE.

When they engage in conversations about a topic, they must frame or reframe the conversation to acknowledge that lack of knowledge. Doing so will help their conversations focus more on making progress and learning, rather than merely proving others wrong.

THEY USE THEIR EXPERTISE WISELY.

When they are an expert on a topic, they can still recognize how much they have yet to learn, but they must also use their expertise to frame problems in ways that will lead to constructive discourse regarding solutions; they should avoid trying to show off their expertise or authority.

HABIT TWO
SEEK REAL LEARNING

On August 25, 1835, in New York City, citizens opened copies of the relatively new newspaper the *New York Sun* to find a story that would have been just as astonishing today as it was then—an astronomer had scientifically proven the existence of life on the moon. The headline looked like this:

GREAT ASTRONOMICAL DISCOVERIES LATELY MADE
BY SIR JOHN HERSCHEL, LL. D. F. R. S. &c.
At the Cape of Good Hope

The story that followed that headline, along with five additional stories the *Sun* printed in the coming days, claimed to be excerpted from a supplemental published by the *Edinburgh Journal of Science,* whose editors had been made privy to the explorer John Herschel's marvelous discoveries on the moon and were allowing the *Sun* to use them. The excerpts included fantastical accounts of fauna, vegetation, oceans, and all manner of interesting lifeforms, including unicorns and humanlike creatures with bat wings. Herschel had reportedly observed all of this through his revolutionary new telescope while studying the southern skies in the Cape of Good Hope. The *Sun* included notes with the excerpts that seemed to be written in Herschel's style and were purported to be from his close traveling companion, Andrew Grant. Drawings accompanying the articles claimed to capture what Herschel was witnessing through his marvelous new telescope.

1. *Illustration for the New York Sun. 1835.*[1]

The public ate it up. Sales of the *Sun* exploded. For weeks, people across the then-small United States believed an entire civilization of bat people lived on the moon and had built elaborate structures and cities. A team of scientists from Yale University even traveled to New York to inspect the original documents from the *Edinburgh Journal of Science*, but *Sun* employees gave them the runaround, and the scientists left the city unaware they had been duped.[2]

Obviously, all of it was a hoax. Historians today debate precisely what the newspaper's goals were, but many assume the hope was to drive up readership, which it appears to have done. Sir John Herschel was, indeed, a famous and well-respected astronomer and scientist at the time who had recently traveled to South Africa with his new telescope to study various astronomical objects in the southern skies. Being in South Africa, however, he had no means of quickly debunking the stories. The *Edinburgh Journal of Science* had been out of print for two years. Andrew Grant, whom the *Sun* named as the author of the original summary provided by the *Edinburgh Journal*, didn't even exist. Historians today think the author of the entire text was actually a reporter at the *Sun* named Richard Adams Locke, who may have intended the entire thing to be a satire to mock other people of the era who had speculated about massive civilizations on the moon. He may have even regretted that the public took the accounts to be true.

A few newspapers around the country suspected a farce and started calling it a hoax.

Finally, on September 16, 1835, the *Sun* admitted it was all fake.[3] As far as we can tell, no one seemed to punish the paper or its staff for it. The *New York Sun* remained a highly successful newspaper for another 120 years.[4]

But the story is a wonderful illustration of human nature. Then, as now, human beings were susceptible to believing almost anything, as long as it was presented in a convincing fashion. Hopefully your new-found intellectual humility will prevent you from trusting in bat people on the moon the second you watch a professionally done video about it. But recognizing how little we truly know raises an interesting question: How are we supposed to be peacemakers and have conversations about anything of substance if we all recognize at the outset how much we don't know?

The next habit peacemakers adopt is engaging in daily acts of real learning. We can't all be professors and researchers who get paid to spend our days digging deep into a particular subject. And as I've already demonstrated, even those of us who have that luxury don't have time to delve into more than one or two areas at most. But we also don't want to throw up our hands and give up on our civic duty to become informed as best we can. The solution is to learn to be far more judicious about our news sources. This chapter offers advice about how to establish the habit of real learning throughout our lives, or even right in the middle of a discussion about a hard topic.

The first parts of this chapter focus on secular learning; that is, learning about our world through evidence, reason, argument, critique, and trial and error. These sections also focus on the barriers we face when trying to establish the habit of real learning. If you are someone for whom spiritual learning is important, or if you are skeptical of any form of spiritual learning, the final section in this chapter addresses that. I start with secular learning because it applies to all of us whether we like it or not. Each of us, every day, is learning something new about our world. Peacemakers seek to engage in true learning that enlightens their minds and can help them solve the problems around them.

UNDERSTAND HOW WE GENERATE KNOWLEDGE

Have you ever considered how we generate knowledge, versus merely acquiring it? The difference is important. How we *create* knowledge is different from how we *obtain* already-generated knowledge. The first we almost always tend to do in groups. The latter we can do as individuals.

We will focus on acquiring knowledge soon enough, but understanding how we as human beings produce or discover new knowledge is critical for being a peacemaker and having productive conversations. We cannot generate new knowledge without learning from those around us and from those who have gone before us. And that means we cannot be in a state of constant conflict with either group.

Isaac Newton is famous for many things, most notably the discovery of Newtonian physics, also called classical mechanics. The laws of motion Newton developed help explain much of the world around us. But he is also famous for a letter he wrote in 1675 to fellow scientist Robert Hooke, in which he said, "If I have seen farther [than others], it is by standing on the shoulders of giants."[5]

To prove the point, it is interesting to note that Newton does not seem to have created that phrase but was invoking an idea already developed by someone else. John of Salisbury, an English author and philosopher who lived in the 1100s, attributed the idea to another philosopher and scholar from France, Bernard of Chartres. John recounts that Chartres used to say we are like "dwarfs perched on the shoulders of giants" and thus we are able to "see more and farther than our predecessors, not because we have keener vision or greater height, but because we are lifted up and borne aloft on their gigantic stature."[6]

The idea is straightforward enough but crucial to understand. No one is generating new ideas in a vacuum. Almost always, we are standing on the shoulders of those who came before us, benefiting from their work and their knowledge, then adding to it whatever we can while benefiting from those presently around us as well. Our new ideas come from a dialogue we have with both the past and the present. The myth of Newton is that he was sitting under a tree, an apple fell and hit him on the head, and he suddenly came to understand gravity. There is some truth to the story. After witnessing an apple fall, he told a friend that "the notion of gravitation came into his mind. 'Why [should] that apple always descend perpendicularly to the ground,' thought he to himself."[7]

From there, Newton began to work out his theories of classical mechanics. He used mathematics and connected the apple's behavior to that of the moon, ushering in a new way of thinking about the world. But *why* did he think of the moon orbiting the earth and mathematics and the idea of the apple falling *perpendicularly* to the ground? Those were concepts already bouncing around in his head. As noted science historian Patricia Fara explained, "Although Newton was undoubtedly a brilliant man, eulogies of a lone genius fail to match events. Like all innovators, he depended on the earlier work of Kepler, Galileo, Descartes, and countless others."[8]

In other words, the idea that "great geniuses make momentous discoveries suddenly and in isolation" is nothing more than a "romantic notion."[9] Always, like Newton, they are building on the discoveries that came before them. They are adding to them bit by bit, line upon line, precept upon precept.

For the purposes of this book, it is learning the *process* of adding to what came before that is most crucial. It is easy to see how all of us are standing on the discoveries of the past to explore our world today. What is less obvious is how we go about generating new knowledge from our current perch.

Newton's experience is again helpful. He did not watch the apple fall to the ground, enjoy a moment of inspiration, then lock himself away in isolation only to emerge with his three laws of physics and bask in his own brilliance. Instead, he had already been thinking about these ideas. He had already been enjoying a discourse with others interested in many topics, and while he did spend some time in isolation during a plague, he continued those discourses after he emerged.[10] Some of those folks challenged him. Consider again his letters with Robert Hooke. The pair had engaged in a public spat in a series of letters read before the Royal Society of London over their theories, and Hooke decided it would be better to take things private. He wrote to Newton:

> S[i]r,—The hearing of a letter of yours read last week in the meeting of the Royal Society, made me suspect that you might have been some way or other misinformed concerning me. . . . I have therefore taken the freedom . . . to acquaint you of myself. First, that I doe noe ways [I do not always] approve of contention, or feuding or proving in print, and shall be very unwillingly drawn to such kind of warre. Next, that I have a mind very desirous of, and very ready to embrace any truth that shall be discovered, though it may much thwart or contradict any opinions or notions I have formerly embraced as such. . . . Your design and mine are, I suppose, both at the same thing, which is the discovery of truth, and I suppose we can both endure to hear objections, so as they come not in a manner of open hostility, and have minds equally inclined to yield to the plainest deductions of reason from experiment.[11]

Hooke was asking to open a dialogue with Newton to discuss their various experiments, discoveries, and theories on the world. He wanted truth, even if it contradicted his own views, and he wanted to discuss his thinking about the truth with a colleague who shared his interests.

Newton's response is important. We can learn much from it about the discovery of knowledge:

> At the reading of your letter I was exceedingly pleased and satisfied with your generous freedom, and think you have done what becomes a true philosophical spirit. There is nothing which I desire to avoyde in matters of philosophy more than contention. . . . What's done before many witnesses is seldom without some further concerns than that for truth; but what passes between friends in private, usually deserves the name of consultation rather than contention; and so I hope it will prove between you and me.

Newton was telling Hooke that he looked forward to corresponding in private because conversations in front of groups tend to yield contention. In groups, people tend to worry more about things like ego, pride, and impressing those around them than about discovering the truth. Newton, like Hooke, said that he wanted to avoid contention.

But notice that Newton distinguished being challenged in his thinking from contention:

> Your animadversions [criticisms] will therefore be welcome to me; . . . To have at once in short the strongest objections that may be made, I would really desire, and know no man better able to furnish me with them than yourself.[12]

Newton asked for challenges to his proposals. He wanted others to find the flaws in his work. He welcomed it. Newton knew an important principle: by allowing others to inspect our thinking and our conclusions, we come closer to the truth. It is scary and gut-wrenching, but it identifies weaknesses where we are wrong. It inspires new thoughts in others where we are right.

This exchange is crucial because it shows how humanity develops and creates knowledge every day wherever constructive dialogue is allowed to flourish. Both Newton and Hooke were thinking about and experimenting in the same field. Both were standing on the discoveries that had come before them, but both were trying to find new ways of thinking about the world. Rather than work in isolation, they wanted to challenge one another. In short, they wanted to be at peace with each other and those who came before them so they could then discover new truths about reality.

This is how knowledge is created, on small and grand scales. People stand on the shoulders of those who came before, talk about their ideas, test them, submit them to criticism, refine them, listen to the ideas of others, learn from and criticize them—in a never-ending cycle that generates more and better information about our world. In his book *The Constitution of Knowledge*, Jonathan Rauch summed up this process well. Referring to someone engaged in the process of creating knowledge, he said:

> You will expose your ideas to peer review and public debate, and critics will suggest questions and experiments and alternatives; in seeking to recruit others to your view, you will refine your ideas, adapt them, incorporate amendments, meet objections, and try out other ideas. You will be forced to adjust your thinking and your strategy, and as the process is repeated millions of times a day across the reality-based network, the whole system becomes a dynamic web of mutual persuasion: critical persuasion, so to speak, a social process of continuously comparing notes and spotting errors and proposing solutions.[13]

Don't think this process is just for scientists and professors. Sure, for those in academia, the process occurs in formal settings. But in everyday life, it occurs any time two or more people work together to solve a problem.

A simple example: we recently had an outdoor heating unit break on us. It just stopped working. I took off the front panel and fiddled around with some of the wires, hoping that the problem would be so obvious that even a writer could detect it. No luck. I tried resetting it and pressing a few buttons. My theories as to what may have been causing the problem reflected my ignorance, but, in my defense, I feel like the solution to nine out of ten problems these days lies in unplugging and resetting things.

I called in a repair service. The technician, a young man not much older than my teenage son, fiddled with a few controls, then, with a scared look on his face, told me he thought maybe it was the gas valve. It would cost me close to $500 to replace it.

He was free to speak. It was obvious he was guessing. He had developed a theory no better than any of mine, and he had no evidence to support it.

I told him I would think about it, then immediately called in a second opinion. This new man, a seasoned and sharp technician who clearly knew what he was doing, looked at the wiring and the equipment and said, "Huh."

"Another guy told me it was the gas valve," I said.

"That's nonsense," he said. "This is electrical. Let me look around some more."

I left him to it, and an hour later, he approached me with something in his hand. "Found out the problem."

"Yeah?" I asked.

"Right here," he said. "The control board had an invader that shorted it out." In his hands, he held the motherboard to the heater, and fused to it was the burned, dried-out corpse of a small frog. It had somehow crawled up into the motherboard housing and electrocuted itself, shorting out and damaging the motherboard in the process.

Completely unexpected, but some new knowledge was generated:

sometimes, small animals like frogs crawl into tight spaces and cause real damage to electrical components. You see the process working: trial, error, theories tested and proven false, new theories proposed, people speaking freely and proposing nonsensical theories that others prove wrong, discussion and discourse—all building on itself until finally some new piece of knowledge is created.

Billions of people all over the globe are doing this, on matters that concern all of humanity and on those that trouble only a handful of people. Along the way, as Rauch points out, this process is generating, accumulating, and disseminating "knowledge at a staggering rate. Every day, probably before breakfast, [this process] adds more to the canon of knowledge than was accumulated in the 200,000 years of human history prior to Galileo's time. . . . There is no reason to think the pace will slow."[14]

For all of this to work, people must be able to communicate. We need legal regimes that allow for freedom of speech, but that is just the starting point. We also need people capable of using that freedom responsibly, building bridges to others who think differently from them, and engaging in constructive discourse. Otherwise, we will squander the opportunity we have to generate new knowledge and better the world around us.

Contributing to these conversations in a productive way requires that we acquire some of the knowledge others have generated. After all, Newton would never have developed his theories if he had not first learned the mathematical concept of perpendicularity or that the earth revolves around the sun, the moon revolves around the earth, and other laws of planetary motion. Like never before, we can tap into the vast treasure of truths humanity has amassed. It is, quite literally, at our fingertips. There are a multitude of ways we can do that, especially in the era of smartphones and the internet. The problem we have is that along with all the knowledge now available, there is a staggering, almost incalculable, amount of false information. The giants who came before us serve no purpose if we are prevented from standing on their shoulders. Or if we refuse to climb on that perch. Both are problems. The remainder of this chapter offers advice for how peacemakers can overcome them.

If we are to seek real learning in our effort to become peacemakers and contribute to solving the world's very real problems, we must know how the world around us is manipulating us. We must also know how to take a world of untrustworthy sources and use them to our advantage.

RECOGNIZE THE FORCES YOU ARE FACING: DOPAMINE, TEAMS OF PSYCHOLOGISTS, AND FOREIGN ACTORS

Achieving any goal requires knowing what obstacles are in the way. For the purpose of seeking real learning that will help us become peacemakers, we need to understand the forces we are up against. And they are formidable. One of the great ironies of our age is that we have more information available to us than any humans who have ever lived, yet many of us fail to access even the small amount we could retain. Historically, what prevented people from real learning was a lack of resources: time, money, available knowledge, access to that knowledge, and good health. Today, many of us face far fewer of those obstacles. Instead, our barriers to real learning are far more complex. They include our own bodies' chemical reactions to stimuli, teams of doctorate-level psychologists and mathematicians who understand our bodies and brains better than we do, and nefarious foreign actors and companies intentionally trying to manipulate us. The good news is this: once we know people are trying to manipulate us, we will understand the obstacles in our way and we can do something about them.

Dopamine

I am not a neuroscientist, and this is not a book about brain function. But we can't understand what keeps us from real learning in the twenty-first century if we don't first understand just a bit about how our brains work, and in particular how they react to smartphones and related technology in our lives.

As the image below shows, two parts of our brains create a chemical known as dopamine.

DOPAMINE PATHWAY

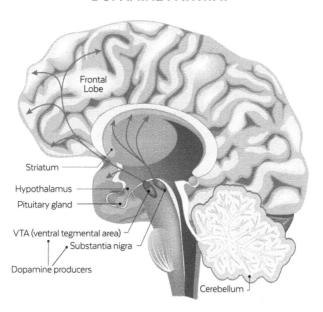

Dopamine serves many functions in the brain, the most important of which is to carry signals between neurons. When one of our neurons wants to send a signal to another one, the message is carried by neuro-transmitters like dopamine.

But it also plays an important role in our brain's reward system. When we encounter something that brings us stimulation, our brains release do-pamine. The effect of dopamine is usually pleasure, euphoria, the thrill of anticipation, and the desire to want to pursue the stimulant. When we eat a sugary treat, or have sex, or drink alcohol, or take drugs, or do anything else that stimulates us, our brains create dopamine. As Stanford addic-tion researcher Doctor Anna Lembke explains, "The more dopamine a [particular stimulant] releases in the brain's reward pathway . . . , and the faster it releases dopamine, the more addictive the drug."[15] And once our brains release dopamine, they immediately begin to rebalance themselves by reducing the amount of dopamine they are creating. This is why we often feel additional cravings for something after enjoying it. As soon as the effect of the dopamine wears off, we find ourselves in a dopamine deficit, which causes us to want to seek out another hit of dopamine.

This is an important component to addiction. We experience something, our brains release dopamine, we feel euphoric (high), we crash, then we seek it again. This process becomes even worse if what we are addicted to is easily available.[16] Research has proven this again and again. From drugs, to digital addictions, to alcohol, to pornography— the easier we can access a high dopamine-producing substance, behavior, or content, the more likely we are to become addicted to it.

All of this relates to smartphones and social media and their interference with our ability to engage in real learning and to be peacemakers. Every time we see a notice—of a like, a text, a comment, some interesting piece of news, a million other things—our brains release a shot of dopamine.[17] It feels good. So we look for the next one, and the next one, and the next one. Give anyone a smartphone, and within a short period of time, you will see them regularly grabbing and checking it. They are seeking, often subconsciously, that next hit of dopamine. So much so that many of us cannot go more than a few minutes without at least glancing at our phones to see if something is waiting for us. We see drivers do it at every red light. We see people do it during movies at the theater. It can be such a distraction that, for me, every time I sit to engage in an extended period of writing, I have to slide my phone, upside down, across the room to keep it out of my field of vision and out of reach. Otherwise, it will pull me away from my project.

The most important source of those hits, for the purposes of this book, are news and information that get us riled up about the hot topics of the day. Notices about something that has happened in the political landscape that interests us will trigger a dopamine release. If we have commented on a news story or someone's political post on social media, reactions to our comment will release dopamine.

Like rats in an experiment, we will continue to seek it out.

But unlike many addictive substances or practices, which must be done in private, smartphone use and reading and commenting on the news has yet to cause any social backlash. It is perfectly acceptable in our environment to pick up our phones and seek that latest dopamine hit, from a text, a like, an article, a video, a stock report. We can't do that with illegal drugs, but we do it all day long with our phones.

And it is in that milieu that every single one of us is operating. At a moment's notice, we can pick up a small device to keep our addictions going. As you will see, that destroys our ability to connect with others and engage in productive conversations with them.

Armies of Psychologists, Mathematicians, and Scientists

While smartphones and social media appear to be major impediments to becoming peacemakers, they are only the tip of the spear. We can't really know what we are up against in trying to establish a habit of real learning unless we know who is controlling the spear.

Every time you pick up your smartphone, you should picture in your mind's eye teams of psychologists, mathematicians, computer programmers, and psychologists whose entire job is to keep you hooked on that device. I do not mean that rhetorically. I am not using hyperbole. One of the major goals of many tech companies—the phone manufacturers like Apple and Samsung, the app developers, the social media companies—is to keep you on your device for as long as possible. Their business model depends on keeping your attention. The longer they can trap your eyes on their product, the better the chance they can sell you something or lure you to buy other products. For these companies, everything we just explored about dopamine and the reward center of our brain is not just an interesting fact about the human experience—it is the necessary feature of their business model. For all the good smartphones and computers do for us, those who create them need you addicted to them. They are meant to imprison you.

A sad irony is that if peacemakers become who they are based on their habits, technology companies are hoping to mold you into what they want you to become by forcing habits upon you. In his bestselling book *Hooked*, industry insider Nir Eyal states this explicitly. "Forming habits," he writes, "is imperative for the survival of many products." In other words, the "economic value" of almost any tech company affiliated with smartphones "is a function of the strength of the habits they create."[18] Eyal wrote his book with one goal in mind: to teach tech entrepreneurs how to develop products that would hook and addict consumers. The goal is to create habits in you that you do "with little or no conscious thought."[19]

What Eyal teaches in his book, and what larger more powerful tech companies were already doing, is hardly novel. Long before smartphones, the gambling industry pioneered getting people addicted to gaming. Especially with computer-controlled games like slot machines, their goal was to hook users, hold them with a series of expertly timed rewards (just enough wins or other dopamine-triggering events), until their interactions with the machine resulted in a "downward spiral . . . a continuous, rapid, responsive interaction with the machine, precluding pauses or spaces in which she might reflect or stop."[20] In other words, the goal was for gamblers' play to become habitual, mindless.

Given how successful the gambling world was at snaring people, it is hardly surprising that other industries would want to follow the model. To give you a sense of what you're up against, consider what one mathematician who works for the gambling industry told researchers for the book *Addicted by Design*: "'Math is the sharp end of my spear,'" he said. He uses math to both hook people and catch them. "'Once you've hooked 'em in, you want to keep pulling money out of them until you have it all; the barb is in and you're yanking the hook.'"[21] And lest you think that what you're up against is just one math nerd who couldn't possibly manipulate you, consider this:

> To strengthen the holding power of games' math, machine manufacturing companies staff *departments* of advanced mathematicians who run so-called math

farms to simulate the efficacy of different payout sched-
ules. . . . By adjusting the mathematical configuration of
their games, designers seek to address an ever-wider
range of human preferences within the human-machine
environment of the gambling arena. "We understand
humans and are creating math for them," [one mathe-
matician] said.[22]

I put the key word in that passage in italics: *departments.* Picture
rooms of mathematics geniuses and psychologists—not working to solve
some disease or place human beings on the moon but focused solely on
keeping you hooked.

Schull wrote her book about the gambling industry in 2012—the
first year the majority of Americans owned a smartphone and five years
after the debut of the original iPhone, according to psychologist Jean M.
Twenge.[23] Imagine all the progress that has been made since then. Phone
and technology companies, like Newton, have built off the knowledge
that came before them, except that the giants upon whom they stood were
focused solely on how to get people addicted. They have developed sophisticated methods that trigger action in their users, which inevitably lead
to rewards that are variable and timed specifically to keep people using,
which then cause users to invest their time and effort into the product,
which then leads to a new trigger to start the entire process over again.[24]

You can picture this in how you interact with your favorite social
media app. You see a photo from a good friend (the trigger), you click on
it and make a comment (your action), your friend likes your comment
(the variable reward), you like the dopamine rush you feel when you see
that notification of a like, so you make another comment hoping for the
same feeling (your investment), which leads to your searching for similar
feelings again (new triggers). Eventually, you reach the point that any
time you have a lull in your life or an instant where a sense of depression can sink in, you reach for that phone and the dopamine cycle it

provides. The cycle is endless, it is intentional, and we can escape it only if we are fully aware of it.

How does all of this relate to the ability to establish a habit of real learning that will allow you to be a peacemaker? One of the ways these various companies keep you addicted and keep triggering dopamine is through outrage. In his important book *Outrage Machine: How Tech Amplifies Discontent, Disrupts Democracy—And What We Can Do about It*, technologist Tobias Rose-Stockwell explains:

> For the first time, the majority of information we consume as a species is controlled by algorithms built to capture our emotional attention. As a result, we hear more angry voices shouting fearful opinions and see more threats and frightening news simply because these are the stories most likely to engage us. This engagement is profitable for everyone involved: producers, journalists, creators, politicians, and, of course, the platforms themselves.[25]

In other words, fearful opinions, frightening news, stories of threats to you and your family—these create the same dopamine hits in our brains as much less nefarious things like "likes" to our photos. So, we return to them. We consume them more and more. In time, we come to see the world not as a complex system with equally complex problems in need of sophisticated solutions. Instead:

> When we are shown what's wrong in the world, we feel the desire to correct it. We want to share these transgressions with our networks. If we see more problems, these problems *must* have perpetrators who are responsible for them. These enemies are now everywhere, and we feel the need to call them out.[26]

When we share a news story that gets us enraged or engaged, we receive rewards—and dopamine hits—as our friends and others interact with the story. They make comments. They offer likes. They share it with their friends. The algorithms running our feeds offer us even more similar stories. We share those, and the cycle starts over again. Soon, the only news we read relates to what we have already shared, and if it is about a controversial subject, it gets us angrier and angrier. In time, we cannot comprehend how anyone could see the world differently than we do. The only possible explanation must be that they are evil or fools, something we'll discuss more in a later chapter.

Cable news is no different. Turn on any news network, and, within minutes, you will see an eye-catching "Breaking News!" alert. If new, important events were happening at the pace cable news channels wanted us to believe they are, the world would have ended decades ago. The reality is that those stations need to keep as many eyeballs as they can on the screens for as long as possible. Their entire business model depends on it. They sell airtime to advertisers, and those advertisers pay based on the number of people watching. That is why Super Bowl commercials cost so much, and commercials airing during a 2 a.m. rerun of the 1961 television show *You're in the Picture* cost so little.

Cable news has learned that their primary tools for keeping people tuned in are breaking news and anger. The breaking news alerts are strategically timed to keep viewers tuned just at the moment they might be inclined to leave. Watch a channel for any length of time, however, and you'll find that most of the breaking news alerts are nothing more than rehashes of the same news the channel has been discussing for hours.

Because there is so little actual news, the channels must look for other methods of filling the airtime and keeping us engaged. They have turned to anger to do this. Talking heads pick the most divisive topics of the day, then offer their opinions on those topics in a way they know will be provocative. They provide us either bombastic opinions with which we are already inclined to agree, or they point out to us threats from which we do not dare turn away our eyes.

Every time we pick up our phones or turn on a news station, we need to remind ourselves what those teams of psychologists and mathematicians are doing. They are not trying to pass on real information. They are not interested in our learning anything or becoming better citizens or being peacemakers. Whether we like it or not, they are trying to manipulate us, from the moment we let our eyes fall upon any screen in our lives. They are a formidable opponent in our efforts to engage in real learning.

And if departments of people in our own country controlling us isn't infuriating enough, there are far more nefarious actors in this world trying to turn us against one another.

The Foreign Actors

Beginning in the 1940s, America's enemies decided to use America's racial and religious diversity against us. As I wrote in my book *The Immortals*,[27] one of the first to perceive America's diversity as a weakness was Adolf Hitler. At the outset of the United States' involvement in World War II, Hitler remarked to those in his closest circle: "I don't see much future for the Americans. In my view, it's a decayed country. And they have their racial problem, and the problem of social inequalities. Those were what caused the downfall of Rome, and yet Rome was a solid edifice that stood for something. Moreover, the Romans were inspired by great ideas. Nothing of the sort in England to-day. As for the Americans, that kind of thing is non-existent."

He droned on, remarking again on America's racial and religious diversity. Then he said, "My feelings against Americanism are feelings of hatred and deep repugnance. . . . How can one expect a State like that to hold together?"[28]

His theory and expectation were that a Germany united through force under Naziism would defeat an America fractured by diversity. Obviously, the United States and its allies proved him wrong. Hitler committed many horrors and made numerous strategic blunders, but one of them was that he rested his theory on a belief. In other words, he anticipated that America's diversity would be its undoing all by itself. He never tried to weaponize it.

That came next. After the United States and its allies defeated Hitler and the Nazis, the next nation to try to turn our diversity into a weapon was the Soviet Union. This began in the 1950s. The Soviets adopted a specific, long-term strategy to try to sow social discord in the United States. They had some success, but it was slow going given the technology of the time.[29]

Fast forward to the 2010s and the burgeoning popularity of the internet and social media; foreign operatives focused on creating internal strife within the United States never had it easier. They no longer needed to send spies. They didn't even need to be in the United States. It was enough for Russian operatives to sit back on computers in their home country and use social media platforms and our own dopamine against us. We now know that their aims were not to support a particular party or presidential candidate; they were much bigger than that. According to documents released through the Dossier Center, a London-based investigative project funded by Russian opposition figure Mikhail Khodorkovsky, Russia's hope was to "'undermine the country's territorial integrity and military and economic potential'" by turning Americans against one another. In short, the documents made it clear that Russia wanted to "'destabilize the internal situation in the U.S.'"[30]

To this end, they set out to influence all sorts of groups in the United States, from every side of the political divide: animal rights groups, gun rights supporters, Black Lives Matter activists, LGBTQ rights advocates, anti-immigrant factions, and more. They were not hoping to help any of these groups succeed so much as they wanted all the groups fighting one another.

As Cailan O'Connor and James Owen Weatherall detail in their book *The Misinformation Age*, the operatives' plans were to "get close" to whatever group they were hoping to manipulate by pretending to be concerned about the same causes or interests. Through fake "personalities, voices," groups, and social media pages, they would "get close, pose as a peer, and then exert influence. After convincing users that they shared core beliefs and values, Russians used these platforms to widen the gap between right and left."[31]

The most blatant example of this was in 2016, when Russian actors used social media to organize two events at the same time and in the same location. One was sponsored by a supposed pro-Muslim group, the other by a supposed anti-Muslim group. Russian operatives in St. Petersburg, Russia, created a Facebook page called Heart of Texas. To outsiders, it looked like any other group we might see on social media. It included the tagline "Texas: homeland of guns, barbecue, and your heart." It also posted all sorts of false information, including stories written to convince its followers that Muslims posed a threat to the safety and security of the state of Texas. It then organized an event outside the Islamic Da'wah Center in Houston. The event's claimed purpose was "to stop the Islamization of Texas."

The Russian operatives also created a separate page on Facebook. This one they named United Muslims of America. It organized an event called "save Islamic knowledge" at the same place and time as the Heart of Texas protest, presumably to create a counterprotest.

Both accounts then paid for targeted Facebook ads that reached thousands of people in the Houston area. The result was exactly what you might expect. Two groups of competing Americans—relatively small in the grand scheme of things—screaming at one another in the streets of Houston, leading to near-violent conflict.[32]

The point in all of this is that everyone involved was operating on bad information and sources. The power of social media, controlled by people who know how to stimulate our brains, convinced one group of Americans that Muslims were a threat and needed to be stopped from taking over Texas. The same operatives convinced another set of Americans that a large group of people in Texas hated Muslims and were coming to attack them. These foreign actors were manipulating everyone involved.

It isn't stopping. In 2023, in the run-up to the 2024 election cycle, Microsoft engineers warned that both China and North Korea were increasing their capabilities to spread misinformation campaigns that could "go viral across social networks in the U.S. and other democracies."[33] This included creating bots that engaged with real human beings across social media platforms, even responding and carrying on conversations with Americans while posing as other Americans.[34] China's goal is clear. According to Chris Watts, general manager of the Microsoft Threat Analysis Center:

> We have observed China-affiliated actors leveraging AI-generated visual media in a broad campaign that largely focuses on politically divisive topics, such as gun violence, and denigrating U.S. political figures and symbols. This technology produces more eye-catching content than the awkward digital drawings and stock photo collages used in previous campaigns. We can expect China to continue to hone this technology over time, though it remains to be seen how and when it will deploy it at scale.[35]

Human beings are susceptible to believing misinformation. These foreign actors know this, as do many activists here in the United States. Their goal is to use the freedoms of speech and expression against us to sow distrust: of each other, our institutions, our history, and the foundational concepts that give us strength, such as belief in democracy, liberty, and equality.

As indicated by the research into China and North Korea, the problem will only get worse with the invention of artificial intelligence, which can create an infinite number of misleading posts and information at a pace no team of humans could ever match.

The bottom line is this: we are all being manipulated to see everyone around us as enemies and conspirators so a few companies can make obscene profits or infamous actors can sow discord. Most peacemakers find a way to mitigate that manipulation, even if they can't escape it entirely. In the coming sections, we will see how.

WE MUST ACKNOWLEDGE WE ARE
ALL SUSCEPTIBLE TO MISINFORMATION

It may be tempting to think that we, individually, are the only ones on earth for whom the above challenges will not be a problem. Everyone else has to worry about dopamine, tech-company psychologists, and foreign actors, but not us.

Peacemakers avoid such hubris. One habit they develop is being wary of misinformation and recognizing that they, just like everyone else, are susceptible to it. Researchers have learned that we can all fall prey to the "illusory truth" effect, which is that "repeated claims are more likely [to] be judged as true than non-repeated (or novel) claims." This is because of something called processing fluency: "The more a claim is repeated, the more familiar it becomes and the easier it is to process."[36]

The result is something we should all take seriously:

> (1) prior exposure to fake news increases its perceived accuracy; (2) illusory truth can occur for both plausible and implausible claims; (3) prior knowledge does not necessarily protect people against illusory truth; and (4) illusory truth does not appear to be moderated by thinking styles such as analytical versus intuitive reasoning.[37]

In other words, the world is filled with people who want to manipulate us, and we are all susceptible to that manipulation. This can happen, some research has shown, because we are too often in too much of a hurry to truly process all the news with which we are bombarded online. So we tend to make decisions with our intuition and gut, instead of by processing information to see if it's accurate. It also happens because, too often, we seek information with a goal of finding information that will confirm the conclusions we have already reached. Consider this research finding:

> Other research has found that politically conservative individuals are much more likely to (mistakenly) judge

misinformation as true when the information is presented as coming from a conservative source than when that same information is presented as coming from a liberal source, and vice versa for politically liberal individuals—highlighting the key role of politics in truth discernment.[38]

In other words, we tend to be skeptical of news when it comes from someone with whom we disagree and trusting when it comes from someone with whom we agree. That's hardly surprising. The question is what to do about it.

Peacemakers try to inoculate themselves from these very human tendencies. The result is real learning that can make dialogue fruitful, not destructive.

HOW TO BREAK FREE FROM THE MANIPULATION

Now that we know we're being manipulated constantly, the question arises: what can we do about it? One thing we know is that many of us are incentivized to engage fully in the very behavior that is causing so much discord in our society. As Rose-Stockwell summarizes,

> Often, if you *don't* do the bad thing, you're at a disadvantage to those who do. If you don't say something divisive, you are often outcompeted in the attention marketplace by someone who does. If you don't accrue followers and attention by using moral and emotional language, you're at a disadvantage to those who do.[39]

I have experienced this in my own profession. I have watched as others in my same space have amassed larger followings on social media mostly through use of divisive and emotional language and claims that stoke outrage and generate likes and followers. And I have been tempted to follow suit. My desire to be a peacemaker keeps that temptation at bay, but what should I do?

I want to stay informed. I want to seek education and real learning. I want to pass on what I have learned to others and have them do the same for me. But I don't want those armies of manipulators to win. Many of us would like to hope that some entity larger than ourselves will materialize out of the cosmos to disrupt this situation. We desire either government or market forces to create a scenario in which people are incentivized to discuss issues civilly and with trust. But until that happens in a way that is consistent with the freedoms of speech and thought, peacemakers recognize they must take matters into their own hands.

They know they have more options than (1) engage in social media and on our devices or (2) fail at life. As they seek real learning, they are not afraid to set their devices aside for other pursuits. Often, they recognize that if they want to learn something new and valuable, they will rarely find it through a social media scroll or by reading an angry op-ed.

They also spend time seeking dopamine hits from sources other than technology. One of the saddest aspects of our modern world is that we have more luxury and leisure time than any humans who have come before us, yet we seem unable to benefit from it. Many who came before us dreamed of a day when advancements in technology would allow humanity to do more than focus on survival. This, they hoped, would allow them to spend more time pondering the meaning of life, exploring spirituality, enjoying nature, considering their place in the world and universe, and (to use more modern phrasing) embracing more mindfulness.

Increasingly, more and more people have reached that place, even many considered poor in the United States. Yet how do we spend that additional time? Staring at screens, binge-watching shows, fighting with others.

One important habit peacemakers master is freeing themselves from that endless cycle and instead pursuing what the masses of humanity dreamed about for so long. They engage in activities like prayer, meditations, walks, fishing, reading long-form works like books (that includes listening to them), talking with loved ones, going to church, journaling, practicing mindfulness, enjoying peaceful music, serving others, observing nature, visiting museums, or learning from lectures available in person or online.

Many of those activities may seem boring to you. In fact, I would fully expect them to be if you, like almost everyone else, have trained your brain to expect a release of dopamine from your devices every few minutes. But if you can reimmerse yourself into the joyous waters this world has to offer without a screen, you can free yourself from technology addiction and begin to engage in real learning—about yourself and the world around you. Try it for short periods if you must. Go for a walk without your phone and note what you see and enjoy. Force yourself to go an evening without a phone in reach and watch in surprise at how your evening changes.

THE PEACEMAKER'S RESPONSE
TO CATCHPHRASES AND HEURISTICS

Even if we can free ourselves from technological manipulation, we still need to know how to process all the information we might bring into our lives. Now that we recognize how little we truly know, doesn't it amaze you that any of us can function? It seems that every single one of us should be paralyzed given how much information our brains need to navigate the world. The cognitive load required to make any sort of decision, given how many choices and options really are before us, should make our brains short circuit. But they don't. Why?

The short, imperfect answer is that we use something called heuristics. The word comes from the ancient Greek *heuriskein,* which means "to find, discover." Heuristics are the strategies we create to navigate practical problems based on previous experiences. For example, when you walk into a dark room, the number of choices in front of you is enough to make your head explode if you were to actually think through each one. But you don't need to explore every choice every time you enter a dark room. You know from previous experience that, most likely, there is a light switch on the wall near the door. If you reach for it and flick it, a light will come on. You do it and move about your day. Most of us have no idea how a light switch works. We don't need to know. We know just enough to solve the practical problem: achieving light in darkness.

Consider a time in your life when you have not been able to use heuristics as much as you would like. A good example is the first time you made a big purchase on your own, without anyone you could trust to help you with the process. In that situation, you likely spent days or weeks researching the pros and cons of the various options, agonizing over where things could go wrong, clicking through multitudes of websites looking for information to help you. Eventually, you likely found trustworthy sources and decided. The next time you bought a similar item, your process was much faster. You learned which websites you could trust. You developed subconscious shortcuts that made the decision-making process much easier the next time around.

Heuristics are incredibly valuable in life. They help humanity do everything from complex computer programming to going to the bathroom (do you really know how a toilet works?). But they can also get us into major trouble when it comes to engaging in conversations about hard topics. The problem with heuristics is that they can be imprecise. They help us find solutions to problems so we can operate in a complex world, but they are often only accurate enough to find a solution that is satisfactory, not perfect. It is enough for us to know that if we flick a switch, a light will come on. We do not need to know all the physics, chemistry, legal regulations, engineering, and testing involved in that act. But when something breaks in the process and the heuristic doesn't work, we are also not able to fix what is broken.

Marketing experts, foreign operatives, and activists long ago realized that heuristics were a crucial tool for getting people to buy products or support certain causes. Think of shoes. For many of us, once we find a brand we like, we stick with it. Marketers know that, so they work tirelessly to lure us into equating their shoes with the best product available to us. They don't want us to think. They want us to think heuristically: "I need running shoes. Just do it. I'll buy some Nikes."

For the important issues of our day, all the forces I discussed in the previous section, including well-meaning activists and nefarious actors from foreign countries, are adept at using heuristics in the form of slogans. The well-meaning activists want you to join their cause. The nefarious actors want to pit you against your neighbors. They don't want you to think or dig deep to acquire knowledge. Catchphrases achieve both aims, because, on the surface, and depending on your personal views, you couldn't possibly say no to them. Here are just a few:

- Black Lives Matter
- Make America Great Again
- Hands Off Women's Bodies
- Love Is Love
- Protect Our Border
- Gender Pay Gap
- Pride
- Build the Wall

- Antiracist
- Lock Her Up
- Me Too
- Power to the People
- Don't Say Gay
- Stop Groomers
- Speak Truth to Power
- Defund the Police

As with marketing heuristics, these catchphrases are effective at drawing people in and helping them quickly align with a particular opinion about a given subject. The problem is that, as with all heuristics, they are imprecise. Because of that, invoking them inevitably leads to arguments. Unless we know how to respond to them.

First, we should be wary any time we hear a phrase like any of the above. Our first thought should not be to argue with or affirm it but be to understand what the person means when they say it. Because these catchphrases can be so imprecise and emotionally charged, it's entirely probable that both you and the person invoking them place different meanings on them. It's entirely probable the person invoking them knows exactly what the catchphrase means and has thought long and hard about that meaning. But it's also likely that a person repeating the catchphrase isn't sure they know what they mean by it. Because they are using a heuristic, they think they know what it means, just like we all like to think we know what a light switch is doing when we flick it. But upon reflection, they are likely to realize they haven't really thought it through.

Your first order of business must be to determine what someone means when they invoke a catchphrase. Only then can you know if you actually disagree with them. More importantly, the two of you will zero in on precisely where you do agree and where you don't. Then you can have a fruitful discussion. Your questions should be sincere, intended to gather information, not to score a rhetorical point.

Let's use one of the most polarizing phrases of the last few years as an example. The phrase "Black Lives Matter" first burst onto the scene in 2013 after the death of Trayvon Martin and the acquittal of George Zimmerman. It means different things to different people. Lest readers accuse me of choosing "Black Lives Matter" for nefarious reasons, I want to be clear: I could have chosen any of the catchphrases listed above and probably plenty of others. No matter which slogan I use, those who are passionate about it will struggle to see there may be different meanings from their own. I chose this one because I was a aware of a public story that reflects the many ways different audiences are interpreting its meaning. I do not share it to question its validity or to police people who use the phrase. That is a separate conversation.

Consider the example of the then-highly ranked Clemson University football team and their head coach, Dabo Swinney. In the example that follows, I will continue to place the term "Black Lives Matter" in quotation marks, because the purpose of this anecdote is to show just how ambiguous a heuristic slogan can be. During the fall of 2020, Swinney was hesitant to allow his football players to include any messages on their uniforms, including "Black Lives Matter." This was, he explained later, because he was a traditionalist regarding uniforms—he felt they shouldn't be changed in any way. In response to this, he received intense ire from those who support "Black Lives Matter." They accused him of not caring about Black lives, police brutality, or the gaps in wealth between white and Black Americans.

In response, Swinney tried to clarify his position. "Black lives more than matter," he said. "Black lives are worthy. They equally matter. . . . Absolutely Black lives matter. That's common sense. I've lived my whole life making sure that that's something that hopefully my actions have shown. Not something I've just said."[40] In time, he allowed his players to put on their uniforms messages that mattered to them, including words like "Love," "Equality," or "Black Lives Matter."

His players' support for "Black Lives Matter" triggered a response from a different set of Clemson fans. One of them called into Coach Swinney's radio show three weeks into the season and asked him if his team would dial back some of their support for "Black Lives Matter" because the "Black Lives Matter" group "was built predominately on hate . . . for all law enforcement" and was pushing for violence against officers.

This forced Swinney to emphasize that his brother had worked as a police officer and that he very much supported the police. In other words, his support for "Black Lives Matter" did not mean a lack of support for police organizations. He also emphasized, "I'm on board with a lot of the messages, but I'm not on board with political organizations."[41]

Swinney managed to navigate all of that without losing his job. Many others did not. In that story, we see three very different meanings of the term "Black Lives Matter." It is being used as a heuristic so people can talk about an important social issue, but because of its imprecision, different people use it to mean very different things. We know from that anecdote alone that the term has come to have at least three very broad meanings:

1. The literal meaning of the words: black lives matter, and our society should not have or support any system that treats black lives as if they do not matter.
2. A nonliteral meaning of the words: hatred for law enforcement.
3. The political activist organization that calls itself "Black Lives Matter," which has a number of stated goals and beliefs

different, or at least more complicated, than either of the other two meanings.

We also know from watching conversations around us that the phrase has even more meanings than that—probably as many interpretations as there are people in the United States. When people engage in conversations using a heuristic with that many diverging meanings, it is inevitable that arguments will emerge. If one person understands it to mean hatred for law enforcement, and the other person understands it to represent the literal definition of the words, they have zero hope of having a fruitful discussion about an important topic in American society.

Their first move, then, must be to make sure they are on common ground when they use the term "Black Lives Matter." Are they talking about the organization? If so, they can get on the website, look at all the claims and arguments the organization is making, analyze its history and what it is or is not doing in society, then have a conversation about whether they support it and its various activities and claims.

Are they talking about the literal meaning of the words? If so, they can talk about whether society is in fact not treating Black lives as if they matter, and if so, what to do about it.

Are they talking about a movement that is hostile to police and law enforcement? If so, they can discuss policing in the United States, what it's doing well, what its challenges are, how to improve it, and whether it is appropriate to be hostile to police officers in any way.

Each of those subjects is filled with potential blow-up points. But it is also far more productive to take on one of those issues on its own than have two people arguing about two different topics while thinking they are discussing the same thing.

All of this is meant to emphasize how dangerous catchphrases and heuristics can be. They are short and catchy, so activists and marketing gurus love them. Like any heuristic, they allow us to align ourselves with a cause without having to do the heavy work of thinking. And that is precisely why they are so dangerous for productive dialogue—we adopt them readily, considering ourselves informed. In truth, they prevent us from engaging in any real learning.

They send us into unknown and vague territory where we likely do not know what dangers await us. The next time you encounter one, think of the old cautionary phrase that appeared on the Hunt-Lenox Globe, built in 1510, one of the first globes ever created: *Hic sunt dracones*—Here be dragons.

And proceed with caution.

DON'T SEEK NEWS THAT ISN'T NEWS

As explained above, news channels and tech companies have every incentive in the world to manipulate you into staying locked into their products. They are not going to change. Any laws that might force them to do so are quite likely unconstitutional, and financial structures urge them to keep up their practices.

While I encourage and applaud those trying to push for systemic change to our tech and media world, and I hope they can find a way to fix things that still comports with First Amendment principles, the bottom line is this: peacemakers do not allow themselves to fall for the manipulation. They take charge of what they consume. They act, and are not merely acted upon.

What this means is that they are very deliberate and conscious of the news they take in, and they always distinguish between opinion and real news.

There is nothing wrong with reading opinion pieces. I have written many of them myself, and I hope people will read them. In many instances, they can provide information and viewpoints that are just as important and valuable as any dry news story, but we must always be mindful of when we are leaving news and when we are entering into the realm of pure opinion. We must also be wary of watching endless hours of opinions and hot takes that do not provide any new information. In most instances, this is not news. It is opinion journalism masquerading as news.

For many of us, the time of day when we are most likely to digest news that isn't news is during our off hours. This is often in the evening for those of us who work for a living. Sometimes it is in the morning when we are getting ready for the day. The next time you find yourself with that discretionary time, you might try something different. Instead of watching hours of Fox News or MSNBC, consider reading in-depth news stories instead. Or, even better, grab a good book from the library and learn about something entirely new in this world you had never considered before.

Remember one of our earliest discussion points, about how a "little learning is a dang'rous thing." Watching evening cable news provides only a little learning about the world's most complex topics. It gives its viewers just enough information to argue with others but never enough to understand the nuances of any given issue.

Audio books, in-depth interviews on professional podcasts, lectures on a topic from a variety of viewpoints—these are far greater sources of real learning than news that isn't news.

DON'T GET NEWS FROM SOCIAL MEDIA—AT LEAST NOT THE WAY SOCIAL MEDIA FEEDS IT TO YOU

Part of real learning is knowing where to get your news. Most peacemakers are very deliberate in how they use social media. As the social psychologist Jonathan Haidt has documented, one of the biggest shifts in our society occurred when social media companies began adding news feeds, "like" buttons, and resharing options to their offerings.[42] People no longer explored social media just to catch up on friends' lives. Instead, they learned about the day's events, world controversies, important and trivial happenings, and anything else the social media companies decided to show them.

That last item is the most important, and the most troublesome. The teams of psychologists we explored earlier came to realize that people using social media experience a dopamine rush when exposed to news stories they're already interested in. They began developing algorithms to keep you on your phone, and one way to do that was with the news feed. If they could continue to provide users with dopamine rushes by sending them headlines that they knew already intrigued the users, they could keep people on their products for longer periods of time.[43]

The task was quite simple. If a user clicks on a news story about Michigan football, it suggests they are interested in Michigan football. If they keep reading the article for any amount of time, the algorithm can track that as well. The next time the user opens their social media app—which can include everything from Facebook to X to YouTube to Instagram to Snapchat to TikTok—they will find even more stories about Michigan football. Sometimes just the sight of the stories will give them a dopamine rush. Clicking on a story's link may provide even more. And, if they do, the algorithm notices. As long as it can, it will continue to feed users whatever will keep them in the app.

Think about what effect this has on our experiences as users. Many have heard of the marketplace of ideas. The concept first appeared in the United States in a 1919 dissenting opinion by Justice Oliver Wendell Holmes, who explained that "the ultimate good desired is better reached by free trade in ideas—that the best test of truth is the power of the thought to get itself accepted in the competition of the market."[44] Thirty-four years later, in 1953, Justice William Douglas coined the phrase with which we are now all so familiar. In a case involving a committee of Congress demanding to know who had purchased books from a specific publisher, Justice Douglas agreed with the majority of the court that the First Amendment protected the names of the purchasers. He then said, "Like the publishers of newspapers, magazines, or books, this publisher bids for the minds of men in the marketplace of ideas."[45]

The metaphor of the marketplace is apt. We can all imagine walking into a crowded market. All around us are people in booths, clamoring for our attention. Each has a different message. We are free to roam about, to stop at those booths that interest us, to engage with the people there, or to move on and find someone else more interesting or more persuasive. We find people with opposing views and hear what they have to say. As we do, we form our opinions and come to understand the world a little better.

But imagine a different market. We amble into it. We see booths for as far as the eye can see. One piques our interest so we step to it and start asking some questions. Right then, a ghostly figure appears, without our even noticing it. It places its hand on our shoulders and guides us closer and closer to that first booth. While we're there, it builds a tent around us, shielding from our view all the other booths in the area. In time, the ghostly figure ensures that we are aware of only that first booth. Sure, we can push our way out of the dark tent it has built around us, but we don't. Inside the tent, we don't see or hear any of the other booths. We're interested in the message and the messenger in that first booth, so we stay and listen. And we are surrounded by other people who are trapped in the same tent.

And the ghostly figure does that for everyone in the marketplace.

That story sounds like something out of an Edgar Allan Poe horror story, but it is precisely how modern social media feeds us the news. The result is that, to some degree, we are all living in different realities. Social media has manipulated us into our own closed tents or echo chambers. Too many of us see and hear and interact with only those voices with whom we initially expressed some interest.

On the rare occasion when someone else breaks into our dark tent, we see them as a threat or as something beyond our ability to comprehend. We cannot talk to them. Their ideas have become foreign, even hostile.

All of this comes from relying on social media to provide us our news, and it is why social media has been such an utter disappointment. For many, we initially saw it as an opportunity to expand knowledge at an exponential rate, and in some instances, it has done that. Too often, however, by using its algorithms to shield people from ideas and talking points that contradict them, it has stifled the development of knowledge. Ideas—often outlandishly false ideas—are shared within most communities with no one to challenge them. Theories that could be debunked in short order in a properly functioning marketplace of ideas instead fester, and only among the people who already believe them.

I suspect many who read this will think of people they know who have fallen prey to social media's algorithm. They will think of the many people in their lives who are trapped in their own dark tents, clueless as to the other perspectives available. Not enough will look at themselves to see if perhaps they are stuck in their own echo chamber.

Peacemakers will. They will recognize that no one is immune to the manipulation of the modern information marketplace. It affects us all, unless we choose to break free from it.

If we would seek real learning, we must break free from the shackles of that ghostly social media algorithm and take our gathering of knowledge more seriously. We must seek our own news sources and not rely on what social media feeds us.

That said, social media can be a useful tool for finding important and helpful news. The next section discusses how.

DIVERSIFY YOUR NEWS SOURCES

Once we recognize we must do the heavy lifting of finding our own news sources, the obvious issue is whom to trust. The short answer is: no one.

Some years ago, I had a conversation with a scientist named Reid Grigg, who was one of the world's foremost experts on carbon sequestration—the process of capturing carbon dioxide before it gets dispersed into the atmosphere and inserting it back into the ground. With a PhD in chemistry, Grigg had developed a niche expertise that made him valuable both to those worried about greenhouse gases and those in the fossil fuel world. Both groups wanted to stop carbon dioxide from being emitted into the air. Those concerned with climate change felt that limiting the amount of the gas we pump into the atmosphere would slow anthropomorphic damage to the climate. The fossil fuel industry saw carbon dioxide sequestration as a way to repressurize long-dead oil deposits to allow us to extract even more oil from them—think of a half-empty water balloon with a small pinhole punched in the side. The hole does not leak water when it's just sitting there, but when you blow air into the balloon and it gets sufficient pressure, water starts shooting out of the pinhole again. Many oil deposits are similar. Lots of oil, but the deposit is only half full with no pressure. They need something to push the oil out, and captured carbon dioxide can provide that pressure. It is more effective than other gases because it also helps separate the oil from the rocks and soil in which it is mixed.

Given how valuable Grigg was to both sides of the political spectrum, he became one of the leading scientists in his field. He was also a man of deep religious faith. (See the next section on spiritual truths for more discussions of people who find knowledge through spiritual means in addition to secular ones.)

On one occasion, he and I slipped into a conversation about the media and news sources generally. He said, "You know. There are only three topics I really know a lot about: carbon sequestration, my family, and my religion. And every time I read a news story about any of them, no matter what the source, I find they get something wrong. It makes me skeptical of anything I read from the media."

I suspect we have all had a similar experience. On those rare topics about which we are true experts, we probably find that newspeople who are covering them generally miss important nuances that make their stories less than trustworthy.

So what are we to do?

Let me be clear. I respect the media. And by the "media" I mean anyone trying to disseminate what they believe to be the truth about any topic under the sun. This includes everything from legacy outlets like the *New York Times* and the Associated Press to the neighborhood journalist trying to draw attention to important legal issues via their Facebook page. It includes right- and left-leaning media groups. It includes fringe groups who hyper focus on hyper specific issues. It even includes opinion writers trying to share their op-eds with the world.

Love them or hate them, they all play a vital role in our country. Earlier I quoted a portion of a comment once made by Judge Learned Hand. Now allow me to provide the entire quotation:

"The [news] industry . . . serves one of the most vital of all general interests: the dissemination of news from as many different sources, and with as many different facets and colors as is possible. That interest is closely akin to, if indeed it is not the same as, the interest protected by the First Amendment; it presupposes that right conclusions are more likely to be gathered out of a multitude of tongues, than through any kind of authoritative selection. To many this is, and always will be, folly; but we have staked upon it our all."[46]

I think Judge Hand got it right. The more voices and sources there are, all checking and cross-checking one another, the more likely we are to expose the truth. I respect anyone and any organization dedicated to that mission. That respect does not extend, however, to those who would try to intentionally mislead people, such as the foreign actors trying to destabilize the United States or domestic actors who have learned they can monetize disinformation campaigns.[47]

All that said, the robust media and information sources we now have in our country raise a serious problem for all of us. What do we do in the face of everything that is out there? Where do we even begin, especially when we know there are deliberate misinformation campaigns, journalists who get things wrong even when acting in the best of faith, and bias everywhere?

In an ideal world with unlimited time, we would be able to take it all in and allow the truth to bubble to the surface in our own minds. But we don't live in an ideal world. For the time-pressed normal human being with a thousand to-do tasks and not enough minutes in the day to complete them, who wants to stay informed, you can adopt a relatively simple formula.

Pick at least two news sources that have stood the test of time and that you know are reputable—that is to say, they at least pretend to adhere to the normal standards of objectivity and reliance on trustworthy sources. You know they will be biased, but that's okay—it's actually why you're choosing at least two. Your goal should be to select two news sources that you know display different biases—one on the left and one on the right.

For instance, you might consider reading the *Wall Street Journal* and the *New York Times*. Research has shown that the *Journal* tends to skew right, and the *Times* bends left.[48] That's no surprise to anyone. Or, if you're going to listen to NPR, which leans left, on your way to the office, you'll want to balance that by listening to news or a podcast that leans right or libertarian on your way home, such as something produced by the Hoover Institution. If you prefer more extreme online news outlets, such as the Daily Wire on the right, there is nothing wrong with that, but you'll want to balance it with something equally extreme on the left, such as HuffPost.

To give you a sense of how valuable this can be, consider Russia's invasion of Ukraine in the winter of 2022. What baffled me more than anything else about that entire scenario—except for the fact that it was happening at all—was that state-led media in Russia had managed to convince many Russian citizens that the invasion was actually an act of defense. Indeed, one research fellow at the center I direct had actually moved to the United States from Russia. His family back home were convinced that Ukraine was the aggressor, because the only news source available to them said so.

For just a moment, I wondered: what if I am being manipulated? How do I know that my perception of things—that Russia was the aggressor in an unjustified land grab against a peaceful neighbor—is right? One reliable indicator for me was that I could turn on two news channels with very different biases and see the same information. I was not hearing two completely different stories from outlets with different political preferences. While that wasn't a perfect guarantee that my perception of reality was correct, it gave me as much confidence as I was going to get.

If you're not sure which outlets are biased or not, at least one good resource as of the time of my writing this book is the website AllSides.[49]

One of the services AllSides provides is ranking news sources based on their political biases. They do not purport to rank how good the sources are or how accurate they are in their reporting, only where their political slant lies. They have created an easy-to-follow chart, which they update each year, that at least gives us a hint of the bias in various national potential news sources. Their methodology is available and clear on their website so you can check whatever biases might have crept into their own assessments of these media companies. Note they are focused only on national media outlets and do not rank every news source in the country, including local papers for specific cities, but they do provide a useful service for news sources focused on national and global reporting.

Try a few. Dip your toes into the waters of news sources you have never explored before. You may be exposed to ideas that make you uncomfortable or that you disagree with, but that's okay. By reading different sources from different ideological perspectives, you will get a better sense of what's happening in the world while still remaining informed.

Another option available to you is to use social media in a productive way. While relying on their algorithms is harmful, social media can be a goldmine for finding different perspectives on the news of the day. For example, in my own field, I am often interested in news regarding the legal world. These are stories that are less likely to appear in normal papers with any depth. I am also aware of which people in my field lean left and right, and which are independent. When I am interested in getting different perspectives on a current matter, I look to see what news stories those various people are posting on their social media feeds. Inevitably, someone on the left posts a story from a left-leaning news source. Someone on the right does the same.

Note what you are not doing. You are not consciously choosing to do what social media is doing through manipulation. That is to say, you are not deciding to stay in your own echo chamber. If your only source of news is NPR, on the one hand, or conservative talk radio, on the other, then you don't need the algorithms of social media to force you into a dark tent with no exposure to the rest of the marketplace of ideas. You're doing it to yourself. You are denying yourself real learning, and you are putting yourself in a position where constructive dialogue with anyone who learns from different sources is all but impossible.

The good news about finding a few sources from different perspectives is that when you're done reading them, you can move on to more productive activities. You've already learned that allowing social media algorithms to corral you into an echo chamber is no good. You now know that most of what is out there is not really news, just commentary. The reality is that you don't need to consume hours upon hours of what appears to be news to be informed. Read your two solid sources from either side of the political spectrum, then go do something productive. When we aren't being manipulated by social media, we will find there is a whole world available to us worth exploring.

THE BLESSING OF ACQUIRING KNOWLEDGE IN REAL TIME

There was a time, not that long ago and for eons prior, that humans needed to argue about small facts because they didn't have information at their fingertips. No longer. Most people these days have access to a smartphone or a computer. This section is short because it doesn't need any theoretical groundwork or scientific research to confirm it. The next time you find yourself in a conversation with someone and you are debating a fact that could be easily searched by punching a few words into your phone, stop fighting, punch the words into your phone, then move on.

Someone's age. The distance to a certain location. Where a particular university is. When the Civil War began. How many calories are in a Twinkie—the list is endless, and it's all available.

Probably half the stupid arguments around the dinner table could be resolved with this one tip.

BE SLOW TO COME TO CONCLUSIONS

Most of us don't know this, but wherever we are in the world, we likely owe our existence as we know it to a man named Vasili Arkhipov. His ability to be slow to come to conclusions prevented catastrophe.

October 27, 1962, is known as Black Saturday. It is, arguably, the day the world came closest to a nuclear war between the United States and the Soviet Union.

The setting is familiar. Eleven days earlier, the United States became aware of the Soviets building nuclear missile sites in Cuba, ninety miles from U.S. territory. As part of its response, the United States formed a naval blockade to prevent any additional Soviet ships from reaching Cuba. Tensions were high. Fidel Castro, the Cuban president, urged the Soviets to fire nuclear weapons first.

By October 23, U.S. ships had moved into place in the Atlantic, quarantining the island of Cuba. Soviet vessels approached, then turned away.

But beneath the surface, Soviet submarines, at least one armed with a nuclear-tipped torpedo, sought to find a way past the American blockade. The Americans, meanwhile, were searching for submarines and were doing what they could to stop any of them from sneaking by.

On October 27, the Russian submarine *B-59* needed to surface to recharge its batteries. Its captain was Valentin Grigoryevich Savitsky. When *B-59* emerged, it found itself surrounded. Among the U.S. forces waiting to greet it were "an aircraft carrier, nine destroyers, four airplanes of Neptune type, three of Trekker," and circles of coast guard forces.[50]

On the submarine, Savitsky and his men were emotionally spent. For three days, they had endured grueling conditions that had worn away at their minds and spirits. The interior of the submarine was hot, as much as 60°C (140°F) in parts. The humidity was oppressive, forcing men to sweat even while resting. Fuel and oil vapors, combined with elevated levels of carbon dioxide, poisoned the air. They were running low on drinking water. Equipment was failing. To top it all off, the Americans had bombarded them with every type of radio and sonar signal available, along with depth charges filled with grenades meant to force the submarines to the surface. All day long, explosions rocked the hull, as if some watery giant were outside pounding on the metal with a hammer.

As that kind of stress wears a person down, rational decision making becomes more and more difficult. When *B-59* finally came to the surface to see its enemy in such force, Savitsky started to panic. He had no radio contact with his homeland, so he was unsure of where the negotiations between the Soviet Union and the United States stood. For all he knew, the countries were now at war, and he had already received permission to fire his weapons—including his nuclear torpedo—if he deemed it necessary.

The first thing Savitsky saw when his submarine emerged from the depths was a blinding light. An American plane had blasted the submarine's communications tower with a beam so bright Savitsky and none of his men could see. Even when he turned away, he was momentarily blinded.

Gunfire followed the light. The planes were only twenty to thirty meters overhead. They and the destroyers were firing all along the side and around the submarine.

To Savitsky, it appeared the war had started. It was kill or be killed. He followed his immediate gut reaction and made an instinctive decision. He bellowed for an urgent dive, which was the first required step before firing the ship's weapons. He also called for the nuclear torpedo to be prepared for firing.

But there was a minor delay. To give those orders, Savitsky needed to navigate down a narrow staircase through the conning tower for his men to hear him. His signaling officer was in the way, which forced him to pause for a few seconds.

In that moment, Captain Second Class Vasili Arkhipov, who was just a bit slower to come to conclusions than Savitsky, noticed that the Americans were not firing directly at the submarine but around it. And the bright lights seemed to be signaling the Soviets, not trying to blind them or spotlight them for destruction. He called to Savitsky, "Calm down. Look, they are signaling, not attacking. Let's signal back."

Savitsky hesitated, surveyed the situation, calmed himself, then ordered his men to signal back. Doing so confirmed that the Americans were warning the submarine to proceed no further toward Cuba. They were not attacking as part of an all-out war.

Years later, another officer on board the ship noted that two other officers would have had to agree with Savitsky before they could have launched the nuclear warhead. But had his instinctive command to force the submarine to dive been conveyed and followed before Arkhipov calmed the situation, the other officers would have had no reason not to agree with Savitsky. As Arkhipov noted, "After the first salvo from an aircraft cannon, the commander could have instinctively, without contemplation ordered an 'emergency dive'; then after submerging, the question whether the plane was shooting at the submarine or around it would not have come up in anybody's head. That is war."[51]

We cannot overstate the importance of that situation and what it means to us. Our world as we know it exists today because one man on a Soviet submarine was wise and in control enough to slow down before coming to a conclusion. That decision saved the world from nuclear war and the inevitable radiation fallout that would have followed. In short, it prevented earth from deteriorating into an apocalyptic dystopia. When others would have moved rashly, Arkhipov called for calm. When others saw only one possible outcome, he asked them to reassess.

Arkhipov's actions prevented nuclear war in a moment of crisis, but we should not dismiss the importance of a similar mindset in our daily interactions. Too often, our instinct to come to quick conclusions on too little information leads to battles and warfare in our interpersonal relationships. This is especially true when dealing with the controversial political topics of our day. Consistent with the Dunning-Kruger effect we studied in the last chapter, too often, we reach conclusions much too quickly on too little information.

Part of seeking real learning is recognizing that whatever conclusions we have reached may be proven wrong as we learn more than we know now. That should make us slow to come to conclusions and hesitant to dig in our heels once we do. Even in areas of life that seem to have been settled for decades, or even centuries, it is possible that our conclusions are wrong. To return to a previous example, consider what happened to Newton. His conception of physics ruled our understanding of how things work for hundreds of years, until a new set of scientists came along and started challenging some of his theories.

Between 1905 and 1915, Albert Einstein started to question whether Newtonian physics was correct in all circumstances. He theorized that at the small scale—at the quantum level—and at the very large scale—at the level of the universe—Newton's laws might be wrong.

Time has continued to prove Einstein correct. It turns out that Newtonian mechanics does a superb job of explaining our world around us for many of our practical needs, but it is not exactly correct at all scales. It has now been superseded by Einstein's theories of special and general relativity. What we thought we knew about the world—a scientific idea considered by many to be an ironclad *truth*—turned out to be only partially correct.

For many of the scientific discoveries humanity is making today, it is a good thing that Einstein was slow to come to and accept conclusions.

Peacemakers tend to do this naturally. It's part of their makeup, most likely a mix of their genetics and the environment of their upbringing. So where does that leave the rest of us? Can we train ourselves to slow our cognitive pace and our mind's tendency to race to conclusions? New research suggests yes.

First, if you find yourself in the camp of people who jump to conclusions too quickly without engaging in real learning, take comfort. You are not alone. The reason so many of us struggle to have productive dialogues or to engage in continued learning is simple: lots of us make the same mistake. But in recent years, leading cognitive scientists have found that while many of us tend to jump to conclusions too hastily, we can engage in what is called "metacognitive training" to train our brains to recognize our biases and to tame our unwieldy overconfidence.[52]

This type of metacognitive training can include online puzzles that help people identify specific biases. It can also help people see other ways of thinking about problems so they can realize there may be more than one way to approach an issue.

The idea of "metacognition" has arguably been around for millennia, but psychologist John Flavell coined the term in the 1970s. He defined it as a learner's knowledge of their own cognitive processes.[53] In other words, it is a person's knowledge about how they think. The word *meta* in this context means "showing or suggesting an explicit awareness of itself or oneself."[54] We are practicing metacognition, then, when we become explicitly aware of how we think. Once we achieve that, we can then change some of our thought processes and, most important, change how we learn.

So how do we get there? Several techniques are available, and more are popping up every day on the internet. Practice searching for some online and you're likely to find many helpful sources, many from universities across the country.

If you are inclined to work the old-fashioned way, don't fret. Many of history's tried and true traditions are actually forms of metacognition. Journaling, for example, can be a powerful tool for becoming aware of how you think and how you learn. One technique that is helpful is to use your journal to think through your conclusions. The next time you find yourself reaching a conclusion about something, before arguing about it with anyone, try the following:

1. In your journal (or anywhere), write the conclusion you have reached.
2. Beneath the conclusion, write all of the facts you know that support it.
3. Beneath that, write all the facts you know that do not support it or even might undermine it.
4. Beneath that, write everything you think you might want to learn to help you confirm your conclusion is correct.

What you will find from engaging in this process is that it allows you to get outside of your own mind and think about your conclusions objectively. It will also help you identify whether your conclusion is sound or whether it is something psychologists refer to as thought distortions. Such distortions are exactly what they sound like—distorted ways of thinking about the world. We are all prone to them. *So and so hates me . . . I'm going to lose my job . . . I am worthless because I ate that piece of cake I shouldn't have . . . I'm now going to gain thirty pounds be-cause I ate that piece of cake I shouldn't have. . . .* We are prone to them in our personal lives, and we are susceptible to them when thinking about society's most pressing issues.

Practicing metacognition will help you slow down, analyze your conclusions, and realize that, in most cases, you need more information and more learning.

Have you ever noticed that when someone comes to you for advice, you are often able to diagnose the problem and give them helpful tips? You may even be able to see the solution in a way they could not. But when dealing with your own problems, sometimes even very similar is-sues, you struggle to do the same. This is because it is very difficult to get outside of our own thoughts. We can often see thought distortions in others, but realizing when our own thoughts are distorted is much more difficult. We are not driven by emotion when we analyze someone else's thoughts, but our emotions cloud our judgment when we are dealing with our own thinking. Metacognition is a way to help with that. It al-lows us to treat our own thinking the way we might a different person's. Once we create that emotional distance, we can begin to pull back on the very human instinct to jump to conclusions too quickly.

SPIRITUAL LEARNING

In all of this discussion, I do not mean to denigrate those who be-lieve they can seek and obtain knowledge and truths from metaphysi-cal sources. Billions of people on this earth believe in a divine being who not only created our world but who can, in fact, communicate with us. And contrary to what some may claim, many of those people also believe in the other methods of generating and acquiring knowl-edge we have explored in this chapter. Consider, for example, Francis Collins. Born in 1950, he earned a PhD in physical chemistry from Yale University and an MD from the University of North Carolina at Chapel Hill. He then was a professor of internal medicine and human genetics at the University of Michigan. As a physician-geneticist, he discovered the genes related to a number of diseases and led the Human Genome Project. He served as director of the National Institutes of Health for more than twelve years, under three U.S. presidents. He dedicated his professional life to science and scientific inquiry.

He is also a man of deep faith. A Christian, he believes there is a God in heaven who created this world and whose son died and was resurrected to save all of mankind. He clearly seeks for (and has found) numerous scientific truths. He also believes he has sought (and found) important spiritual truths. He has no qualms with holding both at the same time and does not see them as being in tension.[55] There are millions of people all over the globe with a similar outlook on the world.

The mistake when it comes to spiritual truths is made equally by those who believe in them and those who feel belief in them is naive or ignorant. There are those in this world who believe the only way to generate knowledge is through the scientific method, deep inquiry, observation of our natural world, reason, logic, and the challenging of current ideas—all the concepts I discussed in this chapter. That belief, by itself, need not lead to conflict. Where they go wrong is when they attack those who disagree with them as simpletons or fools. A better approach is to recognize good faith differences, not attack individuals.

Professor Douglas Laycock provides an excellent example of this. He is one of the leading legal scholars of the twentieth century. To give you a sense of his accomplishments, most scholars dream of just being respected in one field. To be arguably the leading academic in one field is beyond the reach of most of us. Laycock is arguably the leading scholar in *two* fields: the study of religion law and the study of something called remedies law.[56] In addition to being a prolific researcher and academic, he has enjoyed tremendous success as a litigator as well, securing several victories in the United States Supreme Court. He always represented people of different religious backgrounds, from Christians to Hare Krishnas to Catholics and Jews to Santeria. Over the decades, people who did not know him personally always assumed he must be a member of the faiths he was defending or at least strategically aligned with them in some way. After decades of silence, he finally explained in a scholarly article his own religious beliefs.

"I am agnostic about matters of religion,"[57] he wrote. He acquires knowledge not through spiritual means but through the other methods discussed in this chapter. "I am a rationalist," he said, "a reasoner, an empiricist. . . . I am a direct intellectual descendant of the Enlightenment, comfortable with Enlightenment methodologies and with no other."

But that is not all. For our purposes, this is what he says that I find most important:

> Hostility to theistic religion need not follow from this worldview. I went through my period of hostility to theistic religion, went through my period of stick figure caricatures of believers, and I learned better. I learned that highly intelligent and accomplished people are devout believers—indeed, that they believe that they have personally experienced the presence of God. I learned that believers reason just as well as nonbelievers on average, and that most believers do not see the conflict between faith and reason that [many secularists posit]. I learned that religious faith is a powerful force for good in the lives of many believers. I learned that the great religious traditions often embody accumulated wisdom, whatever its sources and whatever the accumulated baggage of positions that seem to me mistaken.[58]

I do not share Laycock's story to promote agnosticism or to place religious people on a pedestal above others. I share it as an example of someone who holds firmly to his own beliefs in reason and evidence as the only sources of truth without feeling the need to denigrate or disrespect those who disagree with him. It is possible to be a secularist who does not look down on those who believe in spiritual truths. Note what Laycock is not doing. He is not abandoning his core beliefs. He is not yielding an inch of his conviction that the only way to find truth is through Enlightenment epistemological methods. And he would gladly discuss that conviction with anyone who would like to challenge him on it. What is important is that he is also treating those who think differently with respect.

Those who believe in spiritual truths can be equally guilty of the same offense, different in direction only. For them, there is more to this existence than what we can identify with our primary physical senses. The spiritual truths they have found are not just convenient or reassuring. In many instances, they see them as far more valuable and important than the knowledge they have acquired through scientific or observational methods of gaining knowledge. These spiritual truths include some of the great wisdom of the ages of many religions. Still others have found escape from life's most desperate situations by following spiritual paths, not secular ones. Consider the case of Al Smith, whom I wrote about in my book *Deep Conviction*. At age thirty-seven, his alcoholism had left him drunk in an alley and on death's door. He overcame that by returning to the spiritual roots of his Indigenous religious traditions. Once he turned to his Indigenous spirituality, for the rest of his life, he never touched another drop of alcohol.[59]

For those who believe in spiritual knowledge, those truths are often at the core of who they are as individuals. As Laycock noted, many of them do not see a tension between faith and reason. They use reason, evidence, logic, and the scientific method in their professional and even personal lives to acquire knowledge, but they also believe that knowledge and wisdom can come from spiritual sources.

While they can be on the receiving end of those who view them as "religious nuts," they can also struggle to respect the views of people who do not share their spiritual understandings of the world. This is the same mistake made by pure secularists but committed in the opposite direction. For some, their spiritual truths are so obviously true that they cannot comprehend why anyone else would not believe them: those who don't must be evil, fools, or (at best) ignorant.

For those who believe in spiritual truth, two practices can be helpful. First, acknowledge that not everyone recognizes the same spiritual truths you hold so dear. In a world with as many diverse religions as ours, that should not come as a surprise. That does not make them your enemy or someone for you to persecute. They hold to their own spiritual (or secular) truths as strongly as you hold to yours. When you are able to think of someone in this light, you can realize that they are not the enemy and shouldn't be treated as such.

Of course, some believers will want to expose others to the same truths they hold dear. If they want to be successful in that, that leads to the second practice, which is showing respect. How we expose people to our spiritual truths matters tremendously. I will have more to say on that in Habit Four, but for now, suffice it to say that we need not reject or condemn reason or science if we also believe in religion. Francis Collins is a powerful example because he is a man of science who does not reject faith. But it is equally valuable to be someone of deep faith who does not reject science and rational inquiry. Collins fits into that camp, obviously, as does the carbon sequestration expert Reid Grigg, whom I mentioned earlier, and millions of others like them; but consider also the late great scientist Henry Eyring.

He earned degrees in mining engineering and metallurgy from the University of Arizona, then a doctorate in chemistry from the University of California at Berkeley in 1927. He held academic appointments at Princeton University and the University of Utah. He was a prolific researcher and won some of the most prestigious prizes the scientific world has to offer, including the Wolf Prize in Chemistry (1980), the Priestley Medal (1975), the Elliott Cresson Medal (1969), the Irving Langmuir Award (1968), the National Medal of Science (1966), the Peter Debye Award (1964), the William H. Nichols Medal (1951), and the Newcomb Cleveland Prize (1932). He also developed something known as the absolute reaction rate theory or transition state theory of chemical reactions, one of the most important developments in chemistry in the twentieth century.[60]

Eyring was also a man of deep faith. He was a devout member of

The Church of Jesus Christ of Latter-day Saints. One of his great fears was that people of faith would be hostile to other forms of acquiring knowledge, including science. To him, there was no tension between faith and reason, and he expressed concerns that too many people of faith discard all scientific truths and methods merely because there sometimes appears to be conflicts with their deeply held beliefs. That, he lamented, was like throwing the baby out with the bath water.[61]

Someone who believes in certain spiritual truths but who also can accept other methods for acquiring knowledge can become a powerful ambassador to the reason-only community. Professor Laycock explains this well. In his article where he admitted his conversion to seeing people of faith in a better light, he went on to explain why:

> The preceding [is] a statement of tolerance and re-spect for beliefs that I cannot begin to share. . . . The source of my respect for religion was frequent contact with sophisticated believers.[62]

In other words, Professor Laycock spent time with believers who helped him see them in a better light. Those who believe in spiritual sources of truth should strive to be that type of believer. Our best method of persuading others is to present the truths we hold dear in the most wonderful light possible.

For both secularists and spiritualists, condemning people, calling them names, cursing them, accusing them of behavior they have not done, trying to take away their civil rights, using the law to force your beliefs upon them, denigrating their own methods of acquiring knowl-edge—history has shown repeatedly that such techniques never work in persuading people. Rather, we want to persuade people through the power of our doctrines, the spirit people feel when they hear us teach or visit our places of worship or talk with us about our experiences. Perhaps most important is what we express through our examples. When we treat others with compassion and kindness, they will want to know more about what makes us who we are. Then we can talk with them in positive ways.

HABIT TWO: WHAT WE'VE LEARNED ABOUT SEEKING REAL LEARNING

In this chapter, we learned that peacemakers engage in the habit of real learning. This means:

THEY UNDERSTAND WE GENERATE KNOWLEDGE TOGETHER.
They know we create new knowledge through constructive dialogue, so they value that skill.

THEY KNOW WHAT OBSTACLES WE FACE.
They recognize that foreign actors and technology companies are constantly trying to manipulate us using the dopamine reward system in our brains.

THEY BREAK FREE FROM TECHNOLOGICAL MANIPULATION.
They free themselves from their devices, apps, and social media and seek dopamine from more natural sources.

THEY ARE CAUTIOUS WITH CATCHPHRASES AND SLOGANS.
When they hear a slogan or catchphrase, they seek to understand what it means to the person with whom they are speaking, rather than reacting to its potential meanings.

THEY ARE INTENTIONAL ABOUT HOW THEY GET THEIR NEWS.
They seek news not as fed to them from social media and are deliberate in diversifying their sources.

THEY ACQUIRE KNOWLEDGE IN REAL TIME.
They take advantage of their ability to use smartphones to acquire easy, already-generated knowledge in real time.

THEY ARE SLOW TO COME TO CONCLUSIONS.

THEY RESPECT SPIRITUAL LEARNING.
They respect that some people value learning through faith and religion, and many practice that themselves. Those who do believe in the spiritual and those who do not, recognize they need not be hostile to one another.

HABIT THREE
ASSUME THE BEST ABOUT PEOPLE

Some time ago, I received an unusual email. It was from two high-level federal judges serving on a court just below the United States Supreme Court. One had been appointed by President Barak Obama, the other by President Donald Trump. They informed me that once a month, they and a group of other justices and judges met together in their private capacities for a prayer breakfast. This was not a public event, not a spectacle where politicians and media showed up to try to garner favor with the voting public.

It was private. Most people never learn of it. The judges—of different faiths and very different political and judicial ideologies—met together throughout the year to enjoy breakfast and pray with one another, usually about people in their lives who were suffering. They were wondering if I would be willing to come and talk with them about one of my books.

I agreed. I traveled to Washington, DC, and met them in the courthouse early one morning. Outside, several news outlets were setting up cameras for a story about a case some of these jurists would hear later in the morning.

As soon as I entered the building, one of the judicial assistants lead me through security, down a narrow hall, and into a small conference room, where all the judges eventually joined. To see them all sitting together, people who are often portrayed as being at one another's throats, was touching to me. Despite their very real differences, they recognized the good in one another and the parts of their identities they had in common, and they shared those over a bite to eat. Like everyone else in our world, they worried over their loved ones, they expressed concern over people they personally knew who were suffering, and they shared empathy with each other over their very human struggles.

I wish everyone could see people like this in that setting.

Their example provides a valuable lesson. This may come as a shock, but the world does not look like this:

- Those who agree with you
- Fascists or despotic communists
- Fools

Yet far too many of us have come to see reality this way. The social media silos mentioned earlier have contributed to that attitude. We are convinced that if someone does not come to the same conclusion as we have about a particular issue, then the only explanation must be that they have nefarious motivations or are ignorant. We are so self-assured of our own righteousness and vast knowledge on a particular topic that we have decided anyone who disagrees must be either a bigot, a buffoon, or worse. If we pause to get out of our own heads for just a moment, we will realize that such a view of the world can't possibly be true.

The people around us with whom we would like to have productive conversations are, we know, often good people. They are family members, coworkers, longtime friends. We know they strive to do right for their children and parents and siblings. We know they try to do a good job for their employers. But for some reason, on the most divisive topics, they transform in our minds to some sort of sinister actor we cannot trust. That type of thought distortion is nonsensical, but we all are guilty of it from time to time.

To be clear, I am not naive. The world does have racists, bigots, despotic communists, fascists, criminals, power-hungry tyrants, and any other manner of evil actors; and fools do abound. But remember who we're talking about in this book: our family members, coworkers, and close associates—the type of people with whom we can have fruitful dialogues. The chances that any or all of them fall into one of those categories is slim, unless you are hanging around with a very different crowd than I am. The very fact that you are reading this book suggests to me that is highly unlikely.

That brings me to an important habit of peacemakers. They assume the best about people and their intentions. If they disagree with someone, they squelch the urge to assume the person has bad motives. They recognize it is possible that the person in question has less information than they do. All of us can do the same. With our newfound intellectual humility, we now know that it is just as likely that the person in question has more or different information. They may also be aware of concerns that never crossed our mind given our limited perspective. If our goal is to be a peacemaker who can find solutions to the problems that trouble us most, then our purpose should be to learn and understand where other people are coming from and why. At worst, we'll discover arguments or information that challenge our views and that we need to take into consideration. At best, we'll come to understand the world better and will be even more equipped to tackle its problems.

ASK QUESTIONS

If you assume the best about your interlocutors, your goal in any conversation with them will shift. Instead of trying to persuade them of their bigotry or foolishness, you will want to increase understanding for everyone involved. Asking sincere questions helps others better understand their own positions and it helps you better understand others' motivations. What you will usually find is (1) people are often not as firm as they think they are in their own views; and (2) they generally hold good motivations. One of the fruits of this will be to better understand where you disagree. Sometimes you will find you don't disagree at all.

Helping Others Understand Their Own Views

In our earlier example of Uncle James and his niece, Gabby, it might be tempting to assume that James either wants a world where women get paid less for the same work, he just doesn't care about living in such a world, or he's so ignorant to reality that he needs proper education. Too often, even if we don't explicitly state it, those are the assumptions we're making about someone who responds as James did when Gabby raised the wage gap. So, after Gabby and James turn to you and you reframe the conversation, as we discussed earlier, your next move might be to see where James and Gabby are coming from. You might turn to James and say:

> Just to make sure we're all on the same page here. James, is it fair to say you would want to fix this problem if there was evidence it actually existed?

It's entirely possible, even likely, James will come back hot:

> Well, yeah, but it doesn't exist. It's all just made up.

Gabby, of course, at that point, will want to start arguing, but you can keep things calm. This is not the point to argue. You've established something important. James does care about the issue if it exists. His problem is that, for reasons you still don't understand, he thinks the issue of the gender pay gap is fiction, not a real problem that requires a real solution.

To know for sure, you need to ask additional questions, so you might say something like:

> So I have to admit I don't know a lot about this. Gabby, you say there is a gender pay gap. James, you say there isn't. What sources do you guys have? It seems we all would want to fix the problem if it exists, so we just need to understand it better.

Note what you've done. You have not attacked anyone. You have not accused either James or Gabby of acting in bad faith. You also did not ask a rhetorical question—that is, a question masquerading as a statement to make a point. You have asked a reasonable, sincere question that will hopefully keep both of them on their toes. Sincerity is key. This is not feigned humility on your part, or an attempt to back your way into your mic-drop moment where you put them both in their place. You are trying to get information. Suddenly, they must look inward. Rather than focusing on proving the other person wrong, they must now look to their own knowledge and question or support how sound it really is.

This is another side benefit of asking questions. Yes, it leads you closer to the truth, but it also forces those with whom you're talking to check their own assumptions. As legal scholar Ward Farnsworth explained in his book *The Socratic Method: A Practitioner's Handbook*, "A question puts pressure on whoever receives it. . . . That's good. Stating an opinion is roughly the opposite. It releases pressure. . . . Every time you ask and answer good questions, your understanding gets a bit deeper. You better understand the other side and the weaknesses on your side. You see more complexity."[1]

Research bears out Farnsworth's claims. Cognitive scientists Steven Sloman and Philip Fernbach conducted studies in which they asked participants to think of a policy they wanted to implement. They then asked participants to try to explain "what the direct consequences of that policy would be and what the consequences of those consequences would be in turn." Forcing people to do this had the effect of calming extremism because it helped participants gain a sense of intellectual humility—forcing people to provide "a causal explanation made the extremists more uncertain about their positions, and this uncertainty changed their behavior. Realizing the limits of their understanding made them less likely to want to take action to push their position forward."[2]

Note, however, that the softening effect occurred only when people were asked to think through the natural steps of what their preferred policies would cause. Asking them to explain their reasoning for coming to a certain position did not cause them to back away from extreme positions. It only hardened them. So you must be mindful of the questions you ask. The right ones can lead people to back away from extreme positions.

Learning Others' Motivations

Asking sincere, nonrhetorical questions of those with whom you are talking about the world's important topics is one of the best ways to understand who they are and what makes them tick, to realize they probably are not monsters just because they disagree with you, to understand precisely where you do disagree, and, if you're lucky, to realize you may not disagree at all. This matters, because in too many of our conflicts, our arguments have little to do with what we truly care about. Uncle James and Gabby may be arguing over the gender pay gap, but it's quite possible they don't really disagree about anything and their underlying motivations are the same: if it exists, they would both like to fix it. Understanding others' deeper motivations can help us all speak to each other in a way that will have real meaning.

This is one of the important insights developed in Jonathan Haidt's groundbreaking book *The Righteous Mind: Why Good People Are Divided by Politics and Religion*, its underlying research, and the studies he and others in his field have done since its publication.[3] What they have learned about humans is that we tend to reach conclusions based on our gut reactions to any given set of facts, then reason backward to justify those conclusions. *Why* we reach those conclusions is important. It has to do with our underlying moral psychologies—what Haidt calls moral foundations. Using empirical research, he and others initially identified five different moral foundations people tend to have naturally. In other words, these are psychological foundations we have as human beings whether we like it or not. Over time, they did some reconfiguring to include a sixth foundation. Each is explained in detail at a website Haidt and others developed to both teach others and gather continuing research:

>Care: This foundation is related to our long evolution as mammals with attachment systems and an ability to feel (and dislike) the pain of others. It underlies the virtues of kindness, gentleness, and nurturance. . . .

>Loyalty: This foundation is related to our long history as tribal creatures able to form shifting coalitions. It is active anytime people feel that it's "one for all and all for one." It underlies the virtues of patriotism and self-sacrifice for the group.

>Authority: This foundation was shaped by our long primate history of hierarchical social interactions. It underlies virtues of leadership and followership, including deference to prestigious authority figures and respect for traditions.

>Purity: This foundation was shaped by the psychology of disgust and contamination. It underlies notions of striving to live in an elevated, less carnal, more noble, and more "natural" way (often present in religious narratives). This foundation underlies the widespread idea that the body is a temple that can be desecrated by immoral activities and contaminants (an idea not unique to religious traditions). It underlies the virtues of self-discipline, self-improvement, naturalness, and spirituality. . . .

>Equality: [This foundation involves] "intuitions about equal treatment and equal outcome for individuals."

>Proportionality: [This foundation involves] "intuitions about individuals getting rewarded in proportion to their merit or contribution."[4]

According to Haidt's research, people who tend to align with the political left more frequently rely on the equality and care psychologies, while people who tend to align with the political right manifest all of the psychologies.[5] And those underlying psychologies dictate their immediate reactions to any situation they see.

Note that none of these underlying moral psychologies are inherently bad. The lesson you can take from this work is that when people disagree about important topics in our society, it is often not because they are "good" or "bad" or "foolish." It's because they have a different psychological reaction to information presented to them. What is fascinating is that those different psychological reactions may be what make our society work. Those on the left—primarily driven by care and equality—often push for changes and improvements that need to happen. Those on the right—motivated by all six categories—often ensure that while we're making changes, we are not doing so too hastily, in a way that could result in outcomes even worse than where we are now.[6]

I see this dynamic playing out constantly in my own field of research and will use it as an example. Scholars are all over the map regarding how they feel about religion law and free speech. For years, I watched them argue and debate one another about what the law should be. What I noticed was that very few ever changed their minds about anything. It happens, but it is rare. No matter what arguments were made, no matter what evidence was presented, people had dug in regarding what the law should be and how certain cases should be decided.

This, of course, led me to wonder why. My observations were consistent with Haidt's work, at least to the degree that it seemed surface-level arguments were not driving people's positions. Something deeper motivated them. Consider the following diagram related to legal disputes concerning religious freedom law. We could create a similar diagram for any issue on which people hold strong beliefs, from taxes to abortion to immigration to gay marriage to how to address race in schools:

SOURCE OF VIEWS ON RELIGIOUS FREEDOM

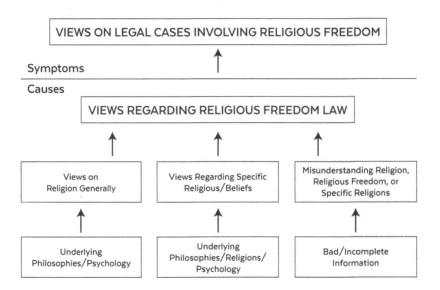

Figure 1. Sources of Views on Religious Freedom

The level at which most scholars and other thought leaders debate the law occurs above the symptoms-causes line. That's certainly where most media personalities spend their time. They argue over how individual cases should have come out. They criticize or support the rationale judges or Supreme Court justices used to reach their decisions. They complain about or cheer the outcomes of cases.

Certainly some scholars and pundits engage in deep theoretical and philosophical discussions,[7] but in the everyday course of things, most disputes are happening above the symptoms-causes line. What is interesting is that we can predict the positions many people will take and how those conversations above the line will play out long before they ever occur. The reason we can do this is because of everything below the symptoms-causes line—aka the topics and ideas rarely discussed on cable news programs and in social media. A person's view regarding how a particular case should be decided has less to do with the specifics of the case and more to do with their underlying moral psychologies or philosophies. They will have strong feelings regarding what religious liberty law should be. That, in turn, is informed by many factors: their views on religion generally; their views on specific religions or specific religious beliefs; their philosophies about the world and how the law should operate; their underlying moral psychology; or their misunderstandings regarding religion generally, specific religions, or religious freedom law and how it works.

When I speak around the world, I often do an experiment—more accurately, a trick—with my audiences, where I provide them a list of religious freedom cases percolating around the United States. It changes each year, but it usually looks something like this:

- Indigenous nation wants to stop mining on one of its sacred sites
- High school drama teacher wants to make girl attend drama practice on Sundays against her religion
- Seventh-Day Adventist can't work on Sabbath day
- Coach wants to pray after football games
- A florist, citing devout religious beliefs, can't service a same-sex wedding
- School principal won't let students form a religious group at school
- Amish ask not to use technology against their religion
- Hindu not allowed to protest for animal rights in park
- Predominantly Black church has property taken by government
- Prisoner on death row asks to have minister pray at moment of execution
- School posts "In God We Trust" signs on campus
- Church offers sanctuary to immigrants in country illegally

I ask the audience to decide how they would rule if they had to determine the outcome of the cases. After I give them a moment to scan and think about the list, I tell them that if they have already decided how courts should rule on these cases without knowing any facts other than what I provided on the list, they are probably committing a grave error. Then I say, "At least half of you right now are thinking: 'Darn, he got me.'"

The audience always chuckles because they know I did fool them. I led them into a common trap. As Haidt and similar researchers discovered, people tend to make decisions based on their gut reactions to whatever is presented to them. This is because their underlying philosophies and moral psychology, not a dispassionate analysis of facts, tend to be driving them. So, an atheist who believes deep down that religion is harmful will almost always say that a coach should not be able to pray after football games, without knowing a thing about when or under what circumstances the coach may want to do it. A person who has strong feelings about the importance of maintaining stability in our country and preserving order will likely react strongly against a church who claims a religious freedom right to offer sanctuary to immigrants in the country illegally—again, without knowing any other facts. And, generally, once people reach those conclusions, they are highly unlikely to change their minds.

I share all of this to make the point that when we are engaged in conversation with someone regarding a difficult topic, those conversations are often centered on issues well above the symptoms-causes line. The reasons such discussions are often fruitless and filled with contention is because neither we nor our interlocutor know what is truly motivating the other's position. In some instances, we may not even know what is driving our own position.

Two people who have spent their days arguing about how the law should apply to a church allowing immigrants to stay in its properties can volley endless arguments; but in reality, they care very little about those arguments. They care about something deeper that is never brought into the discussion. They are like people trying to mail letters but always sending them to the wrong address. The messages are arriving somewhere, but never where it matters.

Asking questions of the people in your life helps you to better understand their concerns. As you ask questions, keep Figure 1 in the back of your mind. Allow it to direct the types of questions you ask. Your goal should be to continue to dig until you understand the true, bedrock concerns of the person—their underlying moral and psychological foundations. Are they worried about unfairness in our society? Are they worried about people's suffering? Are they concerned about preserving our foundational institutions for stability? Do they have incomplete or bad information? Once you know what truly motivates them, you will have come that much closer to having meaningful, problem-solving dialogue because you may be able to come together to solve a problem in a way that satisfies both of your underlying moral concerns.

You can do this no matter who the other person in the conversation is. We need not reserve questions for those who have some expertise or maturity beyond our own. Consistent with the intellectual humility we are hopefully developing, asking questions of someone, anyone, may yield important insights we have never considered. In fact, it may help if the person with whom we are speaking is *not* an expert.

We are trying to have productive conversations that can help solve the world's very real problems. If we limit ourselves to asking questions only of those people we deem worthy, we will be depriving ourselves of unique and potentially helpful perspectives that can refine our thinking and open our minds to solutions we had never considered. We do need to hear from people who have studied things deeply, and we do need to engage in real learning, but we should not underestimate the value of different perspectives from a variety of sources. It may well be that a teenager provides the answer that opens our minds to a whole new way of thinking.

Finally, a word of warning on questions. Sometimes, forcing people to explain their positions too much will only frustrate them. Consider Sloman and Fernbach's findings again: "Exposing people's illusions can upset them. We have found that asking someone to explain a policy that the person doesn't really understand does not improve our relationship with that person. Frequently, they no longer want to discuss the issue (and indeed, often they no longer want to talk to us)."[8]

In all your inquiries, it's important to remember *why* you're asking questions. Remember: you are not trying to prove a point. Sloman and Fernbach engaged in their research to try to show people that they really did not understand a particular policy for which they were advocating. That was their goal. It is not yours. You are not trying to show people they are fools. You are not trying to prove a point. You are trying to understand them better so that the two of you can seek ideas and solutions that will speak to both of you.

Along the way, you will find that most people in your life are genuinely good. They care about the same things you care about. They are driven by legitimate concerns that deserve to be taken seriously: equality, rewarding people proportionally to their effort and merit, caring for others, being loyal to people and good causes, liberty, and preserving what is positive in ourselves and society. Where your disagreements often lie is not in the underlying concerns, but in whether the solutions offered will truly address them.

ACTIVE LISTENING

All the questions in the world will do you no good if you are not listening to the answers. Peacemakers ask genuine questions, and they listen for complete answers. They do not listen with the intent of poking holes in the response. They do not listen for an opening where they can make their counterpoint. They do not ignore someone once they have asked them a question. They listen to learn.

If you're unsure of how to do this, a practical method is to ask questions (and listen to the answers) until a question is asked of you. You may have points you want to make. You may have opinions you want to share. Hopefully, as you're listening, those points and opinions are growing more sophisticated. Eventually, as you ask more questions, the person with whom you're speaking will realize they haven't asked you anything. When they finally do, you now have your window to share your thinking.

WHAT ABOUT WHEN PEOPLE
ASSUME THE WORST ABOUT YOU?

If life were as clean as the pages of this book, we wouldn't need the book in the first place. But life is messy and rarely cooperative. Nowhere is that more evident than when people assume you are something you are not. And let's face it: that happens all the time.

At least two practices can help you overcome this challenge. First, don't always assume that other people are assuming the worst about you. Read that sentence again if you need to.

Some years ago, a very senior and successful attorney named Carol told me a story: When she was younger, she had joined the board of a local nonprofit, hoping to get involved in some community service. She was a partner at a major law firm with a healthy book of business, but when she arrived at the first board lunch, she noticed she was the only woman at the table. This made her insecure, and she assumed that the men would discount what she had to say simply because she was a woman.

Each month, as she attended the board meetings, she felt this. She assumed they would not listen to her and would not care about her perspective, so she often ate her lunch quietly, not contributing much to the conversation. After nearly a year, a thought slipped into her brain one day while she was walking from her office to the lunch board meeting. What if this is all in my head? What if they actually don't care that I'm a woman? So she tried an experiment. She decided she would go into the lunch and act as if all the other board members were eager to hear her perspective. She wanted to see if that changed how she perceived their behavior.

It did.

What she found was that they really did want to hear what she had to say. She spoke up and shared her thoughts, they listened intently and responded positively, and she realized she had been projecting onto them her own insecurities the entire time. "From that day on," Carol told me, "those board meetings were some of the most fantastic meetings I ever attended, and the other board members became some of my closest professional friends."

The lesson she learned was that her assumption that those men were assuming the worst about her was wrong. What Carol was engaged in was a form of "confirmation bias." In the 1960s, a psychologist in England named Peter Wason coined that now familiar term. In a series of tests, he found that people often ignore information that can potentially refute their beliefs.[9] Later researchers have confirmed this very human tendency. The bottom line is that we tend to favor, hunt for, remember, and interpret information in a way that confirms and supports the beliefs we already have.

In Carol's case, she believed the men on the nonprofit board were biased against women, and she interpreted all their body language and comments in a way that confirmed that belief. Only when she consciously became aware that she may have been engaging in that practice did she start to see things differently. She was able to see and hear the exact same body and verbal language but she intentionally gave it a different meaning. It turns out that was the right way to think.

You can take an important lesson from all of this. We all have insecurities, and we are all subject to confirmation bias. We often project onto other people what we think about them, instead of discovering what they actually think. When we're dealing with someone who we think is assuming the worst about us, our first step should be to ensure we aren't just heaping upon them our own insecurities. We can do what Carol did and try to reinterpret the situation. It's possible the person may be a bad actor with the worst intentions, but don't start there. If you do, you will never be able to have a constructive conversation.

Of course, sometimes people do assume bad things about us. What then? That brings us to the second practice: our goal must be to assuage their fears. We will explore this with more depth in the next chapter, but consider a few tips here for dealing with someone who clearly has the wrong impression about you.

Do your best to find and emphasize the common ground you enjoy with people. It may well be that the first step to productive dialogue about hard topics is to avoid discussing hard topics and instead focus on all the other commonalities you have with people. Do you both have children? Do you both enjoy pickleball? Do you both enjoy the NBA? Do you both hate or love the Lakers? Do you both find happy hour at work an annoying obligation? Poke around about all the daily activities that have to do with living, and you and your interlocutor may just find that you're each dealing with a normal, rational human being, not a monster.

Jonathan Rauch makes an interesting point in this regard. He regularly publishes on a variety of topics, including politics, culture, LGBTQ+ rights, and public policy. I am certain he has much about which he could disagree with people. Yet in his book *The Constitution of Knowledge*, he writes, "In my own career, I have spent more time agreeing with other people than disagreeing with them. When I do criticize someone, it is often after first stipulating the grounds on which we agree."[10]

Your common ground need not be limited to trivial topics either. More likely than not, there are more weighty public policy topics on which you agree than you realize. Too often, too many people allow their few points of disagreement to dominate their relationships, but if you pause long enough to think about your doubters, you will realize that you share much in common. Here's a simple example: despite all of our disagreements over Donald Trump, Joe Biden, Barak Obama, or George W. Bush as presidents, we can probably all agree that it is a good thing none of them started a nuclear war with China. You're welcome—you have something in common with everyone (or at least almost everyone—I'm sure there is someone, somewhere who disagrees).

But let's consider a more serious example. A new colleague recently joined the faculty of the law school where I teach. In the first two minutes of our first conversation, she made comments that told me she was making assumptions about me that were just wrong. I didn't see an obvious way to correct her directly, but I waited for an opening.

During the conversation, as we danced around other topics, she mentioned her frustration that too many students refuse to come and talk with professors with whom they think they disagree. I agree with her. That phenomenon has been one of the great frustrations of my academic career. We talked about it at length, exploring possible solutions and sharing ideas that have worked for us. By the end of the conversation, we agreed to have lunch and talk further. When we did, we were finally able to delve into other topics, such as constitutional interpretation, but this time she was no longer assuming the worst about me. She had come to see me as a reasonable person who shares many of her concerns about the world, even if we may disagree on some of the solutions.

Finally, perhaps one of the best ways to help assuage the fears of those who think we are bad actors is to do whatever we can to lift them up and help them with their own hopes and dreams. As a law professor, I have taken on the task of training the next generation of lawyers, among other things. That involves giving them practical skills they can use on the job, but, perhaps more importantly, it involves helping them think about the law in a new way. I want them to understand more than just what the law is on a given topic, but *why* it is that way. To do that, I have to engage in lengthy discussions with students about the theoretical and philosophical foundations for various aspects of First Amendment jurisprudence.

One of the early challenges I faced when I joined my faculty was that a subset of students decided they didn't want to take my class or get to know me because they assumed they disagreed with me on many issues. They also assumed that I would not help any students with whom I differed. Their second assumption was categorically wrong. Their first may or may not have been correct, but the only way any of us would know was if they got to know me.

I knew I needed to break the ice. My first move was to reach out to the student organizations most likely to include those who felt this way. I offered to help them put on events and invited them to get involved with the center I direct so I could help them get jobs after law school. I also tried, whenever they asked, to assist them with their various projects and to speak at any events they asked. Over time, word has spread that I am someone who wants to help those around me thrive, whether I agree with them on every issue or not. I still have work to do in that regard, but we have made important progress.

You may disagree with people in your life on important issues, but you can treat them with kindness despite your differences and without sacrificing your core principles. My book *The Immortals* tells the true story of five American servicemen in World War II who sacrificed themselves to save hundreds of others after a Nazi U-boat torpedoed their ship off the coast of Greenland. They were each of a different religion or race and could have used those differences to justify being harsh to those around them. Instead, they did the opposite. They selflessly sacrificed to save others, despite very important and real differences.

I have often wondered why that story resonated with me so much, and why it has resonated with so many others over the years. It captures the imagination of everyone who hears it. The five men have received awards. Congress has designated days in their honor. Foundations have been built and named after them. Yet even as I wrote the book and did all the research on it, I struggled to articulate why the story meant so much to me. After it was published, in dozens of radio, podcast, and television interviews, I still labored to provide a coherent explanation.

Then one day, it dawned on me. The story is powerful because it reflects a paradox that many of us know is true but that we too often lose sight of: we find ourselves when we lose ourselves in the service of others. It is not necessarily intuitive that we will find contentment and happiness by losing ourselves in acts of kindness for others, yet that is what happens. Again and again.

The story of the men in *The Immortals* is powerful because each lost himself in the service of others but never once sacrificed who he was in his core. They did not renounce their religions or races. They did not yield on the essential beliefs by which they differed from one another. They learned to treat each other and the men they served with respect despite their differences.

If you would like to engage in constructive conversations with the people in your life, lose yourself in serving them and lifting them up. In doing so, you don't need to give up those beliefs you hold so dear. You will find yourself. You will find that all boats tend to rise together. As they do, you will find others are far more willing to talk with you about hard subjects.

REFRAMING PEOPLE'S COMMENTS IN THE BEST LIGHT

It is one thing to assume the best about people in a vacuum or before they do anything obnoxious, but what about when they launch a subtle or explicit attack at you? One of the hazards of my career is that this happens to me all the time. Usually, the volley occurs in the form of a hostile question or statement from someone in an audience I am addressing.

In addition to asking questions and finding common ground, one of the best habits skilled peacemakers use is one we have already explored: reframing. In this situation, however, peacemakers are not thinking about the end goal of the entire conversation but are instead focusing on reframing the attack against them.

When attacks come, it is easy for us to get defensive and to immediately respond in kind. Or we might feel the need to repel the attack on its own terms. Rather than take offense, peacemakers look behind that hostility to determine what is motivating it. They take that motivation seriously. Sometimes, they already know what it is. If they do not, they engage in asking nonrhetorical questions like we discussed above (For example: "May I ask a follow-up question before I answer? Are you worried that if churches grant immigrants sanctuary it might lead to chaos, or do you have a different concern?"). Once they have determined the concerns of the person pushing the attack, they then focus on responding to those concerns rather than to the attack itself. To do so, they reframe the person's statement or question to capture their concerns. They do so without sarcasm or snark. And, if able, they reframe it in the absolute best light possible. That reframing is then what they respond to. We will discuss in Habit Five the importance of finding the best arguments against your position and how to do that. Assume for now that we know the best argument, and we know we're dealing with someone who has not stated it. Oftentimes, they may not even know what that argument is. Instead, they are speaking from their gut, allowing their emotions to drive the conversation.

Peacemakers bring the conversation back to the highest level of dialogue, while not dismissing or disrespecting their interlocutors.

To see this principle in practice, consider the following story.

Shortly on the heels of the COVID-19 pandemic, after the world had reopened in-person meetings, I was scheduled to speak to a large audience about the fundamentals of religious freedom law. Like most scholars, my views in my field are nuanced and complex, and I don't fall cleanly into any ideological camp. The goal of this address was to discuss just the basics of the law in the United States, where it has been, and where it is going, without injecting any of my own opinion into it.

After I finished and opened the session up for question and answer, a middle-aged woman in the front row raised her hand.

I smiled and nodded for her to go ahead.

"I don't think the law should be used to justify being able to do whatever you want, like all these churches that claimed they didn't have to follow COVID protocols but everyone else did. That's all religious freedom is—it's just an excuse by people who hate science to justify breaking the law." She crossed her arms as if the conversation was over.

What she was expressing was something many feel and fear, and that is not surprising. With the limited information they have, the media often report only on religious liberty cases if those cases intersect with highly controversial issues. And the few personalities in the media who do have some in-depth knowledge of religion law usually have highly controversial takes.

It would have been easy for me to express frustration, or even anger. It was as if she had not listened to a thing I had said in the preceding thirty minutes. I had tried to explain all the situations in which religious liberty law applies, and almost none of them had anything to do with the pandemic. In fact, almost all of them showed that religious liberty law protects all of us, regardless of our beliefs or nonbeliefs, and it doesn't allow people to do whatever they want regardless of other laws. I think I could have felt justified in snapping at her, perhaps by saying, "You didn't listen to a thing I just said."

But it was incumbent upon me to think through what was motivating her, and to take those concerns in their most serious form. I had heard them before. I knew the arguments. I also knew I was dealing with someone who had limited knowledge on this important topic but who felt very passionately about it.

"So you've raised an important issue in the world of religious liberty law," I said. "How should the law treat religious institutions when governments are trying to stop the spread of a virus?"

My first move was to acknowledge her comment and her concerns. Notice I did not respond to her attack directly but instead focused only on what worried her. When she nodded, telling me I had hit the nail on the head, I continued, "Most of the cases involving churches were not that controversial. Many involved instances where government said movie theaters could be open at 50 percent capacity but not churches, and as soon as the churches complained, the government officials realized their mistake and allowed churches and theaters to be open to the same degree. But you're worried about those instances where churches claimed the right to be open at full capacity without masks regardless of how the law treated anyone else."

She nodded again.

At that point, I was able to address her real concern. "Those situations were relatively rare," I said, "but a few of those cases came up and they are important because they represent a situation that needs addressing. The churches were claiming that the First Amendment allowed them total license to ignore government limitations, and they lost in pretty much every case. Religious liberty law doesn't extend that far, and the governments could show they needed to place some restrictions on gatherings."

Her accusation—that religious liberty law does nothing but let people who hate science ignore the law—was not supported by facts or logic. I would have been justified in addressing her tone with an equally aggressive one, but behind her not-so-well-formulated declaration lurked a legitimate concern.

So I reframed her comment in its best form, then addressed that. It led to a productive exchange, and when the meeting was over, she came up and we talked even more. We ended by exchanging cards and with a feeling of mutual respect. We can all do the same.

KNOW WHEN CIVIL DISCOURSE IS NOT POSSIBLE

In all this talk about assuming the best about people, I do not wish to appear Pollyannaish. There are some people for whom positive dialogue is not possible. Someone better trained in psychology than I could probably write an entire book about them. I am not a psychologist, so I write about the two groups that I think you are most likely to encounter: (1) those who are incapable of constructive conversations; and (2) those who are capable but who refuse to engage in constructive dialogue. The first is the one you're most likely to come across in your daily life. The second is the bigger threat to productive discourse because they embrace an ideology that is fundamentally opposed to it, at least as to certain topics.

Those Incapable of Productive Discourse

Let's talk about those who are incapable first. To some degree, we all belong in this category some of the time. Some people have brains that make rational dialogue all but impossible, even if part of them might want to engage in it. These include people dealing with substance abuse, past trauma, or low-level executive functioning, among other traits.

If you have someone in your life who is suffering from substance abuse, it is important to recognize that and to realize that the likelihood of productive conversation is low. There are some individuals, of course, who are even better at pontificating about important topics when under the influence. If you know someone like that, feel free to move forward. But many who suffer from addiction often struggle to engage in any real dialogue about hard topics. Their behavior can be erratic. They can lash out. They will often accuse you of things you haven't done. In those situations, it is best not to try to discuss hard topics. In most instances, it will lead only to heartache.

Similarly, some people have had certain experiences in their past that make conversations difficult, at least within those certain topics. They may have been abused. Perhaps they have suffered a particular real trauma related to the issue that has come up in conversation. They may have other mental issues that make it impossible for them to discuss certain topics while regulating their emotions. You need to be mindful of these folks as well. If you have tried many of the habits in this book with someone like that in your own life and have found again and again that they are just incapable of productive discussion, you may be better off leaving the hard topics for a different day. Focus instead on those areas of life where you can agree. Let them discuss the harder topics in a professional environment with a trained therapist.[11]

Finally, some people have various forms of executive functioning issues. In some instances, this can make them thrive off argument. They enjoy it, as do some who just enjoy the dopamine and adrenaline rush that comes from a fight or who have never lived without it in their lives. Their goal, even if they don't realize it, is not to find productive solutions to real problems. Their joy comes from the debate itself, no matter where it leads and no matter how much it may frustrate or anger the people with whom they are speaking. Each of us has likely met someone like this. If you enjoy debate and argument, then by all means, engage with that person. But if your hope is to talk about difficult topics in a positive, constructive way, recognize when you are dealing with someone like this and try to stay clear. It may frustrate them, because what they want is to engage in the fight. Oftentimes, they don't even see fighting as a negative. They may even walk away from some arguments feeling that the entire exchange was a positive experience that they want to do again.[12] Still, you should not feel it your obligation to feed the beast. If they like argument, there is literally an unlimited supply pretty much anywhere we look online. They need not get their fix from you. If your hope is to talk about deep topics in a positive way, you can politely decline to engage.

In other instances, some people don't necessarily thrive off argument, but they struggle to have the impulse control necessary for productive dialogue. They interrupt frequently. They do not pick up on social cues. They quickly slip into emotional outbursts. Their emotions take over any conversation in which they engage. If you have someone like this in your life, I again recommend that you politely decline to engage in conversations about topics that you know will lead to the above. Find your common ground, and frolic around there as much as you can.

Those Who Reject Civil Discourse on Principle

As for those who are capable, often quite capable, of productive discourse but who refuse to engage in it, they present an entirely different problem altogether. Consider the story of Coleman Hughes. He is a graduate of Columbia University. A Black man, he started college decidedly on the far left when it came to racial issues. At some point in his education, he started asking questions, dug deeper into various claims political groups were making, and has since moved into a position that is much more independent and nuanced.[13]

That shift has brought both criticism and praise, as you might imagine.[14] He wrote articles about his ideological shifts. They gained attention. Over time, he developed enough of a following that he started a widely listened-to podcast called *Conversations with Coleman.** In it, he

---

* I recognize many readers disagree with Hughes and his views on many topics, especially related to race. I considered not referencing his anecdote for precisely that reason. In the end, I opted not to go down that path. His story exemplifies the subject matter we are discussing in this section. If someone disagrees with Hughes, the proper response is not to remove him from my book or to refuse to talk with him. The proper response is to engage with his ideas directly. If he is wrong, then prove why he is wrong and why another view is right. Let him try to prove why he is right. Share your ideas with one another. Talk without personal attacks. Use the methods discussed in this book.

challenges ideas from the people with whom he once agreed. His demeanor is always calm and respectful, and whether you agree with him or not, he models well how to have constructive dialogue.

At the beginning of one of his episodes, he offered the following preface:

> Before I introduce my guest, I'd like to give a short preamble. I often get the critique that I don't get enough guests that disagree with me on my podcast, especially on the issues of race and racism, which is where my opinions have been the most controversial. The idea is that I'm creating a sort of echo chamber of people that mostly agree with me. Now I can see how you might think this if you don't see what goes on behind the scenes.
>
> Behind the scenes, I've invited countless of my critics onto the show, and the near unanimous response has just been a refusal to speak with me. . . . That is the main reason why you don't see more guests who disagree with me. It's not for lack of trying on my part.[15]

The question is: Why? Why do some people refuse to speak with or debate those with whom they disagree? Why will some who disagree with Hughes demand that I not even include a mention of him in this book? This subsection will try to explain that mystery.

Understanding people who adopt a philosophy of refusing discourse is crucial to understanding some of the arguments percolating in the broader culture. There was a time when I would have been disinclined to include any discussion of them in a book like this because the chances of your meeting them were slim to none, unless you were someone who walked the halls of academia, and, even then, only within certain departments. But in recent years, their theories have achieved something quite rare: they have broken free from the cloistered hallways of the university and begun to spread into the broader culture.[16]

This has happened largely through social media. Students and others have read about these theories and adopted the most simplistic forms of them as their own. Twenty years ago, like-minded students may have done the same; but back then, there were few outlets available for any broader discussion. Today, they can turn to TikTok, YouTube, Instagram, and any number of other social media outlets to repeat arguments that once existed only among academics, and then only as thought experiments. Because of that, the worldview needs addressing.

You may find yourself stating what feels obvious to you: that talking constructively about tough problems is a common good we should pursue. If what you hear in response is that civil discourse is bad and that we should not be pursuing it at all, you will know you are dealing with someone who refuses on ideological grounds to discuss certain hard topics with anyone who disagrees with them.** As with those who are incapable of constructive dialogue, you are best off walking away. Pushing the point, no matter your demeanor, methods, or rationale, will likely be fruitless.

I address the philosophy of refusing civil discourse here in the hopes that you can develop the tools to identify it when you see it. If you can, you will have a better sense of when a productive conversation is unlikely and therefore not worth the effort. You will also be able to avoid adopting for yourself an ideology whose foundational premises reject constructive discourse as a positive activity. These ideologies are all branches from the same trunk and share the idea that dialogue on certain topics can never be constructive. They are dangerous because their arguments are sophisticated and sound plausible at first blush. Only when we analyze them carefully do we realize how problematic they truly are.

Consistent with one of the habits I will provide later, I will do my

---

** I want to emphasize that many of the folks who subscribe to the philosophy we will explore here are not opposed to civil discourse on every topic. They are opposed to it on certain topics, which I will flesh out in this section.

best to present these philosophies in their best light. I want you to understand how their proponents frame them, because only then will you see why they are enticing to some people. For most of us, we have grown up in a world where it has become intuitive to appreciate the good and the importance of civil dialogue, even if many of us are less skilled at putting it into practice. Given how second nature that understanding has become, how is it that a sizeable swath of people now believe that it is inherently wrong, even evil?

For our purposes, the story begins in France, in the 1960s, with the rise of two philosophies now known as postmodernism and poststructuralism.[17] As you might imagine, both topics are complicated and controversial. They were obscure academic theories that were nearly impossible to understand for anyone who did not live and breathe them every day. And even then, they were still confusing, in part because those who created and advocated for them wanted them to be.

Although different in nuanced ways, the philosophies shared two core ideas: (1) the premise that the only truth is that there is no truth; and (2) the notion that any narrative whatsoever can be deconstructed and dismantled to show that it actually has no meaning at all.[18] Academics took the foundations of these theories and studied them, applying them in some contexts but not in others, critiquing them, analyzing them, distancing themselves from them, modifying them, and obfuscating them.

Over time, poststructuralists began dismantling literature, with the aim of showing that it was impossible to prove any definitive—or superior—reading of any text. For example, if someone were to strut into a classroom and declare they knew the definitive meaning of Shakespeare's *Romeo and Juliet*, a poststructuralist would dig into the text to present a dozen other possible meanings. They'd then tell you they could go on doing this forever. Their goal would not be to declare any one theory correct but to make you believe that there is no one true meaning to any text.

Eventually, scholars began applying this same technique in every area of life. All the world is a text, they posited. This was a crucial intellectual move.

One of the ideas they developed is critical to understanding why regular people, outside the halls of academia, have taken hold of what seems to be an esoteric exercise in rhetoric. That idea was that language is the key to everything. As that key, it enjoys tremendous power. It controls society. It controls how we think. It preserves or breaks down power—between the classes, races, people of different sexual orientations, sexes, genders, and many other groups in society.

Postmodernists suggested that because language can be interpreted in endless ways—just like the text from Shakespeare's *Romeo and Juliet*—it doesn't inherently mean anything. Instead, it means whatever the people in power want it to mean. In the 1970s, the French philosopher Michel Foucault coined the term *discourses* to describe language's ability to gatekeep power. According to Foucault, the discourses used in every system in society developed based on the power dynamics that exist within it.[19] In other words, those with the most power in any discursive situation prescribe the rules by which discourse may occur, as well as the criteria by which we should consider legitimate any knowledge or truth that comes from that discourse.[20]

The bottom line for us is that there is a subset of people today who believe these types of discourses are everywhere and that they are all about preserving power in various orders of society. These discourses, according to this view, are any systems that produce knowledge and meaning, and they usually involve language: texts, books, films, political dialogues, everyday conversation, the names and titles and pronouns we give to one another, the way we dress—the list is all encompassing and includes any way in which human beings communicate, even our clothing. Foucault's important insight is that all discourses are a product of the culture and historical period in which they arise. Because they have no true meaning, they must be based on something else. For Foucault and those who came after him, that something else was power.

To better understand how some modern proponents of this idea think, let's go back in time for a couple of examples. In Europe, before the Reformation and the birth of Protestantism, much of the power on the continent lay in the Catholic Church.[21] Many conversations of the day would have been framed through that lens. The Church enjoyed not just ecclesiastical power over its members, but civil secular power over everyone. Heresy against the Church, for example, was considered an offense on the same level as homicide or rebellion. In that environment, you can imagine that people were careful how they spoke, and they certainly would never have wanted to convey messages that suggested they were heretical. Indeed, these power dynamics likely prevented conversations about some topics from happening at all. The conditions of the times dictated the discourse of the day.

Or consider another example. This one illustrates how power dynamics dictate not just *what* is being discussed but the *way* it is discussed. During the Middle Ages, after the fall of the Roman Empire, much of Europe descended into battles over land. Whoever was most physically powerful controlled the land and the villages surrounding that land. The wealthiest landowners dominated and protected the villagers, cultivating loyalty among their subjects through both fear and a sense of safety. They often worked to align themselves with the Catholic Church. This gave them spiritual legitimacy to go alongside their physical prowess and helped them create a sense of nobility. True to that noble sense, they came to be known as monarchs.

In many regions, men with less power than monarchs but enough to be considered lords would often come to control specific, smaller areas of land within a monarch's domain. Because these men used warfare to seize their power, they have been referred to as warlords. As you might imagine, this arrangement had the potential to result in all-out warfare if a lesser lord decided he wanted to expand his estates or felt that the monarch wasn't treating him well. Lesser warlords would come to the royal court and try to overthrow the monarchs.

To preserve their own power and keep warlords in check, monarchs developed elaborate rules—courtesy codes—that dictated the behavior of their subjects and how their subjects were allowed to interact with the monarch. Over time, they developed a culture of restraint that repressed certain behaviors and tried to cultivate others. They developed courtesy codes that dictated how warlords should behave when arriving in the monarch's court. These codes required all sorts of formalities that worked to moderate behavior and reduce the chances of violence: a requirement to set weapons aside, dismount from one's horse and bow when entering the court, for example. There were even rules about the tone of voice used to address a monarch.

Those who wrote the code understood that many warlords would not be receptive to this on its face, so the writers included wording in the code that flattered warlords. The wording suggested that such lords were a higher class of human who deserved to behave and be treated in a more dignified manner, and that manner required endless protocols. The result was that warlords did not come to the court ready for battle when they had a grievance with a monarch, but instead they came believing they could resolve their concerns through formal, courtly dialogue. Monarchs were able to maintain a semblance of peace and control over the various lords in their regions this way.[22]

History like this is why some scholars have come to see civil conversation not as a good worth pursuing but as a way to maintain power:

> There is a long tradition of using civility to silence dissent, excluding people and issues from public discussions. Promoting civility can close down debates, often recasting disagreement in terms of etiquette and manners, silencing heterodox views and draining disputes of passion and agonism. . . . Civility from this perspective is a conservative favoring of the status quo, standing opposed to all forms of dissent, rebellion, and revolution and in doing so forecloses radical change.[23]

In other words, according to this view, *how* we talk is as much about preserving power as *what* we discuss. And the various discourses in which we all engage daily are formed by those in power to preserve the power they enjoy. Those who adopt this view to the extreme believe that all discourse must be seen through a power struggle—at least as to certain topics.

While the original postmodernists pushed the idea that there is no truth, their intellectual grandchildren have come to adopt something more coherent. The problem with postmodernist thought for modern activists was that it ultimately achieved nothing. A well-trained post-modernist might be able to deconstruct any discourse or text to show it has no meaning and serves no other purpose but to promote the interests of those in power, but what they are left with is a pile of linguistic rubble out of which nothing can be built.

This became untenable for many scholars who wanted to see change in the world. For them, it was not enough just to deconstruct the narratives of the powerful. They also wanted to uplift those they saw as oppressed. This idea gave birth to activist scholars, many of whom adopted what are now called "critical theories."[24] Critical race theory, critical gender studies, postcolonial theory (also known as critical colonial theory), and critical queer theory are the most prominent. Proponents of these theories see the world as one in which oppression is ever present. It always exists. Every discourse is not just about power, but it is about whoever is in power oppressing those who are not.[25]

Society, they say, is all about the power dynamics between oppressors and those they oppress. There can be no other way of thinking about it.

Their goal, then, is to break down discourses to reveal the nefarious nature of unnoticed power dynamics and to reveal the underlying oppression.[26] It is to look "critically" at every discourse in society to reduce the oppression as much as possible. Then, if possible, the final aim is to change the discourses so that those who have been historically oppressed rise to power.[27] For critical race theorists, this means uplifting minority races. For critical gender theorists, it means raising up the voices of women. For the queer theories, it means dismantling what they call "heteronormative" discourses and lifting up sexual minorities. For post-colonial theorists, it means looking critically at all discourses that were a product of colonizers and instead spotlighting the voices of the colonized. There are others as well.

The irony is that some of these critical theorists—the intellectual descendants of postmodernism—reject postmodernism's defining feature. Whereas postmodernists found no truth anywhere, many critical studies theorists have become so confident of at least one truth that it dominates all others. In their view, once they have determined who is oppressed, that truth supersedes every other consideration. No discourse is valid unless it acknowledges the oppressor-oppressed relationship and involves the oppressor confessing their power and ceding it to the oppressed.[28] Debates, "civil discourse," constructing knowledge by challenging one another's ideas, presenting evidence and counterevidence, allowing a robust culture of free speech—these are all forms of discourses created by oppressors that have the effect of oppressing those without power. Because of this, there can be no debates. There can be no constructive dialogues to find truth. All that matters is dismantling power structures and granting power to the oppressed.

I have been careful in this book not to take sides on the specific hot-button issues of the day. My hope has been to provide tools that will allow people to explore those problems without devolving into fighting and bitterness, not to push any of my own current positions. So, it is with tremendous caution and only after much thoughtfulness that I take a stand on these theories.

Note that I am focused on the theories as I have laid them out above. Not all critical theorists or postmodernists subscribe to everything I have described above, and many do not subscribe them to any policy area outside their particular field of study. I am not addressing those scholars. I see in their work many ideas that can be helpful to a continued pursuit of knowledge. For example, the notion that how we talk and what we discuss is sometimes determined by those in power is worth exploring and likely does have some truth to it. The idea that many of our discourses keep certain people in power and others oppressed is a falsifiable claim that scholars should examine and research. The concept that many of our discourses might be different if traditionally marginalized groups were allowed to speak more and had not been silenced over the centuries strikes me as provocative and powerful and worthy of testing. The view that any given text can have numerous, even endless meanings, strikes me as worthy of debate. Looking back on history through a critical lens, such as through race, gender, sexual identity, or colonialism, seems to me a powerful way to discover new truths, even profound truths, about where we are today and about how people different from us experienced the past.

I have tried to paint the theories in their best light possible, setting forth their strongest arguments and ignoring the weaker ways of formulating them. I have also tried to present them without a hint of sarcasm or disdain. If I am going to reject them, it should be because I have carefully considered them in their strongest form, supported by their best reasoning, and still do not find them persuasive.

That is the case. I reject the theories to the degree they claim that any and all dialogues are about power dynamics only and are therefore void of truth, are incapable of discovering truth, or cannot lead us to solve real oppression around us. I reject the argument that once an oppressed group has been identified, we can no longer have any discourses related to issues surrounding that group. I reject the argument that the only people allowed to speak on a given topic are those who belong to historically oppressed groups.

My reasons are straightforward. Those aspects of these theories are opposed to truth-seeking. They are opposed to vetting ideas. They are opposed to intellectual humility and the admission that any of us, at any time, can be wrong, no matter our identity. They are opposed to the notion that many minds, working together and challenging one another is more likely to yield truth and progress than one person declaring truth from a position of authority. In wanting to highlight the plights of historically oppressed groups, they have gone too far and risk throwing the baby out with the bathwater. We can work toward rectifying past wrongs and oppression without jettisoning all the progress we have made toward understanding how we develop knowledge through constructive dialogue. In fact, we must do so.

It does seem to be true that the rules of civility for feudal warlords helped to preserve the power of ruling European monarchs. But seeing civil conversation only through that lens ignores another important purpose of the rules of civility. They not only preserved power; they also preserved peace and allowed dialogue that resulted in progress for all of humanity. Lord Chesterfield, a statesman in England in the 1600s, noted in a letter to his son that courts must be "seats of politeness and good-breeding; were they not so they would be the seat of slaughter and desolation."[29] It may be tempting to think that progress cannot be made through discourses that have been framed by the powerful to preserve their power. That assumes, of course, that the postmodernists and critical theorists are correct and discourses are about nothing but power—a claim upon which they have built their foundation but which they have never proven.

Even if it were true, if we remove the possibility of discourse, of productive conversation, of challenging those in power through measured discourse, we abandon all hope of conversation at all. The only option aggrieved people feel at that point is violence.[30] That may, at times, be necessary for progress, such as with certain revolutions or some civil wars. But more often, it only achieves the growth of the graveyard. Warlords who entered the courtly environs of the monarch did come away with some of their goals. They moved toward a brighter future, and we are all beneficiaries.

The better approach if we fear that a particular conversation is being framed in a way that preserves one side's power at the expense of others is to point out the unfairness of the dynamic and politely request the conversation be framed in different terms. Or, as we discussed earlier, you can take charge and reframe the conversation yourself. Abandoning the conversation altogether, or silencing one side of it, achieves nothing.

It is also too casual to conclude that just because the rules of civility in feudal Europe helped preserve the powers of monarchs that polite, constructive conversation is doing the same today. Those were different times. People were just as likely to strike with a sword as they were to greet a stranger with a head nod or a handshake. Indeed, time seems to have proven just how constructive civil conversation can be. Humanity's ability to engage in problem-solving dialogue has resulted in some of the greatest achievements in our history. It was through constructive dialogue that humanity discovered an understanding of physics sufficient to send people to the moon and populate earth's orbit with satellites that allow most of our modern travel and communication. It was through constructive dialogue that we developed all the science we benefit from today, including medical knowledge. It was through constructive dialogue that much of the successes of the Civil Rights Movement came to pass.[31] There is a reason Martin Luther King praised so many of the principles of the First Amendment:

> If I lived in . . . any totalitarian country, maybe I could understand the denial of certain basic First Amendment privileges, because they hadn't committed themselves to that over there. But somewhere I read of the freedom of assembly. Somewhere I read of the freedom of speech. Somewhere I read of the freedom of the press. Somewhere I read that the greatness of America is the right to protest for right.[32]

Productive dialogue produces results that benefit all of humanity. To reject it for fear that it may preserve oppression is, in my view, a grave mistake.

Nevertheless, there are those who feel differently. We may not be able to do anything about that, but we can still employ some of the principles in this book. When we meet someone who refuses to engage in dialogue because to do so would be to justify or support oppressors, we will have a better sense of where they are coming from. But, no doubt, I won't have captured all their beliefs here, so we can still ask questions to better understand their mindset and motivations. We can still learn how they think and ask them questions about the implications of their views, assuming they will let us. We can probe to see if there are other topics on which they will engage in dialogue—I think you will find that is often the case. We may never receive an opening to express our own ideas on certain topics, and, if so, the world will be a little poorer for it. That is unfortunate, but my hope is that it will be less frustrating for you than it otherwise might have been because you'll understand why.

FORGIVENESS

Forgiveness, both grand and miniscule, is a habit peacemakers engage in regularly.

When I was a young man, just starting in college, an older gentleman with at least five more decades of life experience encouraged me to be forgiving. "It will make you a strong and mighty man," he said. I didn't appreciate how profound those words were at the time, but I never forgot them. As I have grown older and have experienced more of life's inevitable peaks and valleys, slights and harms, I appreciate how much wisdom that small pearl captured.

All of us have been wronged. And if we let them, those wrongs can prevent us from engaging in any sort of peacemaking.

Perhaps one of the more well-known stories to come out of World War II is that of Louis Zamperini. After Laura Hillenbrand's best-selling book about him, there are few in the United States who are not at least familiar with his name. In the Pacific, after his bomber crashed in the ocean, he survived years of torture and neglect at the hands of his Japanese captors. A miraculous part of his story was his physical survival—on a raft floating in the unrelenting sun of the Pacific; in prison camps; through physical beatings and starvation. That he survived all of that for as long as he did is almost beyond belief. It was so compelling that Angelina Jolie made a movie about it, ending it at the moment he was finally rescued from a POW camp in Japan at the end of the war.

But Jolie missed the truly astonishing part of Zamperini's life. Whether she did so because of lack of time or because she didn't fully appreciate the true miracle of his life, I cannot say. Many critics lamented that the movie employed wonderful cinematography and moving moments but lacked a certain emotion or joy. What was missing was Zamperini's internal emotional journey. The truly great stories that resonate with us and stand the test of time show not just a physical plot—like most action movies—but involve the people in them changing and growing, discovering something about themselves that forever changes who they are.

For Zamperini, his story was so much more than surviving unimaginable suffering. Like many veterans, upon returning home, Zamperini suffered from post-traumatic stress disorder (PTSD). Scientists did not have a term for it then, but it has plagued many soldiers and others who have survived intense trauma like war or abuse. For too many men like Zamperini, surviving the horrors of war was only the beginning. Hillenbrand captured it well:

> As bad as were the physical consequences of captivity, the emotional injuries were much more insidious, widespread, and enduring. In the first six postwar years, one of the most common diagnoses given to hospitalized former Pacific POWs was psychoneurosis. Nearly forty years after the war, more than 85 percent of former Pacific POWs in one study suffered from [PTSD], characterized in part by flashbacks, anxiety, and nightmares. And in a 1987 study, eight in ten former Pacific POWS had "psychiatric impairment," six in ten had anxiety disorders, more than one in four had PTSD, and nearly one in five was depressed. For some, there was only one way out: a 1970 study reported that

former Pacific POWs committed suicide 30 percent more often than controls.[33]

Zamperini started down that path as well. In his first years back, he nearly lost himself to alcoholism. Then, something changed, something seismic, and he spent the next nearly seventy years thriving, lifting, and supporting others.

What changed for Zamperini? The key was forgiveness, spurred by his conversion to Christianity. He became famous for returning to Japan and forgiving the many men who only years earlier had beaten and starved and tormented him. He met with them and offered them compassion. This included, even, one man who had made it his mission to try to break Zamperini.

Those acts of forgiveness did something to Louis that changed him and inspired everyone around him. They helped him overcome his alcoholism. They helped his anger at his former tormentors dissipate and vanish altogether. They allowed him to leave behind the nightmares and thoughts of vengeance that stalked him like shadows for months. They gave him permission to look forward to a better life as a husband and father, instead of backward at all the wrongs he had suffered.[34]

Louis's story is compelling because his acts of forgiveness made him a strong and mighty man. They reflect the best of what each of us can achieve. Too often, individuals refuse to forgive because they believe doing so confers a benefit or comfort on someone who is undeserving of it. Louis's story teaches us that the primary benefit of forgiveness belongs to the person doing the forgiving, not the one receiving it.

Of course, the idea of forgiveness is not new. Many of the world's great religions teach the importance of it. It is a central theme in Christianity—believers acknowledge a God who forgives them their sins and who commands that they should forgive others as well.[35] In Islam, it is a powerful principle taught by both Sunni and Shia Muslims.[36] In Buddhism, forgiveness brings harmony to our lives and ends our own suffering.[37] Sikhs believe God is a forgiving being, and those who are spiritually inclined seek to develop that divine attribute in themselves. The stoic philosophers saw forgiveness and justice as two parts of a great whole. Seneca, for example, argued that a forgiving emperor was akin to a loving father or even God.[38]

It seems every major philosophy calls for forgiveness. In recent decades, science and evidence-based research have proven the importance of it as well. While it is often associated with religious teachings, the world of psychology and mental health has repeatedly shown that forgiveness results in better mental health and overall well-being for those who understand it and practice it. Studies have shown that in most instances, victims who can forgive those who have harmed them show elevated mood, improved optimism, and less anger. In one recent study of nearly five thousand participants across multiple and diverse countries, researchers discovered that those who engaged in forgiveness showed reduced symptoms of both depression and anxiety.[39]

Most important for our purposes, forgiveness is a habit that peacemakers engage in regularly. Peacemakers tend to be quick to forgive, especially the minor slights all of us face every day. In most instances, peacemakers recognize that if someone didn't do something to them on a given day for which they could have taken offense, they probably didn't interact with anyone that day. In short, people do offensive things all the time, and peacemakers don't allow that to control their own behavior.

To put it another way, peacemakers do not make a big deal out of small things. Some years ago, I was driving along with a young man who, even at age fifteen, already showed a remarkable talent for being a peacemaker. He turned to me and said, "You know, I have found in my life that I often just don't get the best of small things because I don't think they're worth fighting over." He paused, then said, "But that usually leads to me getting the best of the things that matter." That was a profound comment from a young person. But it speaks to the principle of daily forgiveness, of not fixating on minor slights. When we do this, we often better position ourselves in the eyes of others to deal with more important topics. To use a common phrase, we pick our battles.

The next time you find yourself wanting to argue with someone about something small in your life, ask yourself how important it is. On a scale of one to ten, rate it in your mind. Try to consider how others would rate it as well, so that you can maintain some degree of objectivity. If it scores lower on that scale—below a four, say—let it go. Forgive and move on. You may not end up with the best of small things on occasion, but you will position yourself to be taken far more seriously on important topics when they arise.

Peacemakers learn to forgive the small things, but they also tend to forgive far more egregious wrongs. Doing so allows them to achieve the peace of mind and calmness that then helps them become peacemakers when discussing hard topics.

If you find you are unsure of how to forgive, resources are available. Talking with a trained counselor or a spiritual leader can be helpful. Reading about the power of forgiveness can help motivate you to let go of burdens you are carrying. Scientists have developed self-guided programs to allow people to become more forgiving. For example, Professor Everett Worthington, a clinical psychologist who studied the impacts of forgiveness for decades at Virginia Commonwealth University, has developed workbooks that include prompts and training exercises that help people identify areas of their life where forgiveness could help them, along with tools to engage in it. As of this writing, he has several workbooks available for free online. A simple search for him and the workbooks should guide readers to them.

Another important principle you can put into practice is to recognize that often, you may have misperceived a situation. Forgiveness of daily slights is helpful for all the reasons we have discussed, but it is also valuable because, too often, we see the world through all the misperceptions of our own emotional and psychological baggage, which means we may be perceiving wrongs that never truly happened.

Allow me to share a personal example. When I first entered

academia, I experienced imposter syndrome—defined as feeling like I did not belong in academia because I was not intelligent enough; I was a fraud or phony—to a high degree. In one of the first academic conferences I attended, I sat in an auditorium with some of the brightest thought leaders in my field. I scanned the room, then pulled out my phone and texted my wife, "I don't belong here."

That sensation stayed with me for years. Why I had that feeling, and why it stayed with me for so long, is a topic for another day—I assume it was a product of my genetic makeup, the environment in which I grew up, and the many experiences I've had since. Regardless of how it developed, it was very real. I saw everything through that lens. When I attended meetings, I assumed others in the room knew I was an imposter and felt I didn't belong. I interpreted their mannerisms, idle chatter, glances, questions, and tone of voice through that lens. And what I found were opportunities everywhere to be offended. I was wronged, I felt, in every meeting in which I participated.

Of course, all of that was nonsense, mostly in my head. I'm sure there are plenty of people in my circles who feel that way about me, but most are far more generous than that. At some point, I developed the mental courage to tell myself to enter all meetings under the assumption that others in the room respected me and wanted me there. As soon as I did that, I interpreted their body language and comments differently. I realized that, in fact, many of them were quite friendly. I also behaved in a way that sent positive signals in their direction. Very little had changed in how others were treating me—what changed was how I interpreted their behavior.

I am not alone in experiencing imposter syndrome or in allowing insecurities to dictate my thinking. In a recent study, researchers from Harvard, Cornell, Yale, and Essex universities found that "people systematically underestimated how much their conversation partners liked them and enjoyed their company." This was especially prevalent, the researchers found, when people met someone else for the first time. "People are often biased by their own internal monologues, which, after social interactions, can be remarkably self-critical and negative, especially with the added uncertainty of talking to someone new." The end result is that people tend to "overestimate how harshly others will judge them during social interactions."[40]

I share my story to reinforce why forgiveness is so important. Because I was so badly misperceiving the intentions of people around me, I assumed I was being wronged—in minor ways—at every turn. Only daily forgiveness allowed me to keep functioning. Had I refused to forgive, I could have easily descended into an even worse perspective about the world and those around me. I would have been angry at people in my space. I would have resented them. That would have made dealing with them daily nearly impossible, sabotaging my relationships and, eventually, my career progression. Perhaps the only thing that saved me from my own insecurity was my ability to forgive.

One last story. Years ago, I was teaching a class to a group of teenagers. The focus of our lesson was this principle of forgiveness. I wasn't sure precisely what I should emphasize, so I asked the class as a group why forgiveness was so important. One of the young women raised her hand and said, "Forgiveness helps us because it lets us move on from hard feelings we have toward other people instead of being dragged down by anger toward them."

Pretty profound answer from a fourteen-year-old. I will admit it was not something I was thinking about; I was aware of the idea intellectually, but it was not where my mind had taken me. I liked the answer, so we continued to explore it as a group, other people made comments, the class ended, and we all went about our day.

Later that afternoon, while I was in my office, my cell phone rang.

I answered.

On the other line was a mom of one of the students in the class—a young woman who had not said a word during the entire lesson. The mom was crying.

I immediately thought, *Oh no—what did I do wrong?*

To my surprise, she said, "I just wanted to call to tell you thank you. How did you know that was what Tonya*** needed to hear?"

I asked her specifically what she was referring to, and she told me that her Tonya had been going through a truly horrible period. She was adopted, and she had been feeling a deep, poignant resentment and anger toward her birth parents. How could they have just given her up? It was tearing her up inside, so much so that she had even begun to see herself as less of a human being than her friends. Why were her friends loved by their birth parents but she was not? She had stewed over these thoughts. She felt furious toward her biological parents. Her anger toward them seemed to consume her almost every minute of every day.

After our class, when Tonya got into her mom's car, she turned to her and said, "Mom, I've realized I just need to forgive them. It's not to make them feel better, but it's so I can move on." And she did exactly that. Years later, she told me that lesson helped her move away from deep depression and suicidal thoughts, all because one of her classmates had the courage to say out loud a nugget of wisdom that has stood the test of time and been proven true by both religion and science.

Forgiveness—it will allow you to move forward, no longer as a slave to someone else's bad choices, but as a peacemaker who can address difficult topics regardless of the person on the other side of the conversation.

HABIT THREE: WHAT WE'VE LEARNED ABOUT ASSUMING THE BEST ABOUT PEOPLE

In this chapter, we learned that peacemakers engage in the habit of assuming the best about people. This means:

*** Name has been changed.

THEY ASK QUESTIONS OF OTHERS
TO UNDERSTAND THEIR TRUE MOTIVATIONS.

They know that most people—especially those in their lives—have good motivations. They ask questions to understand those motivations before stating opinions.

THEY LIFT UP THOSE WHO ASSUME THE WORST ABOUT THEM.

They do not overreact when people assume the worst about them. Instead, they seek to lift up others who assume the worst and find common ground with them.

THEY REFRAME OTHERS' NEGATIVE
COMMENTS IN THEIR BEST LIGHT.

They know others often do not state their positions in the best light, so they reframe comments to reflect the best possible position.

THEY RECOGNIZE WHEN SOME PEOPLE
CANNOT TALK ABOUT SOME TOPICS.

They know some people are not capable of discussing some topics without allowing their emotions to take control. They know others refuse to talk about certain topics as a matter of principle. In those situations, peacemakers choose to focus conversations on other topics.

THEY FORGIVE.

They forgive others who have wronged them. This includes major harm, but it also includes the many minor slights all of us face every day.

HABIT FOUR
DON'T FEED PEOPLE'S WORST FEARS

Some years ago, I watched from a distance when an old friend posted on Facebook an article critical of Donald Trump and immigration laws in the United States. I will call her Diane.

Another woman, whom I did not know, commented, tossing out several reasons why she thought we should have stricter controls on immigration. We'll call her Elizabeth. She asked Diane a series of questions and was sincerely hoping for real answers. The questions focused on crime rates of immigrants.

Diane responded in a respectful way. The two were engaging in a productive dialogue about an important topic and clearly enjoyed a respectful relationship.

Soon, a third party joined in. We'll call him David Goliath.

"Elizabeth, I support strong immigration regulations and laws," he said. "but I don't support your racist and incorrect stereotyping of undocumented immigrants as violent criminals. . . . Elizabeth, you must be insane."

Elizabeth responded quickly, "Please do not attack me and call me names. I don't even know you. My comment was to my friend Diane, who I respect for including her opinion. I was sharing my thoughts, and I do not appreciate being called insane, Mr. Goliath."

David was not done. In a very quick follow-up, he responded, "Elizabeth. No, you don't get a 'pass' on your factually deceitful statements. . . . Your statement is purely deceitful, defamatory, nonfactual. I'm sorry but you HURT people with your lies."

What Goliath was commenting on were not statements Elizabeth had made, but sincere questions she had asked.

Shortly thereafter, Diane turned the post to private. All dialogue about the issue stopped.

BE YE EXAMPLES

Note what happened in the above story. David's attacks on Elizabeth did nothing to change her mind. All it did for the conversation was stop any progress anyone might have made regarding the issue of immigration laws in the United States.

But for David, the results were even worse. His first failure was that he did nothing to persuade either Elizabeth or Diane. His second was to lose all credibility with anyone else watching the exchange. In separate posts, he tried to share data challenging anything that Elizabeth had claimed, but his rhetoric was so hateful and aggressive, it made it difficult for others to want to listen to the valid points—and some of them were valid—he was making, then or in the future.

The worst thing we can do is behave exactly how people fear we will. This means we need to develop habits that help us become someone others can trust. Since most people are inclined to believe that anyone who disagrees with them must be a fascist, tyrant, or fool, the last thing you want to do is give them ammunition that proves their point. David gave everyone plenty of ammunition.

In the United States, we enjoy a long tradition of allowing most speech, with just a few exceptions. But with freedom of speech comes responsibility. Others in our circles can hold us accountable for what we say and how we act. There are many ways people might do that, but the most obvious is that they will choose to ignore or discount us. The bottom line is this: how we behave matters. Peacemakers understand this, either through instinct or painful experience.

Peacemakers know that if they want people to listen to them, they must treat them with respect. They must, by their example, show that they can get along with and be friends with others. When your everyday behavior signals you are someone who values others, they will take you seriously. This does not mean peacemakers do not express disagreement. They do, often, but they do it in a tone that expresses love and caring for the people with whom they are engaging.

Many peacemakers are incredibly intelligent—this means they are the kind of people who could, if they wanted, enjoy a mic-drop, put-people-in-their-place, burn moment every once in a while. They choose not to do so. They know that expressing ideas with kindness and love is more effective than using sarcasm and anger.

In this instance, the old wisdom from Proverbs holds true: "A soft answer turneth away wrath: but grievous words stir up anger."[1]

ALL THE FALLACIES TO WHICH HUMAN BEINGS ARE PRONE

Earlier, we explored all the barriers we face that keep us from real learning. Now, we focus on all those tendencies we have to behave our worst. Becoming aware of them is the first step to overcoming them.

One of the most pervasive is bias. We are subject to dozens of biases. They arise in nearly every aspect of our lives, and research continues to find more and more. We already explored confirmation bias in our personal relationships, but that is just the tip of the iceberg. Consider these other biases to which we are all prone (see if you can't recognize them in your own life):

- Focalism or anchoring bias—the tendency to focus too much on one trait or tool when making a decision, such as when someone begins a negotiation by throwing out a number, which then sets the terms of the negotiation.[2]
- Apophenia—the tendency to perceive meaningful connections between things that are not related, such as when a gambler at a roulette table convinces himself he sees a pattern in how the ball is landing.[3]
- Effort bias—the tendency to place more value on something if we put effort into creating it, such as when someone values a piece of furniture more because they built it.[4]

- Egocentric bias—the tendency to have a higher opinion of ourselves than, well, anyone else, such as when someone is convinced they know more about tax policy than anyone else in the room because they watched one YouTube video on it.[5]
- Logical fallacies—the tendency to commit errors in causal logic, such as when a young boy concludes that because mousse is foamy and puffy, the product he is about to put in his hair must be mousse because it is also foamy and puffy.[6]
- Failures in self-assessment—the tendency to over- or underestimate our abilities, such as when Uncle James is convinced he knows everything about the gender pay gap or Uncle Pete is convinced he is not capable of changing the oil on the car.[7]
- Hindsight bias—the tendency to look back on past events as if they were predictable, such as when a married couple looks back on their engagement and sees it as inevitable.[8]
- Optimism or pessimism bias—the tendency to over- or underestimate favorable outcomes, such as when a child convinces himself he will reach the NBA and another child convinces himself he shouldn't even try out for the team.[9]
- Recency bias—the tendency to believe that because we have finally recognized a phenomenon, the phenomenon itself must be recent, such as when someone learns a new vocabulary word and starts hearing it everywhere.[10]

I could go on. There are as many as a hundred cognitive biases, and many of the ones I listed above have subcategories. Logical fallacies, for example, come in dozens of forms. This is not a book about cognitive biases, so let those examples suffice to prove the point: none of us thinks as clearly about the world as we like to think we do.

That is problematic if one of the habits we hope to adopt is to avoid being the jerk people accuse us of being. It's also unrealistic to expect any of us to overcome all these biases. Many of them serve an important purpose by helping us make sense of and operate in a world that would otherwise overwhelm us if we were suddenly exposed to all its complexity.

But being aware of our biases is an important step. Just knowing that at any time we may be engaged in all sorts of bias can help us tone down our positions. Although I note: many cognitive scientists are not optimistic about our ability to overcome our biases. One of the leading folks in the field, the Nobel Prize–winning researcher Daniel Kahneman, explained, "The question that is most often asked about cognitive illusions is whether they can be overcome. The message . . . is not encouraging."[11]

Even if we can't overcome them, being aware of them can contribute to our ability to engage in positive dialogue. If we know we are likely biased in almost everything we are doing, that should give us pause. We should be a little slower to spout our opinions and a little faster to ask: How am I biased here? How is that bias affecting my thinking? Bias awareness is a cousin, perhaps even a sibling, of intellectual humility. Both encourage us to pause, to proceed with caution, to examine a little bit more what we think we know and compare it to what we might be able to learn.

HOW TO CONTROL YOUR EMOTIONS

One habit that can help us overcome—or at least soften—our natural tendencies is controlling our emotions. In conversation, if someone brings up the question of whether women should have a constitutional right to receive an abortion, most people have an intense emotional reaction. Peacemakers learn how to respond to that reaction before it controls them. To be clear, there may be times when we want our emotions to take control, such as when our favorite college football team finally beats its rival after a long drought; but when discussing complex topics, we are all better off if we do not let our emotions dominate our conversations.

This comes more naturally for some than others. Walking among us are those who feel the same range of emotions as anyone else but do not experience the emotions in the range as deeply. You might describe their emotional experience like this:

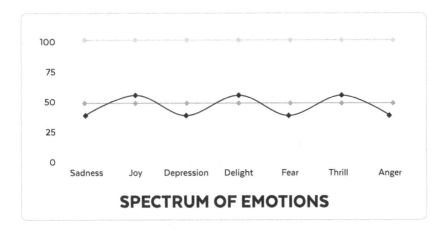

EMOTIONAL BASELINE **INTENSITY OF EMOTIONS**

For them, although they experience the entire spectrum of human emotions, they have an easier time controlling them. Some issues might cause emotional spikes for them more than others, but, generally speaking, they are able to discuss difficult topics while keeping their emotions in check.

Others have a very different experience. We might imagine their emotional journey more like this:

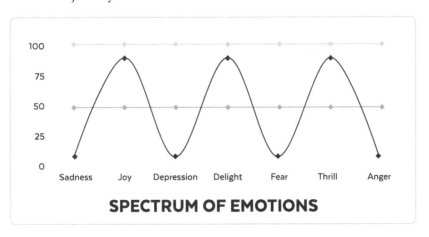

EMOTIONAL BASELINE **INTENSITY OF EMOTIONS**

For these people, emotions tend to hit them like a tidal wave. Often, their emotions cloud their rational thinking and prevent them from processing information and facts.

Psychologists refer to our instinctual emotions as our "elephant" and our rational brains as our "rider." The metaphor emphasizes that, while we generally want the rider to be in charge, we too often allow the elephant to roam around wherever it likes. In other words, we allow our emotions to control us, not our rational side.

The good news is that almost anyone can give their rider more control. It might be easier for the first group, but with practice and development of certain skills, the second group can achieve the same outcomes. The goal is to reach a state of being where you can be exposed to various ideas and discussion topics without your emotions taking total control.

If this does not come naturally to you, the key is to identify topics that cause you emotional spikes, then expose yourself to them a bit at a time. Make a list of all the topics that might cause you an emotional reaction. Abortion, LGBTQ+ rights, immigration, tax policy, the death penalty, gun rights, foreign policy, race relations, family matters, religious beliefs—your topic (or topics) may be any one of these, or it may be something else altogether. List the major issues about which you care and look inside yourself to see which provokes you most.

Once you have identified a topic, the next step is to expose yourself to nuanced conversations about the issue. You can do this a little at a time. The key is to listen to or read discussions about issues from a variety of different viewpoints. If you listen only to people who reinforce your own views, you will be doing little to help with your ability to control your emotions. In fact, you may be making your situation worse. But you also don't need to flood your brain with comments from people who get your blood pressure boiling. Expose yourself a little at a time to debates, conferences, long-form articles, and books—all of which are available today online.

The more time you spend with these issues, the more you will be able to think about them rationally and the less jarring they will be the next time they come up in conversation. After a time, observe yourself when the topics come up in conversation. You should, over time, see your ability to discuss topics rationally increase. Learn this habit of exposure in your daily life, and soon, you—not your emotions—will be in control.

KNOW THYSELF AND WHEN YOU CANNOT CONTROL YOUR EMOTIONS, BUT EMBRACE YOUR DIGNITY

Almost all of us face certain topics about which we cannot control our emotions . . . yet. That topic may be a wayward child. It may be a strained relationship with your father-in-law. It may be because of past trauma from abuse or something else horrific like the death of a loved one. On the lighter side, it may be your favorite sports teams.

You have no obligation to jettison that part of who you are. You likely couldn't immediately even if you wanted to—that is the nature of those types of topics. They have such a powerful hold over us that controlling our emotional reactions to them is impossible, at least for a time.

The challenge, then, is not to change who you are. It is to reach a point where the topics no longer affect you as much. That takes time and slow exposure to the topic over many years, usually through therapy and what we discussed in the previous section.

Until you have done all of that, the mission is to recognize which topics get you so emotionally charged that you simply cannot talk about them in a rational way. Spend some time pondering what those topics might be. One test you might apply is asking yourself if all of your conversations somehow return to that particular topic. I offer one quick example.

A few years after the COVID-19 pandemic, I penned an opinion piece on the eightieth anniversary of the events I brought to life in *The Immortals* and argued that our culture in the United States needed to recapture the spirit reflected by those men.

As a general rule, I don't read the comments for pieces I write. But I took a glance at them for this one. Many were what you might expect:

folks noting what a powerful story it was and how grateful they were for the examples of those men and their families. Some of the commenters, however, immediately devolved into anger, writing how they would never sacrifice anything for anyone ever again because of what they'd seen as tyranny during the pandemic. That, of course, led to the predictable backlash. And then I remembered why I never read the comments section.

My op-ed had nothing at all to do with the pandemic, but some readers could not help but bring it back to that. It held such emotional sway over their thinking that no matter what other subject was on the table, they could not help themselves from thinking about how governments and others reacted to the pandemic.

If you have a topic like that—one your mind goes to immediately in nearly every situation, regardless of its relationship to the discussion, and you find yourself wanting to launch into an opinion with the reckless abandon of an unsupervised toddler jumping into a swimming pool—you should probably consider that a topic with emotional sway over you. When such topics come up, know that perhaps your best way of dealing with them is to refrain from talking about them outside of a controlled environment. Such an environment would include a session with a therapist or with a trusted person who knows the totality of the situation.

That said, a word of caution. Do not devalue yourself. Your ability to talk about hard topics and to be exposed to challenging ideas is part of what makes you human—it is one aspect of who you are that gives you unique value as a human being. In my other line of work, I have done a great deal of research into the concept of human dignity. It holds a grand place in many cultures. It has many different potential meanings, but my research has focused on it in a specific sense: the idea that human beings are unique, different from any other living species on the planet; we therefore enjoy certain rights, privileges, and responsibilities that set us apart from plants and animals. In other words, we enjoy human dignity.

In the Western tradition, there have been three paths for conceiving of dignity in this way: theological, philosophical, and as a reaction to historical events. The first minds to conceive of the idea, though not explicitly, were Plato and Aristotle. They had not developed the word *dignity*, or even the concept fully, but we see in their ideas a kernel of what was to follow. In their view, some humans were unique because they were capable of understanding, self-understanding, loving, self-determination, creating art, and self-expression.[12] They did not believe this applied to all humans, only those Athenians who were like them, but, nevertheless, they had begun to develop the idea that human beings were different from other beings on the planet.

The Roman philosopher Cicero followed and first developed the term *dignitas*. This referred to the idea of "human beings as human beings" because we share in our nature our rationality. Akin to the ideas birthed by the Athenians, this argument rested on the notion that human beings are different because of our ability to reason and to assess and know our world. "It is vitally necessary," wrote Cicero, "for us to remember always how vastly superior is man's nature to that of cattle and other animals: their only thought is for bodily satisfactions. . . . Man's mind, on the contrary, is developed by study and reflection."[13]

Cicero died shortly before the beginning of the Christian era, which ushered in new concepts of dignity that combined the Ciceronian and Athenian notions of rationality and self-awareness with a theological perspective. This took time to develop, but by the Renaissance, it bloomed into full view. Giovanni Pico della Mirandola, in his famed *Oration on the Dignity of Man*, argued in 1486 that humanity enjoyed unique status as creations of God. Humanity, he argued, has dignity as the center of God's creation and as spiritual beings. But he did not abandon the previous ways of conceiving of dignity so much as he added a theological rationale to them. In addition to being spiritual beings, humans also possessed a unique dignity because of our ability to choose; in particular, to choose any form of our existence, including reaching our highest potential. That capacity for choosing between the lowest and highest forms of our existence, or anything in between, set humanity apart from animals and plants.[14]

The Christian rationale continued to hold sway—and still does in many circles—until Immanuel Kant explored the concept from a more secularized, philosophical perspective. Near the end of the eighteenth century, he grounded dignity in humans' capacity for rationality, jettisoning any reliance on humanity's divine nature. In particular, humans' ability to conceive and follow the moral law and to choose their own destiny set them apart from other creatures, making them deserving of different treatment under the law and from each other. Only humans, Kant argued, could identify certain acts that are categorically moral and should be done by everyone simply because they are moral. These are acts that are not means to some other end but are ends of themselves, worth doing because of their inherent worth. Only humans could identify those and act upon them, which also meant that human beings themselves were not to be used as the means to someone else's ends either. Given their intrinsic capability for choice, humans are not objects to be used by others. They should neither be bought nor sold as one would some other living being, and their dignity was intrinsic, with no connection to rank or status.[15]

Kant's ideas found friends in the writings of other philosophers and politicians around the same time. As Kenneth Abraham and Edward White from the University of Virginia School of Law explain, "Republicanism in France and America emphasized the extension of privileges previously accorded only to aristocrats to all citizens and the connection between dignity and the natural rights of man, while anti-slavery literature of the mid-nineteenth century asserted that slavery was incompatible with human dignity."[16] All of this placed an emphasis on dignity as setting humans apart and demanding that they be treated differently than other beings.

Today, we live in a world where everyone in Western countries—and in most other countries—agrees that all humans have dignity. Many still believe in the religious reasons for dignity: that people are different because they carry within them a kernel of divinity. Others subscribe to the Kantian view, even if they don't know it. To the extent we have disagreements, they are over what the implications of dignity are. In other words, we may all have dignity, but what laws should stem from that idea to ensure our dignity is protected? Thousands of questions abound among academics and policymakers.

We will not get lost in those debates here. They are beyond the scope of this book and might bore you to tears. I spent these last few valuable pages on dignity to draw your attention to one important theme. Note that no matter who was doing the pondering about why humans have an inherent dignity, they all seemed to agree on at least one idea. Humans enjoy dignity because of our ability to think rationally about our world, to make sense of it, to ponder its meaning.

You enjoy that dignity as well. It is part of what makes you a special creature in this universe, more so than the lizard scurrying under a bush, or the spider spinning its web. So even as we spend time recognizing that there may be some topics about which we cannot talk yet without allowing our emotions to take over, we should also acknowledge that those topics should be few and far between. If we find ourselves feeling that way about more than a couple of issues, we have likely allowed our emotions to take control of too much in our life. We are rational beings. Part of what sets us apart from other creatures is that we do not act via instinct alone. If we find that our emotions are preventing us from tapping into that part of our identity, the time has arrived for us to embrace our dignity and learn to tame our emotional reactions.

To do so, we can expose ourselves in small doses to others' viewpoints until we can explore certain topics without allowing our emotions to drive us. As I said at the outset, some people have truly experienced real trauma, from abuse or tragic experiences. And those experiences may mean that they can only talk about related topics in the controlled environments of a properly trained therapist. Aside from that, we can all embrace our human dignity and our ability to think rationally about the world around us.

DON'T SEEK RECOGNITION

Often, in some situations, what can lead to discord is a desire by one person or another to compete with everyone else in the room, to seek recognition for anything and everything they have accomplished or contributed. Peacemakers learn that they do not need recognition.

What often leads people to behave in ways that make it hard to take them seriously is a desire to receive recognition. In our day and age, recognition often appears in the form of likes, reposts, and comments, which means too many of us spend our time chasing those, instead of other, more worthy goals.

Consider some of our most toxic politicians, the ones who are consistently doing things to get attention. If we're being objective and controlling our emotions, we can find them on both sides of the political aisle. Note that much of their ridiculous behavior is driven from seeking recognition and fame. Were they to remove that desire from their lives, they may actually spend their time doing work of substance, even, perhaps, being peacemakers.

In your own life, develop the habit of not seeking praise for your own contributions and instead try to highlight the great work of those around you, including those with whom you disagree. This does not come naturally to most of us, so you must practice. In your next interaction where you may be tempted to get credit for something you achieved, replace that habit with praise for someone else. This will be difficult at first. There will be times when someone may dismiss you or not grant you the respect you feel you deserve, but if you keep your eye on the long term, you will find that you are putting yourself in a far better position for healthy conversations. People will trust you because they will know you are not merely acting out of your own best interest. You will also be inclined to make comments that are actual contributions, rather than signals of your own brilliance. That, in turn, will lead people to continue to want to hear what you have to say.

OUR OPINIONS SHOULD BE LIKE UNSTABLE EXPLOSIVES: OFFERED SLOWLY AND GENTLY

Earlier, we explored the importance of training ourselves to slow down when reaching conclusions. A second, equally important habit is being slow to *state* the conclusions we have reached.

We have all been there. The moment we hear someone mention a topic we are passionate about, including one we have thought about deeply, our first instinct is to make a declaration.

Some time back, I was sitting with a small group of folks discussing various contemporary issues, and one person brought up a controversial law in the United States.

Another man announced, "That law is absolutely ridiculous. It's just stupid." Then he got up and walked away.

He might be right; he might be wrong. But making that declaration, dropping his metaphorical microphone, and walking away from the group achieved nothing. He belted out an emphatic conclusion with no specificity, so no one else in the group could respond to it with any specificity. Those who agreed with him would have simply nodded. Those who disagreed would have argued back at the same level of generality with something brilliant like: "No it's not!"

What the statement foreclosed was any opportunity to explore the law itself, its precise provisions, and why those provisions might be problematic or positive. It wasn't just the degree of generality but the emotions behind it. The ardently stated opinion sends a signal to the group that any discussion or pushback could result in a blowup. The message is unmistakable: the safest path is to stay silent.

People did stay silent, for a time, but those who disagreed with him were not persuaded by what he said. He gave them no reason to be. And those who agreed with him found nothing in his comment to bolster their own convictions. All he achieved was casting a shadow over what otherwise could have been a fruitful dialogue. I should add, however, that I did not allow the threatened blow up and silence to last for long. I reframed the conversation to keep the dialogue going in a more positive manner, and the rest of us were able to explore the topic in a healthy way. But the emphatic opinion at the outset almost made that impossible.

Sadly, our current society lends itself to those kinds of comments. Perhaps one of the biggest downsides of social media and comment sections after articles is that they encourage us to state our opinions quickly and often. No one is immune. Academics, athletes, celebrities, some guy sitting on a couch eating potato chips, politicians, everyone—with smartphones at our fingertips, we can launch an opinion into the world with almost minimal effort and thought. And we do so all the time, on any number of topics about which we often know very little.

This is a tragedy for productive conversation. It is almost impossible to have a true and helpful exchange with someone when all they are doing is tossing out their opinions. Yet that is precisely what social media asks us to do. It also undermines our credibility. In my own profession as a law professor, perhaps nothing undermines the authority of me and my colleagues more than spouting out some half-baked opinion on a matter of public concern. I may have written books and articles about important legal and doctrinal issues, but if my readers' first contact with me is nothing more than a few sentences where I went off on some highly charged political topic, the chances of convincing anyone to go deeply into the nuanced arguments I am making in my writing effectively plummets to zero. The only people who will read me are the ones who already agree with whatever I wrote on social media.

DEVELOP SELFLESS LOVE FOR OTHERS

The most surefire solution to avoid acting in a way that reinforces people's worst fears is to not be what they accuse you of. Peacemakers are as much about who they are as what they do. Perhaps the most crucial trait someone can develop is a true, selfless love for others. Of course, if developing that were as easy as typing out the words, we wouldn't have any of the problems our world currently faces.

There are many ways to develop love for others. I struggled over adding this concept to this book for a variety of reasons. First, the concept of selfless love is complex and deserves its own library-length treatment. I'm not sure I can truly do it justice here. Some aspects of it are intuitive and obvious, perhaps captured best in these passages from 1 Corinthians 13:4–7 in the King James Version of the New Testament (and in many similar texts from other religions), with the word *charity* meaning "selfless love":

> Charity suffereth long, and is kind; charity envieth not; charity vaunteth not itself, is not puffed up,
> Doth not behave itself unseemly, seeketh not her own, is not easily provoked, thinketh no evil;
> Rejoiceth not in iniquity, but rejoiceth in the truth;
> Beareth all things, believeth all things, hopeth all things, endureth all things.

We can probably all agree those are traits worth developing in our lives. But what about other more complex questions related to love? Is it love to never give our children any consequences out of fear we might be too overbearing? Or is it love to ensure they have consequences, sometimes even harsh consequences, so they can be better prepared for the world they will enter as adults? Is it love to give children chores and make them work to earn money, or is it love to give them an allowance and focus their time on hobbies and self-improvement? In the arena of politics, is it love to vote for government programs that provide money and welfare assistance to others, or is it love to ensure that any programs require people to stand on their own two feet?

These are not easy questions, and I won't pretend to have all the answers here. The bottom line is that what true love looks like in practice is not obvious and deserves careful consideration.

Second, once we know what love is, *how* to develop true love for others also deserves its own book-length treatment. For some, it comes naturally. For the rest of us, it takes a lifetime of growth and even then, we may never fully get there. Again, I'm not going to pretend to be the expert on how to do it, but I will offer three habits peacemakers work hard to develop.

First, they engage in selfless service. I have found that the more we serve others and seek to lift them up, the more we come to love them unselfishly. Service places us in their shoes. It helps us experience their hardships and the struggles—both mental and emotional—they face every day. In time, through service, you will come to find yourself thinking of those you're serving more than you think of yourself. You will want to see what's best for them for their sake, not for your own. And for the purposes of this book, you will come to appreciate more their point of view, which will lead to fewer arguments and more understanding.

The second habit is related to the first. We will never achieve selfless love by focusing on ourselves and our desire to achieve it. We develop love for others by *thinking* of and *doing* for others. If we spend our days focused on improving ourselves, the paradox is that we may end up not improving in those areas that matter the most. We improve ourselves by focusing on lifting others.

The third bit of advice is that we should never stop trying to develop the attribute of selfless love. If you spend your life doing nothing but working on loving others, it will have been a life worth living.

SOME ROADS ARE NOT WORTH FOLLOWING: REJECT THE BAD EXAMPLES OF PUBLIC PERSONAS

Sadly, the digital world gives us lots of bad examples. Most behavior we see online or on television related to debates about hard topics is not what we should emulate. Comments on news stories are often combative. Media personalities are hunting for attention and clicks, not for the truth. People post stories hoping for engagement, not thoughtfulness. We get a dopamine rush anytime we can leave a snarky comment that causes someone else to like it and applaud us for putting our "enemy" in their place.

Hopefully, as you seek real learning, you will distance yourself from those examples, but to the extent you still see them, I encourage you to recognize them for what they are: divisive behavior that does nothing to solve problems. They are, at best, entertainment meant to amuse, not to be followed. At worst, they are human beings behaving their worst.

So, the next time you see two talking heads on television cutting each other off and yelling over one another, know that their "commentary" is bringing value to no one but themselves. When you see people leaving snarky, rude comments after an article or in response to a post on social media, remind yourself that they are helping no one progress. When you see a person pat themselves on the back for a perfect one-line, mic-drop zinger, know they may have embarrassed their opponent, but they did not help humanity move forward in solving our very real problems.

Look for these tactics, then use them not as examples to follow, but as models to avoid.

HABIT FOUR: WHAT WE'VE LEARNED ABOUT NOT BEHAVING THE WAY PEOPLE FEAR

In this chapter, we learned that peacemakers engage in the habit of not feeding the fears of those who disagree with them. This means:

THEY SPEAK THROUGH EXAMPLES OF KINDNESS IN THEIR BEHAVIOR AND TONE.

They know that the best way to connect with others is through their own kind example and tone, long before any words come out of their mouths.

THEY REMIND THEMSELVES REGULARLY OF ALL THE FALLACIES TO WHICH THEY ARE PRONE.

They know that all of us are prone to bias, and they use that knowledge to tone down their positions on issues.

THEY STRIVE TO CONTROL THEIR EMOTIONS.

They engage in practices to ensure they are thinking clearly about issues, rather than being controlled by their emotions.

MORE OFTEN THAN NOT, THEY DO NOT SEEK RECOGNITION.

THEY ARE SLOW TO STATE STRONG OPINIONS.

They listen more than they speak and are slow to state their opinions. When they do state them, they try to do so gently, leaving open the possibility they could be wrong.

THEY DEVELOP SELFLESS LOVE FOR OTHERS.

They engage in selfless service; they focus on helping others, not on improving themselves; and they never give up on those first two goals.

THEY DO NOT FOLLOW THE BAD
EXAMPLES OF MANY IN THE PUBLIC SPHERE.

They recognize that many of the examples we see in the public sphere are good for TV ratings and internet clicks, but not for following in our daily lives.

HABIT FIVE
HUNT FOR THE BEST
ARGUMENT AGAINST YOU

Sadly, not everyone will read this book, which means (1) I won't be purchasing a chalet in France any time soon, and (2) most people will still be throwing at you much of what I warned against in the last chapter. This brings me to the next habit: always, always hunt for the best argument against your position.

Some years ago, I was sitting in the lobby of one of the nation's most prominent law firms when one of the leading litigators in the nation walked by and sat across from me. His name is Christopher Toll. We were planning to go to lunch together, along with some other folks. He is an atheist and leans left politically. He is also one of the most skilled peacemakers I have ever met. One of the most interesting things about him is that those attorneys against whom he litigates often end up becoming his closest professional friends who later refer him business. He never sacrifices even a millimeter of his clients' interests, but he also manages to turn opposing lawyers into friends. Affable but disciplined, fun-loving but focused, brilliant but humble, hardworking but charitable, principled but open-minded, firm in his beliefs but curious—he models much of what we are discussing in this book.

The first thing he did when he eased into his chair for that lunch was reach out and grab a copy of the *Wall Street Journal*. I had watched him over the years donate to and support numerous Democratic candidates. There were two newspapers sitting on the coffee table; the other was the *New York Times*.

"I'm surprised you grabbed the *Journal* instead of the *Times*," I said, half-jokingly.

"Oh," he smiled. "I like to read the op-ed page in the *Journal*. It's the best place to find the best conservative arguments for the issues of the day."

And there was a man practicing one of the most important habits any of us can master. We can quibble with whether he'd found the right source for the best conservative arguments, but he was clearly walking down the right path.

Years later, when I was drafting this book and asked him about that experience, he immediately pulled out his phone and showed me his news apps. I saw the ones I expected: the *New York Times*, the *Washington Post*, MSNBC. But I also saw the ones that showed he had maintained his habit: Fox News, the *Wall Street Journal*, other conservative outlets.

One of the foundational texts in our current way of thinking about how to acquire knowledge is John Stuart Mill's *On Liberty*. There is much to admire in the tract, and plenty to challenge, but Mill emphasized one principle that has remained true over the years:

> [Cicero] has left it on record that he always studied his adversary's case with as great, if not with still greater, intensity than even his own. What Cicero practised . . . requires to be imitated by all who study any subject in order to arrive at the truth. *He who knows only his own side of the case, knows little of that.* His reasons may be good, and no one may have been able to refute them. But if he is equally unable to refute the reasons on the opposite side; if he does not so much as know what they are, he has no ground for preferring either opinion.[1]

Let's unpack that passage. What Mill hit on is that if we want to understand our own position, we must understand the arguments against it. We have already explored the importance of finding opposing views and differing viewpoints in our knowledge gathering, so on some level, this is nothing new. But what do we do when those viewpoints are moronic? Or are obviously flawed? What if we're left leaning and we finally decide to bite the bullet and tune in to Fox News, only to find the commentary unpersuasive and ridiculous? Or we're right leaning and we have the same experience with MSNBC? Or we're looking at almost anything posted on social media?

The temptation will be to strut about in our own superiority. We see this every day, most often on social media. People find the most ridiculous formulation of one side of a particular issue, post about it or respond to it to show how absurd it is, then sit back in a pleasant trickle of congratulatory likes and retweets.

That is folly.

Return to the opening of Habit Three. The world is not made up of people who agree with you on one side and fools or monsters on the other. Lots of intelligent, kindhearted, reasonable, logical people in this world have reached conclusions other than yours. That doesn't mean they are right and you are wrong. It doesn't mean their conclusions are even as good or as valid as yours. It does mean, however, that there must be strong arguments out there in favor of those positions, persuasive reasoning or intuitions that have attracted large swaths of the population.

One of your habits should be to find those arguments and to explore that persuasive reasoning. You can do that using the methods for real learning we discussed in Habit Two. If for no other reason, it will force you to better understand, articulate, and defend your own opinions. It may even cause you to—gasp—change your mind. Let's see how to do this.

RECOGNIZE THERE ARE ALWAYS ARGUMENTS AGAINST YOU

If you ever want to have your day ruined, talk to an economist. One of the things economists are fond of pointing out is that there is no such thing as a free lunch.[2] What they mean by this is that there is a cost to everything. If you say you're excited to go get a free lunch, and there is an economist around, they will be quick to point out that if you think it's free, you're wrong. You're giving something up to enjoy that lunch: the time to get there, whatever else you could have been doing during the lunch, another meal you might have enjoyed, other people you could have spent that time with. There is, they will say, always a trade-off.

Once they have you depressed, they will emphasize that those trade-offs are often referred to in economic theory as opportunity costs—the value of what you give up when you choose between two mutually exclusive options. This is not a hard concept to understand. Any time we choose to do one thing, we are giving up something else. If I choose to accept my friend's free tickets to an NBA game, I am giving up spending that time with someone else or watching a different sporting event. If I choose to linger after work for happy hour, I am giving up time with my family. If I choose to go home to my family immediately after work, I am sacrificing networking time with potentially powerful connections in my career.

The economists are right: There is no such thing as a free lunch, and everything has a cost, which means for every position on a given topic there are arguments against it. Those arguments may be weak; they may not raise costs so high that you feel you should change your mind, but they do exist. And you should always be aware of them.

For a simple example, consider something like seatbelt laws. Except for New Hampshire, all of the states in the United States require adults to wear seatbelts. (All states require children to wear seatbelts.) The rationale is what we see on road signs anytime we take a trip: they save lives and reduce medical care expenditures related to accidents.[3] Enough of us are convinced this is true; otherwise, all these seatbelt laws would not have passed. They have become so commonplace that few of us even question them anymore. That was not always so. There are costs. One is that people must give up some of their personal autonomy when mandated to wear a seatbelt. Some may use the argument that if people want to choose to risk death when they drive, that is their choice; we don't need a paternalistic government to protect us from every harm to which we might want to subject ourselves. Another cost that not everyone considers is that seatbelt laws disproportionately burden those families who want to have more children. It's no longer the 1970s, when a hoard of kids climbing around in the back of a station wagon was perfectly legal. Requiring that every seat in a car have a belt means that any parents who would like to have more than three kids must incur a greater cost to purchase a bigger vehicle and will be disincentivized from having larger families.

When the various states were debating passing seatbelt laws, those and other arguments were brought to the fore. They obviously did not win the day almost anywhere, but they were real arguments that policymakers needed to take seriously.

Similar arguments exist for any policy position you might adopt. So always ask yourself: what is the cost to what you want to see happen in the world? Once you come to understand that, you will have a better grip on the best argument against your view. You may even come to realize that the cost of what you want is just too high, which may force you to tweak or nuance your position. Doing so will make your viewpoint even stronger.

That is an important point. You are not seeking out the costs of your preferred position only to weaken your arguments. You are seeking them out to find the weaknesses *in* your position. The result will be that you either improve your view, or you realize you were mistaken. Either way, your world will be enhanced.

DO NOT BE AFRAID OF ARGUMENTS
THAT MAKE YOU UNCOMFORTABLE

We live in a society that attempts at almost every turn to protect us from potential harm and discomfort. Psychologists, theologians, teachers, and philosophers have all recognized that some time, over the last sixty years, the wealthy nations of the Western world have shifted culturally.[4] We used to adopt the mindset that people should lose themselves as part of various higher causes. In some instances, this belief was one of necessity. Children born into an environment in which the only option was to produce food or die needed to learn as quickly as possible to contribute to the enterprise of survival. The goal was to help them become contributors at an early age.

But the wealth and luxury of the modern world changed that. Many segments of society now operate with the mindset that we must not only protect children from physical harm, but from any notion of discomfort—mental, emotional, or physical. Instead of asking how we can contribute to society, we have started asking how society can be therapeutic to us. Anna Lembke traces all of this back to Freud:

> [Freud's] groundbreaking psychoanalytic contribution was that early childhood experiences, even those long forgotten or outside of conscious awareness, can cause lasting psychological damage. Unfortunately, Freud's insights that early childhood trauma can influence adult psychopathology has morphed into the conviction that any and every challenging experience primes us for the psychotherapy couch.[5]

With that conviction, many of us have been trained from an early age to avoid discomfort, including the discomfort of ideas or arguments that challenge how we view the world.

If you want to engage in constructive dialogue, if you want to help solve the world's real problems, then you need to overcome that instinct our modern culture has created in us. Peacemakers are not afraid of arguments or facts that challenge their worldview. They seek them out. They analyze them. If arguments or facts make them uncomfortable, they seek to understand why.

Know that each of us is part of a culture that has increasingly trained us to avoid any and all distress. Once you embrace that, you can then prepare yourself to find and embrace ideas and arguments that may prove you wrong.

HOW TO DEAL WITH BAD ARGUMENTS AND STRAW MEN

One of the first steps you can take is to save yourself valuable time by jettisoning from your life one of the more annoying pathologies of our age. If you have fallen into the habit of responding triumphantly to stupid arguments, either online or in your personal conversations, it is time to break that habit and, hopefully, replace it with a better one.

We each have only twenty-four hours in a day. Responding to arguments that we know are less than stellar is a horrible waste of those hours. Recently, a group of scholars discovered that adults were happier when they used their money to make purchases that saved them time than they were when using their money for the purchase of mere material goods. In their article, they noted a new form of poverty in our modern age: time scarcity. Lack of time, they argue, has resulted in a reduced sense of well-being and happiness, "increased levels of anxiety and insomnia," higher rates of obesity, and unhealthy eating and exercise habits.[6] They suggested that individuals gain back time by spending money for others to do time-consuming chores like yardwork and housework.

I don't doubt their results, that many of us don't have enough time, but I wonder if we could combat time scarcity better if we were to spend fewer of our precious minutes on social media responding to arguments that we know are stupid and more of our time on productive things.

The most common type of bad argument used in today's modern dialogues is the straw man. It is a method by which people avoid the strongest argument against their position. The term is a nod to the "battles" in which medieval knights would not fight worthy opponents but would instead build fake foes out of straw and attack them. A straw man is a misrepresentation of a person's argument. After creating the straw man, we then dispute it rather than the stronger position. We use straw man arguments when we want to make someone with whom we disagree look silly. Sometimes, those with whom we are arguing, who are especially unskilled, create straw men for us. Sometimes we reframe arguments with which we disagree into straw men just so we don't have to deal with strong rebuttals to our own positions.

Consider one example from a controversy over the past few years. In the state of Florida, the legislature wanted to pass a law that forbade public school teachers from offering lessons regarding sexuality, sexual orientation, and gender identity to public school children between kindergarten and third grade. After that, they could teach about the subject in "age-appropriate" ways.[7]

Opponents to the bill immediately characterized it as the "Don't Say Gay Bill," then attacked that characterization. Their argument was that the bill forbade anyone from saying the word *gay* in public schools.

Proponents of the bill then attacked the opponents, calling them "groomers" and arguing that anyone who wanted to teach these ideas to small children must be trying to groom them to embrace all things LGBTQ+.

The debate in Florida and nationally homed in on both of those accusations and resulted in countless arguments. I suspect it also resulted in plenty of money flowing into cable news stations, provocative websites, activist groups, and talk radio. What did it not result in? Any conversations about the *actual* bill and the best arguments for or against it. Both sides had created straw men that were easy to attack. The media failed to help because they reported on the entire situation using the same straw-men terms instead of the substance of the proposed law.

If the topic of the bill came up in one of your conversations, hopefully your first steps would have been to engage your intellectual humility. What did the proposed law actually say? What was its text? What specific limits did it place on teachers and administrators? Did it prevent those who are LGBTQ+ from identifying as such? How would it be implemented? Were its provisions too vague for anyone to ever truly comply or enforce them? Why did some lawmakers and a large portion of the voting public support the law? Did they feel there might be serious reasons for not allowing untrained elementary school teachers to instruct youngsters on the subject? Did the law prohibit both right-wing and left-wing teachers from pushing their views? Did it, in fact, prevent people from saying the word *gay*? Did it infringe on First Amendment rights?

Those were the conversations people should have been having over the law. Instead, almost all of the dialogue that made any headlines related to the straw men. That may be how society and the media will deal with things. Hopefully you will develop the habit to dig deeper, to neither create straw men nor attack them.

RESPONDING TO GASLIGHTING

At the end of 2022, Merriam-Webster chose the word *gaslighting* as its word of the year. They did so because searches for the word had increased dramatically—1,740 percent—over the prior twelve months.[8]

The word comes from the 1938 play *Gas Light* written by British playwright Patrick Hamilton. The play was made into a movie of the same name in 1944 in the United States. It involved a husband trying to manipulate his wife into questioning her sanity by, among other things, dimming and brightening the gas-powered lamps in their home and then convincing her that she was imagining the change. She came from a wealthy family, and his hope was to persuade her that she was insane so that he could steal some of her wealth. The word *gaslighting* appeared soon after the film in several television sitcoms. Reporters and others started using it in the 1990s and early 2000s.[9]

Today, there are varying definitions, but we often use the term when someone is repeatedly engaging in tactics to get us to question our reality. An important point to note is that not everyone who gaslights does it intentionally or with nefarious motives. In fact, most of us, at some point or another, can be guilty of gaslighting. As psychologist Jennifer Sweeton has explained:

> If you're looking for scary predators lurking in the
> night, ready to jump out and gaslight you, you'll miss the

real danger. Many writings on gaslighting portray gas-
lighters as vicious and intentionally manipulative, but
this isn't always the case. People who gaslight aren't always monsters, rather, they are friends, romantic partners, parents, and siblings. They are people with whom
we laugh and fall in love, and their identity is more complex than "part-time gaslighter."[10]

In other words, gaslighting is a common human defense in arguments. While it can rise to the level of abuse and extreme emotional
manipulation, it doesn't always, and those situations are not what we are
focused on in this book.

What we are interested in is gaslighting as a form of argument that
almost always takes what could be productive conversations and turns
them into fights. It also almost always distracts from the strongest arguments related to serious issues. Because you are in the hunt for the
strongest arguments against your position, you don't want to be gaslit.

This can happen both when talking about politics but also just in
everyday interactions. Imagine the following scenario:

> Mom to Daughter: Don't forget that you need to
> take out the trash later.
>
> Daughter: Stop yelling at me!
>
> Mom (in a perfectly calm voice): I'm not yelling at
> you. I just want you to do your chore.
>
> Daughter: You're always yelling at me and getting
> mad at me for nothing!
>
> Mom (still patient): I'm just trying to help you to re-
> member to do your chore just like everyone else.
>
> Daughter: You're always yelling at me! And you
> never tell Son to do his chores. You're always telling me,
> but you never tell anyone else.
>
> Mom (now raising her voice): That's not true.
>
> Daughter: Yes, it is. It happens all the time.

Mom: Name one time I've done that.

Daughter: You did it just now. You did it yesterday.

Mom: I tell everyone to do their chores the same no matter what.

If you've ever parented a teenager, you've probably experienced some variation of that conversation. Note that Mom is focused on only one issue: the daughter needing to not forget to take out the trash.

Daughter responds by shifting the topic just a little bit and in a way that might make Mom question her reality. Deep down, Daughter likely doesn't want to do her chore, so she shifts the topic to an accusation that her mom always yells at her. She may even genuinely believe her mom is yelling at her. At first, Mom does a great job of staying on target, but Daughter is persistent. Soon, Mom feels the need to address the accusation.

The moment Mom said, "That's not true," the conversation shifted from the original topic toward something else. Now they are no longer talking about Daughter's responsibility to do her chores. They are in an argument over whether Mom yells at her daughter and no one else. If the conversation were to keep going, the daughter would most likely shift the conversation again, and it could potentially go on for hours. At the end of it, Mom may start to question her reality. Perhaps she does yell at her daughter all the time. Maybe she does single her daughter out. What started out as a mom simply doing the job of a good parent morphs into her questioning her reality and sifting through her memories to see if perhaps her daughter's accusations are correct. Most problematic, if Daughter even did have a good argument for how she couldn't do her chore that day, she will never get to it. Mom will never even get to hear it.

The same thing can happen in political conversations. Consider this all-too-familiar scenario, between Uncle James and his niece, Gabby, who has now returned home from her second year of law school and has learned a little about how the Constitution works:

Uncle James: I think the Supreme Court should rule against the baker and in favor of the gay couple in that *Masterpiece Cakeshop* case.[11]

Gabby: Really? I'm not sure I do. It's not clear to me that a state civil rights law should be applied like that, and I think it might run afoul of the Free Exercise Clause.

Uncle James: Well, you've always been homophobic.

Gabby: I'm not homophobic. I have lots of gay friends. I'm just talking about how I think the law should work.

Uncle James: That's the classic retort of every homophobe and racist in history, to say they have friends of the very people they are oppressing. It's exactly what a homophobe would say.

Gabby (leaning forward in her chair and raising her voice): When have I ever said or done anything homophobic?

Note the same thing happened here as happened between the mom and daughter above. The topic was narrow: should a particular party win in a specific case pending before the U.S. Supreme Court? James started the conversation off by offering his opinion. Gabby's response was right on target, but it was more sophisticated than what Uncle James was likely expecting. After all, she has now been through a couple of years of law school.

James responded in a way people often do when that happens. He shifted the target slightly. His response is no longer focused on the narrow issue of the conversation he started but instead pivots to accuse Gabby of something. It seems related, but it is now a completely different topic, and it will have the effect of making Gabby question herself and her reality.

She takes the bait to defend herself, and the argument is off to the races. By the time it ends, the one thing we can guarantee is that neither James nor Gabby will have explored or changed their thinking regarding how the Supreme Court should rule in *Masterpiece Cakeshop v. Colorado Civil Rights Commission*. Gabby will not hear the best argument against her views on how the Free Exercise Clause of the First Amendment should limit application of state civil rights laws. And, James, if he has such an argument, will not be able to give it.

This form of argument is all around us. People do it by instinct. Social media exchanges encourage it. Many people are naturally gifted at gaslighting others, even if they aren't doing it intentionally.

So how are you to respond? What do peacemakers do? The key is to not take the bait of the initial gaslighting move. You must recognize it for what it is, call it out, if necessary, but keep the conversation on the topic. You do have to be careful, because sometimes when pointing out the gaslighting, you can find yourself in an argument about whether someone actually did gaslight you. Or, now that the term has gained so much notoriety, you might find yourself in an argument about whether gaslighting is even a thing worth discussing or just a made-up term to attack one political party or another. That argument, if raised, would just be another form of gaslighting.

Returning to our examples, here is how Mom could have responded to Daughter after the initial gaslighting move:

> Mom to Daughter: Don't forget that you need to take out the trash later.
>
> Daughter: Stop yelling at me!
>
> Mom (in a perfectly calm voice): I'm not yelling at you. I just want you to do your chore.
>
> Daughter: You're always yelling at me and getting mad at me for nothing!
>
> Mom: I'm sorry you feel that way, but it doesn't change the fact that you need to do your chore, so please don't forget.
>
> Daughter (in exasperation and while slapping her hand on her thigh): I won't, Mom!

Despite the temptation to want to correct her daughter's body language at the end, at that point, Mom should move on and consider it a dramatic victory for not having snapped at the gaslighting bait. Chalk one up for team Mom.

As for Gabby and Uncle James, consider how Gabby could have responded when the topic shift occurred:

> Uncle James: I think the Supreme Court should rule against the baker and in favor of the gay couple in that *Masterpiece Cakeshop* case.
>
> Gabby: Really? I'm not sure I do. It's not clear to me that a state civil rights law should be applied like that, and I think it might run afoul of the Free Exercise Clause.
>
> Uncle James: Well, you've always been homophobic.
>
> Gabby: Well, you started the conversation about what the Supreme Court should do in *Masterpiece*. Why do you feel the Court should rule against the baker? And is that just your gut feeling, or are you basing it on the law the justices have to apply?

In short, Gabby is not going to allow herself to get pulled into the side conversation that makes her question whether she is a bigot. That is a topic for a different day. The temptation is there, of course. Most likely, as soon as the gaslighting accusation hit her, she wanted to respond with intense emotion and defend herself. Her first move was to ignore those emotions. The second was to use her skills at reframing to keep the conversation on topic.

That is crucial. Peacemakers calmly but firmly keep the conversation on topic. They do not allow themselves to be pulled into debates that are different from the issue at hand. They may be willing to address those other issues on another day, but not when they are trying to have a productive conversation about an important topic. For Gabby, it's likely Uncle James may come back with another attempt at gaslighting. Or he may respond in a way that makes it clear that while he has strong feelings about the topic, he just isn't equipped to talk about it at the level Gabby is and is not interested in what she has to say. If that occurs, at least Gabby will know it, and she will learn it may be in her best interest not to stay in the conversation long.

Lest you think this skill cannot work with the people in your life, consider this story involving one of my sons. For years, he was a master at gaslighting. It came naturally to him. Every time we tried to enforce a rule in our home, he would turn the discussion about the rule into some fight that had nothing to do with it.

Finally, once I came to understand the concept of gaslighting, I started to call him out on it. "You are changing the topic," I would tell him. "I'm not going to let you do that. We are talking about why it's important for you to take a shower."

He got upset a few times, but it often worked. It allowed us to stay on topic and not get sucked into a rabbit hole that had nothing to do with the subject at hand. A few years later, after he had matured, he came to me one night with a smile and said, "Hey, Dad—you know all those times you used to tell me not to change the subject when I was mad about something?"

"Yeah?" I said, a bit cautious.

"You were right. That's totally what I was doing. It wasn't on purpose, but I just knew deep down it was a way around you telling me something I didn't like to hear."

That was a win for us parents. Now go out and seek your own triumph. Practice identifying when people are using gaslighting on you and on others. And then practice how you might respond. Soon, you'll be ready to keep conversations on target and productive.

RESPONDING TO FACTS THAT DO NOT MATTER

One of the more common forms of argument we see today arises when people point out facts related to your position that have little bearing on the topic at hand. A fact may be true, but that doesn't mean it proves a broader point or is worth fighting about.

This form of argument plays out on the internet and in homes every single day. Like gaslighting, it distracts from the best arguments either side can muster. It is akin to gaslighting, and can even result from it, but it doesn't necessarily need to.

Consider this argument over Russia's 2022 invasion of Ukraine:

> Gabby: I've been thinking a lot about the war in Ukraine, and I think Western nations should be doing much more to assist Ukraine. If we send the signal that countries like Russia can just invade their neighbors anytime they want, Russia and China will be emboldened to do even more in the future. It's the first line of defense for our own country.
>
> Uncle James: Well, Ukrainian President Zelensky is nothing more than a television celebrity and comedian who happened to get elected and he doesn't know a thing about international politics or war.

Note what happened here. Uncle James is someone who, in his gut, disagrees with the notion that the United States should be involved at all in defending Ukraine. His response back to Gabby reflects that, but it doesn't seem to address her comment directly. The problem is that what James said is true, to some degree. Volodymyr Zelensky was a former comedian and actor who turned into a politician and who didn't receive any formal training in international politics or war. This is different than pure gaslighting. Uncle James is not saying something that is false or accusing Gabby of something that will get her to question her reality. What he is doing is making an assertion that is arguably true but that really doesn't seem to matter or address the point Gabby was making.

This places Gabby in a delicate position. If she engages and tries to defend Zelensky, she may find herself in a lengthy battle over his credentials, his educational background, that of his parents, whether his experiences prepared him for this moment in history, and any number of other issues. Or, if she flies off the handle and yells, "What does that matter?" she may end up escalating the conversation to a fight long before it is necessary.

The way to handle this is to keep the tone civil, not assume the worst about Uncle James, and try to understand a bit more where he is coming from. She could respond something like this:

> Gabby: That's true. I'm not following how that relates to whether assisting Ukraine will make the U.S. more secure in the long run. What are you thinking?

Gabby did not engage in a lengthy debate with her uncle about a fact that did not matter. Instead, she asked a question, and she did it in a way that will not lead to argument. She sincerely wants to know if James has a good response. He may well have. Perhaps he feels that any assistance to Ukraine will be a waste of resources and money because the inexperienced president there will not make good use of it. Perhaps he feels that the war with Russia is more complex than a simple story of one country invading another and Zelensky's lack of training exacerbated the situation prior to the start of the war.

If either of those—or perhaps some other I am not considering— is what Uncle James truly thinks, Gabby will have come closer to the best argument against her position. She can respond to those in substance, and both she and James will be one step closer to figuring out, for themselves at least, the best policy the United States can adopt in relation to the Russian invasion of Ukraine.

But what if James provides no real answer in response. What if his response is something like this:

> Uncle James: I just don't think we should be helping some joker who never should have been a president in the first place.

That doesn't help Gabby get to the best argument against her position. It seems James is arguing from a place of emotions, not one based on information or evidence or logic. But if Gabby is serious about her own ideas and wanting to test whether they are sound, she will respond in a way that will hopefully nudge James to engage her initial claim. She could respond:

> Gabby: Fair enough. I get that. But what do you think about the worries of emboldening Russia and China? I'd love to hear your thoughts on that.

In all of this, Gabby is probing, not to prove her point, but to learn why she might be wrong. She has a strong position on a controversial issue of paramount importance. She should want to ensure she is right.

The key is to keep searching and not allow yourself to be distracted by facts that do not matter. When someone states such a fact, slow down, ask yourself if you can see how it relates to the conversation. If you can't, or if they are not perfectly clear, ask them for that clarity. Make sure you understand their point. If they don't have one, or they aren't sure of it themselves, then continue to ask them questions until they finally land on a solid argument with which you can engage.

REVISITING CATCHPHRASES

We've already spent plenty of time on catchphrases and how, as heuristics, they lead us into trouble. I raise them again here because catchphrases often have the effect of obscuring the best arguments for a given cause. This means that if you express worry about something, you may find yourself frustrated when someone uses a catchphrase to respond to your concerns. We already explored how catchphrases confuse situations and make dialogue all but impossible. Sadly, they are even more problematic than that. They often obfuscate the best arguments for a given position. This means they are bad for their proponents, who risk looking like fools, and for their opponents, who struggle to know precisely what they are arguing against. If your goal is to be a peacemaker, you must take any catchphrase you hear, and then find the strongest form of the argument related to it.

Let us consider another controversial catchphrase from recent years: "Defund the Police." As with any heuristic slogan, it was meant to rally people who saw police violence as a problem. And as with any catchphrase, it evoked immediate and imprecise reactions. Those who saw police brutality and felt law enforcement across the country had become too militarized immediately agreed with the broader concept. Those who saw law enforcement as a crucial component to our society's ability to maintain order and the rule of law immediately recoiled.

Of those two groups, the second seemed to be the larger. Polls showed that most Americans did not like the idea of defunding police departments.[12] This resulted in proponents of the slogan trying to offer the nuance behind what they meant.[13] But by then, it was too late to recapture the meaning in their cause. The cat, as they say, was out of the bag. Online, commentators mocked the idea of defunding the police. Every time a shooting occurred, or statistics showed increased crime in neighborhoods with diminished police forces, critics pounced to show it was a result of defunding the police.

Pause to notice what happened. One group used a heuristic to try to mobilize people behind their cause, and I should note: catchphrases can be very good at doing just that, which is why activists use them. It wasn't the best catchphrase, however, because its unclear meaning caused many people to recoil. The backlash included literal responses to the literal meaning of the words *defund the police*. The heuristic had become an unsophisticated argument for a sophisticated problem.

If you were watching this from the outside, trying to decide what position to take on the issue, you would need to remove yourself a degree or two from the situation, taking your emotional gut reactions out of it. First, you would recognize that "defund the police" is a heuristic, so hopefully your inner voice would be warning you to tread cautiously.

As we discussed in Habit Two, your next move should be to figure out precisely what people mean when they say "defund the police." Of course, the definition of the term could have as many meanings as there are people, so which one should you adopt if you're trying to determine your own position on the topic? In a conversation with other people, your goal is to make sure you're both using a common definition so you can have a productive conversation about the same topic and not scream past each other like ships in the night.

But when you're trying to formulate an opinion, your goal should be to find the strongest argument the heuristic represents. In the case of "defund the police," the heuristic grew out of a concern, backed by some research, that police forces across the United States had become increasingly militarized. That is to say, police departments had received increased funding and supplies for military-like training and weapons: body armor, tank-like vehicles, artillery-like weapons, combat training, heavy-duty assault rifles. The average neighborhood police department was beginning to look, to some, like an army preparing to invade a foreign country, not like friendly cops trying to maintain peace and order. This was especially true in urban centers.[14]

The results, these people argued, were increased unnecessary and excessive violence by police officers in situations that might have called for more nuance.

A related concern involved the policing of Black neighborhoods. Some research has shown that police officers are more likely to become violent with Black suspects during routine stops, even if the same research shows they are less likely to *shoot* Black detainees.[15]

Weak forms of the argument also existed, including those who wanted to abolish police forces altogether,[16] but the strongest form of the argument did not blame police officers or attack their character. It was not anti-police. In fact, if anything, it was sympathetic to the plight of police officers. They are often asked to take on tasks that seem nearly unsolvable, including policing neighborhoods with overwhelming mental health and drug abuse problems, where very real, life-threatening dangers exists.[17]

Rather than attack the officers themselves, the most sophisticated form of the argument contended that in too many cities, the system was designed in a way that put both the police and the citizenry in no-win situations. Funding for police departments was going to training and equipping officers to deal with sophisticated situations in unsophisticated ways. They were being taught to do microsurgery with an axe, and then the government was providing the axe. The result was as disastrous as we all might expect it to be.

Those who pushed this viewpoint were not asking to entirely or literally defund police departments. Certainly, they wanted the police to have the funds and resources and personnel necessary to do their jobs effectively. But rather than spend all funding on increased militarization, their argument was that more resources should be channeled to people trained to de-escalate situations and to help with severe mental health problems. For example, when the police department receives a phone call about a domestic abuse incident in which one woman is physically attacking another in a life-threatening way, the police could send heavily armed officers who are trained in combat techniques and use of any number of firearms. Or they could send mental health professionals with fewer weapons but who are trained to deal with precisely those situations. A trained social worker who can talk a violent person out of a situation might be far better than a heavily armed police officer trained in physically detaining people or firing weapons when necessary. Or, funds could be used to train officers in how to use better techniques for de-escalation. For the people thinking this way, the phrase "defund the police" does not mean truly defunding police forces; it means repurposing those funds toward activities and individuals that will be more effective at reaching the shared goals of peace and safety in the community.[18]

Of course, there are plenty of strong arguments against everything I just set forth. Many would argue that police departments are already doing this, that officers receive more training than anyone on how to de-escalate situations, and that many—if not most—of the situations in which violence occurs are no-win scenarios where the police are forced to use violence or risk allowing someone to harm a third party. The reality, some would argue, is that some situations involve violent individuals who are on the verge of doing severe harm—even murder—to someone else, and all the social workers in the world will not be prepared to resolve those tragic circumstances. In short, sometimes, a well-armed police officer is needed.

Those arguments are all valid and strong. They involve empirical claims that can be tested and falsified. They represent important counterpoints to the narrative that police forces are overmilitarized and undertrained. But we never even get to explore those claims if we don't discover or understand the strongest form of the "Defund the Police" position. Instead, we get memes showing increased murder rates. We get accusations that people hate law enforcement and want to blame them for everything. We hear mic-drop moments from commentators claiming that people actually believe we can live in a world in which police departments do not exist.

In short, we get everything other than productive dialogue about important issues. All because we relied on a heuristic catchphrase to lead us toward weak arguments that do not properly capture the seriousness of the arguments on each side of an important issue.

The next time you hear such a heuristic, hunt for the argument that captures its meaning in the most sophisticated form. *That* is what you should engage.

HABIT FIVE: WHAT WE'VE LEARNED ABOUT FINDING THE BEST ARGUMENT AGAINST US

In this chapter, we learned that peacemakers engage in the habit of seeking the best argument against their position. This means:

THEY RECOGNIZE THERE ARE COSTS TO EVERY SOLUTION.

They know everything has a cost, which means there is always an argument against their position.

THEY ARE NOT AFRAID OF AND EVEN SEEK OUT ARGUMENTS THAT MAKE THEM UNCOMFORTABLE.

They know that they must expose themselves to arguments and ideas with which they disagree.

THEY LEARN HOW NOT TO RESPOND TO
BAD ARGUMENTS AND INSTEAD REFRAME THEM.

They do not waste their time responding to weak arguments; instead, they reframe them into their best form and respond to that.

THEY RECOGNIZE GASLIGHTING AND DO NOT ALLOW IT.

They do not allow others to lure them away from the topic of any conversation but politely return the conversation back to its original focus.

THEY RECOGNIZE FACTS THAT ARE TRUE BUT DO NOT MATTER.

They recognize that while some statements may be true, many are irrelevant to a topic. They listen for such facts and always politely keep the conversation focused on facts that do matter.

THEY FIND THE BEST ARGUMENT A CATCHPHRASE
OR SLOGAN IS DESIGNED TO CAPTURE.

When they hear a slogan or catchphrase, they do not respond to it immediately; instead, they keep digging to find the most sophisticated argument the catchphrase symbolizes. That is what they engage.

HABIT SIX
BE OPEN TO CHANGE

Years ago, newlyweds Mark and Tracy moved into their one bed, one bath apartment.* They were young, in their early twenties, still in college, so neither had lived before in a place where they needed to worry about the maintenance of appliances or fixtures around the house. Their parents had tried to teach them, but as with most young people, Mark and Tracy had only absorbed a fraction of the lessons their parents had tried to pass on.

When they moved into their new place, Mark had been adamant that they not have a plunger in the house. He was a bit of a germaphobe and found plungers disgusting. He didn't want one around, and nothing was going to change his mind.

Tracy thought it was a bit strange. Her family had always had a plunger around, and they had always made good use of it. But she figured it wasn't worth a fight, so she let it go.

One evening, she was in the kitchen cleaning up from dinner. She had not eaten much of her chicken breast that night, so most of it was still left on the plate. Glancing down at the sink, she decided it was too big to shove into the food disposal. Somewhere from the recesses of her mind, she recalled her mother when she was a child telling her that it was okay to sometimes put food down the toilet. (Years after this incident, she realizes that whatever she thought her mother had told her, it

---

* This story is true and shared with their permission, but I'm changing their names to protect their identities. You'll see why soon.

wasn't that; or it was a very specific situation where putting food in the toilet might have made sense.)

She walked to the toilet and scraped the chicken off the plate.

It slid into the water and nestled into the bottom of the bowl.

Tracy didn't hesitate. With two fingers, she pushed the flush handle.

The chicken vanished into the hole at the bottom, but the water started backing up almost immediately. The bowl filled most of the way, then paused.

She instinctively looked to the side of the toilet for the plunger. Nothing. She paused, considering the water, knowing that the chicken breast was lodged somewhere in the pipes. It occurred to her that if she flushed again, it might force the clog down. That must have been what Mark's family did when they faced backups, she figured, since they didn't use plungers.

She reached for the flush handle and pushed it again.

The increased water in the bowl didn't force down the chicken. Instead, the water rose. Rapidly. Its surface reached the lip of the bowl within seconds.

Tracy had no idea what to do. She fiddled with the flush handle, but that didn't slow the flow.

The water spilled over the porcelain.

"Mark!" she screamed. Another memory flashed into her mind. Aside from seeing her parents use a plunger as a kid, she recalled her dad tinkering with the back of the toilet. She yanked off the tank lid and dropped it to the floor.

Mark appeared at the bathroom door. "What's up?" he said in his normal soft-spoken voice. Then when he saw the water flowing over the lip of the bowl and flooding the floor, he raised his voice. "What the—?"

"We have to shut it off!" Tracy yelled. "Help me!" She pulled the float up and yanked it out from the tank.

"What are you doing?" Mark yelled.

"The chicken clogged the toilet!"

"Why is there chicken in the toilet?" Mark said. He stepped in the growing puddle on the floor to join Tracy at the tank. The bathroom was barely big enough to hold both of them. "And why are you yanking stuff out of the tank?"

"I'm just trying to stop it!"

"That's not how you do it!"

"Then help me!"

"Get out of the way!"

Tracy backed against the wall and sidestepped to let him pass.

He immediately bent to the wall and reached behind the toilet. Tracy watched him turn something. "You have to shut off the water at the valve!" he yelled.

"It's still flowing out of the toilet!" she said after he stood straight.

"That's because you ripped the stopper out when you yanked out the float arm!" He plunged his arm into the tank and pressed the flapper against the bottom. The water finally slowed.

"Well, how was I supposed to know!" Tracy said.

"Why were you doing this anyway?"

"I thought I could flush chicken down and it got clogged," she said.

"Why would you flush chicken down the toilet! Put it in the garbage disposal!"

"It was too big!"

"Then put it in the trash can! We need towels!"

"Hey," Tracy said, yanking a couple of towels off the rack and dropping them into the water. "This only happened because we don't have a plunger!"

"It happened because you tried to flush an entire chicken down the toilet and then kept flushing until the water overflowed!"

"I wouldn't have kept flushing if we had a plunger!"

The argument continued for some time. Eventually, they fixed the toilet and cleaned up the mess.

In case you're worried about it, Mark and Tracy are still married. Tracy understands much better how a toilet works and that, whatever her mom was teaching her all those years ago, it wasn't to put giant pieces of uneaten food in the toilet.

And what is important for our purposes is that Mark changed his mind about having a plunger in the house. They now have one in every bathroom. Although he and Tracy may still quibble over who was at fault in the Great Toilet Fiasco of their first year of marriage, he acknowledges that having one available is probably a good idea.

We can all learn from Mark and Tracy. Once we free ourselves from the fiction that anyone who disagrees with us must be a monster or a fool, we need not be so afraid of allowing ourselves to be persuaded. The techniques I have explored so far relate to keeping things civil even while you may want to persuade someone to come around to your point of view or solve a problem together. But being a peacemaker carries with it important responsibilities, one of which is being willing to change. This is a hard concept for humanity to understand. But recognizing we don't know everything, being willing to learn, seeking the best sources for doing so, asking people honest questions—all of those mean nothing if you are unwilling to ponder the new things you are learning and consider changing your views.

LESSONS FROM THE FOUNDING OF THE UNITED STATES . . . AND YOU ARE NOT A POLITICIAN

In recent years, the Constitution of the United States has endured a veritable barrage of attacks. Certainly, it had—and still has—its flaws. I won't dwell on them here or dive into the debates regarding the attacks on the document or its effectiveness in establishing the rule of law. For its time, the Constitution was a remarkable achievement. Despite all the weaknesses of the United States, the Constitution remains the longest-lasting document of its kind in history, and it has allowed the United States to thrive and progress even in the face of dramatic challenges.

Many of us do not spend much time thinking about how it was written, or how the various individuals who helped draft it achieved that goal. It was not easy. Delegates from thirteen states arrived in Pennsylvania in sweltering heat, in an era long before air-conditioning or bug spray. They represented intensely competing interests. This was not the America we know today, where we enjoy a somewhat common culture despite our geographic differences. These men represented interests, ideologies, and ways of life that made any likelihood of achieving any sort of workable agreement highly unlikely.

From all objective evidence, they should not have been able to draft and agree to the Constitution. I will return to this more later but want to focus on one point in particular now. Legal historian and scholar Derek Webb dove into the history of the Constitution's drafting not to look for the meaning behind various provisions but instead to try to understand how these various delegates could have possibly set aside their differences long enough to achieve what they did. By any standard, it was remarkable. As he explains, the delegates devised rules to "free the delegates to float new ideas, change their minds, alter course, and flexibly respond to new arguments, evidence, and proposals without fear of recrimination."

They agreed "not to keep an official record of the votes of individual delegates." George Mason supported the rule because if a record was taken, it "'would be an obstacle to a change of them on conviction.'" As Webb explains, "If delegates knew their votes were being recorded for posterity, simple pride might very well have prevented them from yielding to new information or better arguments."[1]

The second rule was related. All the proceedings were to be secret. Delegates could not publish them in newspapers or write home about them in letters. Finally, the third rule allowed any delegate to "move to reconsider any vote that had already been taken. If new ideas presented themselves or new coalitions formed, any member could ask the Convention to revisit a topic already discussed and voted on."[2]

Think about the effect these three rules had on the convention. No one was watching. No one was waiting with their social media account or smartphone to catch one of the delegates if they changed their mind on a given topic. This made them free in a way too many of us today are not free. They could change their minds, consider new information, listen to increasingly sophisticated arguments, think through the implications of their decisions and adjust accordingly, and search for the best solutions available.

One gem Webb discovered in his research was a remark from James Madison nearly forty years later, in which he recalled the effects of the rules on the convention:

> Opinions were so various and at first so crude that it was necessary they should be long debated before any uniform system of opinion could be formed. Meantime the minds of the members were changing, and much was to be gained by a yielding and accommodating spirit. Had the members committed themselves publicly at first, they would have afterwards supposed consistency required them to maintain their ground, whereas by secret discussion no man felt himself obliged to retain his opinions any longer than he was satisfied of their propriety and truth, and was open to the force of argument.[3]

We may not like all the decisions the founders made when drafting the Constitution, but we can learn from the rules they crafted. Retaining the ability to change our minds is a critical practice of peacemakers. Being open to more truth is pointless if we are not willing to allow that truth to affect our thinking.

I also want to highlight the biggest impediment the delegates faced to changing their mind, as flagged by Madison. Their concern was that once they had "committed themselves publicly," as politicians, it would have been almost impossible for them to change their minds. Then, as now, they would have been accused of inconsistency and flip-flopping. That is a legitimate concern for politicians clamoring for every vote they can get. But here's the key: most of us are not politicians. Some of those reading this book may be, but for most of us, we do not need to worry about public condemnation, or voters being upset that we are pulling the wool over their eyes. For most of us, seeking the truth and being persuaded by it will not lead to career ruin. What it will lead to is progress and dialogue that we allow to be constructive.

LESSONS FROM JUSTICES DOUGLAS AND BLACK

In the introduction, I mentioned the 1943 *Barnette* case, in which the Supreme Court ruled that school districts could not force Jehovah's Witness children to say the Pledge of Allegiance. I return to that now to illustrate an important principle. The case is remarkable for a number of reasons. It represents the foundation and, arguably, the founding of our modern understanding of freedom of speech and thought. It included what is often considered to be some of the most powerful language regarding the limits of government action in the modern era. In addition to what I shared in the introduction, it includes some of these important gems:

> If there is any fixed star in our constitutional constellation, it is that no official, high or petty, can prescribe what shall be orthodox in politics, nationalism, religion, or other matters of opinion or force citizens to confess by word or act their faith therein. If there are any circumstances which permit an exception, they do not now occur to us.[4]

Or this, when talking about our constitutional system and how it limits government from having power in certain areas of our lives:

> Government of limited power need not be anemic government. Assurance that rights are secure tends to diminish fear and jealousy of strong government, and by making us feel safe to live under it makes for its better support. Without promise of a limiting Bill of Rights it is doubtful if our Constitution could have mustered

enough strength to enable its ratification. To enforce those rights today is not to choose weak government over strong government. . . . Observance of limitations of the Constitution will not weaken government in the field appropriate for its exercise.[5]

And, finally, this sentence, explaining the purposes of the Bill of Rights:

The very purpose of a Bill of Rights was to withdraw certain subjects from the vicissitudes of political con-troversy, to place them beyond the reach of majorities and officials and to establish them as legal principles to be applied by the courts. One's right to life, liberty, and property, to free speech, a free press, freedom of wor-ship and assembly, and other fundamental rights may not be submitted to vote; they depend on the outcome of no elections.[6]

It may come as a shock to those not trained in the law, but the above quotations were not well established as part of the American experi-ence until around the time of the *Barnette* decision, in the middle of the twentieth century. Prior to that, government, and particularly state and local governments, enjoyed tremendous power over people's lives. The primary reason we don't often hear about that is because lawmakers for the first one hundred years of our country's existence were less inclined to pass as many laws as they do today.

The *Barnette* decision represented an important shift in American constitutional law and one that paved the way for much of the success and growth—with its accompanying discomfort—of the twentieth cen-tury.

But it was almost not to be.

The first time the Jehovah's Witnesses asked the court to rule in their favor, the justices decided differently. As already explained, three justices then retired and were replaced. Two more changed their minds.

Consider how remarkable that is. It is difficult today to imagine a Supreme Court justice changing his or her mind after only a few years, especially when so much is at stake. These cases arrived at the court during the height of World War II. The impetus for wanting children to recite the Pledge of Allegiance was to instill a love for the United States and the promotion of good citizenship at a time when the nation's very existence seemed to be in question. The cases were controversial, just as many are today. With Nazi Germany in Europe and imperial Japan in the Pacific, the stakes could not have been higher. What the Jehovah's Witnesses were asking was strange to everyone around them.

Yet Justices William Douglas and Hugo Black changed their minds. In doing so, they helped solidify one the most important Supreme Court decisions in modern history. When they did, they said, "It is appropriate that we make a brief statement of reasons for our change of view." They explained that they had been reluctant to apply some of the terms of the federal Constitution to state laws—something courts did not do until the early twentieth century.

Then they offered the important line for our purposes: "Long reflection convinced us that although the principle is sound, its application in the particular case was wrong."[7]

Long Reflection

I am not interested in discussing here why the court ruled the way it did in that particular case, nor in whether we as readers eighty years later agree with the outcome or the court's reasoning to get there. Legal academics have spilled gallons of ink exploring and dissecting those issues. Instead, I want to focus on *how* these two justices changed their minds. They listened to the best arguments the other side could muster. Then they engaged in long reflection. To do that, they opened their minds to the possibility of change. They considered the reality that they may have been wrong. Unlike politicians, they didn't need to worry about losing their jobs for doing so. And unlike justices today, they didn't need to dread endless hours of cable news and social media condemnation for their decisions. Instead, they considered new and more sophisticated arguments and came to believe that the rule they had wanted to apply was not the right way forward.

I pause here to emphasize the importance of both the word "long" and the word "reflection." It is okay to have a high threshold for how much evidence and logic we need to change our minds—it may require a long period of time to explore and examine a topic before we allow ourselves to be convinced. Otherwise, we risk shifting too much too often. But without being willing to change our mind, to at least consider the evidence and logic others might present to us, we abandon all hope of finding better solutions to the world's problems.

This is what peacemakers do. With intellectual humility comes the recognition that there may be more to learn about any topic and that as we learn, our positions may change. Peacemakers do not fear that. They do not see it as selling out or compromising on core values. Quite the opposite. For Justices Douglas and Black, their core values had not changed at all. What they realized was that the rule they had originally adopted was not the right way to achieve their core values.

That is an important point. Being open to changing our minds about many contemporary debates is not a question of changing our values. One principle I have learned when trying Habit Three ("Assume the Best About People") is that as I ask people questions about who they are and what they believe, I find we share many of the same core values. We both want other people to be able to flourish and thrive. Our disagreements are about *how* to achieve that goal. If I change my mind on the method I believe is most appropriate to achieve one of my core values, I have not sacrificed my principles or allowed someone else to change my identity—I have shifted my view on how to bring my principles to fruition.

We do this all the time in our daily lives. Some time ago, my wife and I heard a suspicious sound in our walls. It sounded like every homeowner's nightmare: dripping water. The problem was that it was mysterious. We noticed it only at night, and the sound came from a place in the walls where there weren't pipes. We saw no evidence of water leaking anywhere. Yet, there it was. Night after night. A sound like drip . . . drip . . . drip. Our shared and only goal was to solve that problem. We investigated. I was hesitant to cut a hole in the drywall, so we tried other methods. At first we thought it might be coming from the hot water heater, but we inspected that and found no leakage. We theorized it might be from the air-conditioning unit, which, in Texas, is often housed in the attic. Again, we found nothing. We pondered the possibility it could be something other than water, such as an animal or an electrical problem—both seemed less likely, but at least plausible. We called several HVAC companies, who told us it could not possibly be the air-conditioner. We called a plumber, who inspected the pipes and ran a pressure test on our system to see if water was leaking from any of the pipes. It was not. With each bit of new information, we discarded certain ways of trying to solve the problem and looked for others.

Eventually, one morning, we walked into our kitchen to find a ten-foot-diameter pool of water on the floor. It was time to start ripping out drywall. We brought in another plumber, who tore out large sections of the walls. All of us assumed we had to be dealing with some sort of leaking pipe. Again, he found nothing.

Finally, we ended up back in the attic, staring at the air-conditioning unit. My gut was telling me there was something about it. We had tried theory after theory to solve the problem, and with every bit of new evidence, we were forced to abandon those theories and look elsewhere. I pulled the insulation from around various parts of the air-conditioning unit, and there it was: the culprit. The unit had been positioned in a way so that the condensation that was supposed to drip into a drain pan was instead running into the ductwork, then leaking out a small hole. It dripped through a lengthy cavity in the walls that went from the attic all the way to the kitchen ceiling. The water pooled there for a time, then ran down the walls and across the kitchen floor.

At that point, all we needed to do to stop the drip was adjust how the air-conditioner was sitting, so the condensation would return to its proper path. We still, of course, needed to deal with the wreck it had made in our home. Notice the problem we were trying to solve never changed. Everyone involved wanted to find the drip and stop it. We hunted for more and more evidence and changed our proposed solutions each time the information we found disproved one of our theories.

Regularly, in our lives, we solve problems like this by seeking out new evidence and new learning, changing our thinking until we hit upon a solution. We do this for small daily problems without hesitation. And it is time we do it for the most vexing challenges in our world as well. Peacemakers already know how to do this. They are open to the possibility that no matter how strongly they feel about one solution, or no matter how much they have thought about it, there may be a better path forward. And they constantly, patiently learn about and leave room for that path, without fear that others will accuse them of inconsistency or abandoning their principles.

AVOID TOXIC TRIBALISM

One of the more remarkable pairings in recent years was found in an opinion piece written by Nadine Strossen, former president of the American Civil Liberties Union (ACLU), and Kristen Waggoner, current president of the Alliance Defending Freedom (ADF). The two organizations could not be more different. And, on many of the most divisive issues of our day, the two women hold positions that could not be more dissimilar. Abortion, gay rights, schooling, the role of government, constitutional interpretation, gun rights, taxation, affirmative action, immigration—they likely have as many disagreements on those issues and many others as anyone in the country.

But one thing they do have in common is a belief that government should not regulate speech except in narrow circumstances. Strossen has written several books about it and has become an important thought leader on the topic. One of her primary theses is that attempts to regulate speech almost always result in harming the very people the regulators are trying to protect.[8] Waggoner has been litigating cases on the issue for many years, including in the United States Supreme Court.

Tribalistic instincts shout that these two women should never join forces, that to show they agree on anything would be a betrayal of all the principles on which they disagree. After the U.S. Supreme Court issued a landmark decision related to free speech in the summer of 2023, the two decided to pen an op-ed together that would explain why the ruling was correct.

Almost no major news publisher in the United States would print it, most likely because most of the opinion editors were not happy with its message. Eventually, Bloomberg Law agreed to do so.[9]

Waggoner and Strossen's story is important for two reasons. First, it shows us that there are people willing to set aside their groups for principles they know are true. Second, it reflects an unwillingness to do the same by those who run America's major opinion pages, which is a symptom of toxic tribalism. We can all better follow this particular habit of Strossen and Waggoner. I emphasize the term *toxic tribalism* because not all tribalism is necessarily bad. As Professors Dominic Packer and Jay Van Bavel explain in their book *The Power of Us*, oftentimes, the very human tendency to form and stay loyal to groups is not necessarily a bad thing. Much depends on the nature of the group. For example, human beings regularly align with charities, nonprofits, and religious groups to perform much-needed service all over the world. And staying loyal to those groups allows them to achieve much more collectively than any of the individuals involved could have ever achieved on their own.[10]

Human beings developed an instinct for tribalism for a reason. It allows for protection, social cohesion, group productivity, and achieving in numbers that which would never be achieved solo. Tribalism, by itself, is not an inherent negative. And, in fact, remaining true to our tribe when our principles demand it is another habit peacemakers regularly employ.

Toxic tribalism, however, can be quite problematic. For example, when a tribe adopts the practice of suppressing "dissenting voices" or a "cult mentality in which members seek only to affirm one another's worldview," tribes can become poisonous.[11] If they adopt a worldview that anyone who is not part of the group is an enemy, it can lead to many of the problems we see in today's modern politics.

Strossen and Waggoner's example is important because each woman belongs to a group that arguably includes some people who have adopted a more toxic mentality. But neither woman caved to that mindset. They remain true to their tribe when principle demands it, but are willing to build bridges with others when those same principles demand that.

Peacemakers put principle over group affiliation. Consider again our metaphorical marketplace of ideas, and pretend that you are in a cloistered tent in which the only people who have entered are those who agree with you. The space is comfortable. You neither see nor hear any threats. The messages are soothing because you agree with them.

What would happen the moment an outsider appears and shares ideas that are different from those inside the tent? The most likely result will be discomfort, confusion, anger, and possibly hostility toward the outsider and their ideas. And all of that might pivot onto you if you decide to listen to the outsider. Imagine how much worse it will get if you then decide to follow the outsider out of the tent, even for a moment.

Taking that step is uncomfortable. It risks alienating us from those in the tent in which we feel the most secure. It leaves us alone. It can make others in our tent feel betrayed, even if that is not our intent. In short, it is a terrifying step.

Yet it is what peacemakers do all the time.

The fear that stems from stepping away from our tribe on a particular issue is very real. The consequences can be real as well. Our tribe might turn on us. Other tribes likely will refuse to accept us. The result is that we may end up standing alone. When you find yourself in that situation, know that standing alone is often the mark of leadership. In an article for the *Stanford Social Innovation Review*, researchers Jacqueline Novogratz and Anne Welsh McNulty explored what they found to be the single most common characteristic of people who are leaders who are driven to "direct or redirect their lives, to tackle seemingly intractable problems, and to stay true to their values in the face of enormous challenges." That characteristic was "moral courage."

They defined moral courage as the "commitment to act upon one's values *regardless of the difficulty or personal cost.*"[12] At the end of the day, peacemakers are leaders. They acknowledge how little they know, they seek truth and knowledge from a variety of sources, they listen and ask questions of those with whom they disagree, they are willing to change their minds, and when they finally do reach a conclusion on a particular issue, they stand up for it, even if it means standing alone.

DO NOT FEAR TO CONCEDE REALITY

If fear of our tribe turning on us were all we faced, we might be able to overcome it. Sadly, other terrors lurk in the night. One of the most common is the worry that if we concede a proven reality, it might undermine our deeply cherished positions. This often leads to individuals taking absurd positions even when all the evidence proves them wrong. That, in turn, leads to them losing credibility or resorting to gaslighting to avoid discussing proven realities.

We do not need to do this. It may be our natural tendency, because we're fearful that acknowledging certain facts may prove that our preferred positions are wrong. But peacemakers overcome that fear. Do not be afraid of truth. If someone proves a fact that you know in your heart is correct, concede that it is true. Then engage in whether it is a fact that matters. If it does, be willing to consider changing your mind. If it does not, explain why. But don't lower the level of discourse or make yourself appear to be a fool by denying reality. Taking that road will lead you nowhere.

HABIT SIX: WHAT WE'VE LEARNED ABOUT BEING OPEN TO CHANGE

In this chapter, we learned that peacemakers engage in the habit of being willing to change their mind. This means:

THEY LEARN FROM THE PAST.

In this case, they learn from past lawmakers and justices and their examples of being willing to change their minds to achieve better outcomes.

THEY TAKE TIME FOR LONG REFLECTION.

They spend the time needed to reflect on issues and the arguments presented to them.

THEY AVOID TOXIC TRIBALISM.

While they may stay loyal to groups and causes, they also put principle above tribe, and they are willing to stand alone if necessary when principle demands it.

THEY ARE NOT AFRAID OF REALITY.

On occasion, we are all presented with facts that are true that contradict our preferred positions. Peacemakers are not afraid to admit the validity of those truths. They either change their minds, or understand why the truths do not undermine their opinion.

HABIT SEVEN
SPEND TIME WITH PEOPLE

I have to confess. I struggle more with the advice in this chapter than with any other advice in the book. Not with the concept. I think it is spot on and incredibly important. What I struggle with is implementing it on a consistent basis. The advice is simple and straightforward: spend time with people doing uplifting things and talking about topics other than the hardest issues of the day. That is a challenge for me because (1) I'm somewhat of an introvert; and (2) my mind generally floats toward thinking about the hardest issues of the day. There is a reason this is my career. I genuinely enjoy thinking about things like religious liberty, freedom of speech, academic freedom, civil discourse, national and global politics and problems, and all the topics that branch off from those trunks. I've also learned something as I've matured in life. Most other people don't like talking about those things all the time.

Recall the lesson we studied in Habit Two about seeking real learning. Professor Douglas Laycock said that, as an agnostic, he found respect for religion by having "frequent contact with sophisticated believers." He was forced into that "frequent contact" because he found himself studying and working with people of faith as he progressed along his career path as an academic studying about religion law. But what would have happened had he never allowed himself contact with people who think differently than he does? Would he have ever developed that respect? It seems unlikely.

ANOTHER LESSON FROM THE
FOUNDING OF THE UNITED STATES

Returning to Derek Webb's research on the founding of the United States, we find another important gem regarding how the delegates from the various states managed to draft the Constitution. We already learned that they established rules that freed them up to deliberate and change their minds. But how was it that delegates with so many differing positions managed to work collaboratively to create what is now the world's longest-standing Constitution? They debated the literal legal formation of a new country and somehow managed to pull it off without it ending in warfare.[1] How?

Part of the secret sauce was that they spent time together. Webb explains:

> The first, and perhaps most important, element of this framework was the simple fact that these delegates had physically housed themselves up with each other for four months in the relatively small city of Philadelphia. They stayed in many of the same boardinghouses, taverns, and private homes, all within easy walking distance of the Pennsylvania State House where they met every day. From 10 or 11 a.m. to 3 or 3:30 p.m., they spent all of their time in the Assembly Room, hashing out business around tables squeezed closely together. After every day's business, they ate dinner at various taverns—with names like the Indian Queen, City Tavern, Epple's, or Oeller's—which were sprinkled liberally throughout the city. Eventually, dinner "clubs" formed in which eight or more delegates would regularly dine together at a time. These clubs were open to delegates from all the states, and their informal membership typically cut across sectional and ideological lines. And after dinner, around 8 or 9 p.m., delegates typically would have an evening

tea with each other and other prominent citizens of
Philadelphia.[2]

In an environment where hostility could have easily prevented
anyone from getting along, the delegates worked well with each other
because they were forced to spend time together outside the debating
framework. In short, they became friends.

Peacemakers find a way to do this, often inviting those with whom
they disagree to engage in all sorts of enjoyable activities. The world is
filled with ways to connect with others: dinners, golf, pickleball, sporting events, movies, musicals, operas, game nights, hikes, swimming,
boating, crocheting clubs, trivia nights, bingo night, book clubs, church
gatherings, happy hours, hunting, cycling, running, line dancing—the
list is endless. Identify those activities you enjoy and invite people along.
As you get to know them and realize they are not monsters (always keeping in mind that they may be coming to the same realization about you),
you will find it easier to engage in productive conversation. You may
even find it enjoyable.

IT IS HARD TO HATE OR DISCOUNT
PEOPLE YOU KNOW WELL

There is an old saying of which I am fond: "There are the people we
love, and there are the people we don't know."

On some level, that is obviously and demonstrably false. We can
know someone who has been harsh to us and not feel love for them. On
a deeper level, however, it rings true for a number of reasons. Decades
ago, the philosopher Bernard Williams developed the concept of "moral
luck"—the idea that we often receive blame or praise for our actions
even when we do not have full control over those actions or the circumstances that led to them.[3] A related term is "determinism."

Both terms are somewhat controversial, and if I were in an academic
conference, I have no doubt that scholars could spend hours quibbling
with the definitions. But moral luck works for our purposes. Large

numbers of us, on first instinct, would say that human beings are captains of their own ships, that they enjoy agency over their actions, and that they should be held accountable for them. I see much that is valid in that worldview, but we also know the world is far more complex than many of us want to admit. For example, we can see the concept of moral luck at play when we witness someone who grew up in extreme poverty stealing just to put food in their mouths.

The extreme view on moral luck on one hand is that no one is responsible for their actions, good or bad.[4] Each of us is a product of the environment and circumstances of our birth, biology, and place in the world, which we did not choose, and thus we can receive neither blame nor praise based on who we are. This view can often be used as a justification to support ideas like socialism or communism—if no one is responsible for their wealth or position in society, then the only moral thing to do is for the government to equalize everyone.[5] You can see it in other less extreme—but just as important—societal issues as well. Is capital punishment appropriate if we believe in the most extreme version of moral luck? How about prison sentences and other forms of punishment?

The other extreme view is we are each a product of our individual agency, and moral luck plays no role whatsoever.[6] Regardless of the circumstances of our birth or the environment in which we are raised, we can each choose to use our agency to overcome whatever obstacles luck or biology may have placed in our way. This view believes that an overreliance on the concept of moral luck robs individuals and communities of any concept of responsibility, making them victims, objects that are acted upon instead of actors in control of their destiny.[7] This view rejects moral luck outright and argues that it is, in fact, immoral to rob human beings of the responsibility that comes from moral agency. To do so results only in a society that cannot govern itself.

Those are the extreme views. Between them is a spectrum on which I suspect many of us fall. Most of us probably recognize that human beings can be both a product of the luck of the birth draw and of the choices they make throughout their lives. We need not decide today where best to be on that spectrum. Quite frankly, I do not know. But we can use the concept of moral luck in a helpful way without committing fully to how we think about it.

When we spend time with others and truly get to know them and the circumstances that led them to behave as they do, we tend to be less judgmental of them and more understanding of who they are and why they make the decisions they do. Moral luck—which could be things like the family situation into which someone was born, the nation where they grew up, whether they suffered abuse of any kind, whether they have genetic predispositions, whether they suffer from chronic mental or physical illness, or whether they experienced various forms of societal prejudice— can affect people's outlook on the world. When we understand how moral luck affected others, we can be more willing to hear their point of view.

Rather than swim only in the waters of snobby philosophers, consider this exchange from the 2005 movie *Batman Begins*, in which the narration explains that Bruce Wayne decided to spend time among criminals to understand their mindset more:

> Henri Ducard: When you lived among the criminals, did you start to pity them?
> Bruce Wayne: The first time I stole so that I wouldn't starve, yes. I lost many assumptions about the simple nature of right and wrong.[8]

There is the philosophical concept of moral luck playing itself out in modern entertainment. But it manifests itself in real life all the time. As we get to know why people think the way they do, we tend to feel less hate and more sympathy. We may not agree with what they say, but we will be slower to dismiss them, quicker to consider their words, and more forgiving of their behaviors that we may find distasteful.

A wise friend, who is a brilliant lawyer and also a devout believer in God, once told me, "For those of us who are parents, God seems to give each of us at least one child that will help us become more like Him."

He said it as a joke, as we were talking about various challenges with our children, but I can't help but wonder if it is true more often than we realize. If you don't believe in God, then you can change the concept to one in which we each end up being more understanding of others through the parenting experience. I have seen it in my own life.

I have a family member who committed many wrongs against me and other members of the family over the years. His behavior was the kind that was difficult to forgive. As I raised my own children, I began to see in one of them as a small child the same behavior I had seen in this other family member decades earlier. As you might imagine, it troubled me. But my wife and I had resources available to us that were never available to any other generation prior, the most important of which was the internet and its endless supply of medical websites.

We searched and sought for an answer. Eventually, enough readings led us to discussions with the right medical professionals and a battery of high-level tests. From them, we learned that one of our children was on the lower end of executive functioning. In lay terms (which is all I'm capable of), it involved the prefrontal cortex of the brain not operating as well as it does in others. That is the command center of the brain, so when it is not at a certain capacity, it makes it very difficult for the individual to control things like emotions or impulses. It makes it difficult for them to focus on some tasks, or, when they are hyperfocused on an activity, it makes it very challenging for them to get their mind off it and transition to something else. It can lead to other challenges as well, such as an inability to place certain lessons in long-term memory or to read social cues.

As my wife and I came to understand our child, we realized that we would need to change how we parent. What looked to us as intentionally bad behavior was nothing of the sort. It was merely the behavior of a human being whose brain worked dramatically different from our own. Just one simple example: consider a child with greater executive functioning. When they are young, they hit someone because they are upset about not getting something they want. Their parents place them in a short time-out and explain to them that when they hit, they will go to time out because hitting is not nice. The next day, when the child has an impulse to hit, his brain will recall the lesson he learned the day before. Hitting equals time-out. Out of self-interest, he will control himself. In time, as he matures, he will come to learn why hitting is wrong and will refrain from it for moral reasons.

Children with less-than-stellar executive functioning do not process the world the same way. They hit someone, and their parent places them in a short time-out and explains that hitting is not nice. The child seems to understand it, but his brain does not place the lesson into his long-term memory. The next day, when in the same situation, he will hit again. His brain will not recall that hitting equals time-out, nor will it recall anything the parents taught him about hitting not being nice. Over time, to the parents, this looks like willful defiance. Good parents will be patient, but eventually they will start to treat the child as a bad kid, one who is refusing to obey the rules. In reality, the child does not remember the rules or the consequences from past days. It's almost as if each day is a new experience for them. And they increasingly do not understand why they are in trouble. Why are their parents always picking on them?

As soon as we came to understand this about our child, we learned to parent differently, and it changed everything. That understanding made us more patient. It made us more kind. We learned to parent our child's unique brain type in a different way that would allow them to learn how to thrive.

Perhaps the more important lesson was that we came to see other family members differently as well, including the one who had done so much wrong. We learned that the tendency to have lower executive functioning is often genetic, passed down from one generation to the next. And we saw that in the other family member. What had been anger melted into understanding. What at one time had been resentment yielded to forgiveness. As we learned about what had led to much of that family member's behavior over the years, we offered him the same patience and kindness we had now learned to grant our own child.

In short, we came to see how moral luck was playing a role in the lives of our loved ones. Some of us were blessed with brains with high-level executive functioning. Some of us were not. It was harder to condemn those with low-level executive functioning once it became clear to us that they were often not doing things to harm people intentionally. That didn't justify their behavior or suggest that others needed to suffer abuse at their hand, but it did change how we viewed them and opened our hearts for forgiveness and far more fruitful conversations.

That type of understanding—coming to see how moral luck has played a role in different people's lives and in our own—can happen if we spend time with others. The old refrigerator sticker is true: "If you wish to understand someone, walk a mile in their shoes." Or at least take them out to dinner and get to know them better. That may seem like too much work, but the reality is that it is far less effort—and much more enjoyable—than spending our lives screaming at people over the internet or across the dinner table.

HABIT SEVEN: WHAT WE'VE LEARNED ABOUT SPENDING TIME WITH PEOPLE

In this chapter, we learned that peacemakers engage in the habit of spending uplifting time with others, doing anything other than talking about the hardest issues. This means:

THEY LEARN FROM THE PAST.

In this case, they learn from past peacemakers that uplifting recreation time together with others can help build bridges and allow for true moments of productivity.

THEY LEARN THEY CANNOT HATE OR IGNORE PEOPLE THEY KNOW WELL.

They spend time with people to know and understand them. Once they do, they realize that often, human beings have good reasons and legitimate concerns justifying why they believe what they believe. And peacemakers take them seriously.

HABIT EIGHT
A SLIVER OF HUMOR

For older readers, you will be familiar with how skilled a politician Ronald Reagan was. Even those who disagreed with his policies and thought he was more harmful than helpful to America had to admit that he was a formidable opponent on the stage.

To give you a sense of his talent, consider the following. In the 1980 presidential election, he won every state but six and the District of Columbia. Four years later, he lost only the state of Minnesota and the District of Columbia. Part of what made him so successful and popular was his sense of humor. Perhaps one of his most popular jokes came during one of the first debates of his second run for the presidency. At that point, he was already seventy-three years old. Many Americans had expressed concern that his age might prevent him from doing the job adequately for another four years. Indeed, in an earlier debate, Reagan had stumbled over an answer, even forgetting what he was trying to say midsentence. His Democrat opponent, Walter Mondale, who at age fifty-six still appeared youthful and energetic, wanted to exploit what seemed to him a potential opening in an otherwise losing campaign.

In the buildup to the final debate before the election, Reagan's staffers knew a question would be coming about the president's age. They tried to prep him for it and wanted to feed him what he should say. He waved them off, expressing that he had the situation under control.

When the debate finally arrived, the moderator, the *Baltimore Sun*'s Henry Trewhitt, asked the following question:

> Mr. President, I want to raise an issue that I think has
> been lurking out there for 2 or 3 weeks and cast it spe-
> cifically in national security terms. You already are the
> oldest President in history, and some of your staff say
> you were tired after your most recent encounter with Mr.
> Mondale. I recall yet that President Kennedy had to go
> for days on end with very little sleep during the Cuban
> missile crisis. Is there any doubt in your mind that you
> would be able to function in such circumstances?

No doubt, Reagan's staff were looking on in fearful anticipation.
How would their boss respond? Why hadn't he taken their advice?

Ever the showman, the actor, the entertainer who knew how to play
a crowd, Reagan did not hesitate:

> Not at all, Mr. Trewhitt, and I want you to know that
> also I will not make age an issue of this campaign. I am
> not going to exploit, for political purposes, my oppo-
> nent's youth and inexperience.[1]

The crowd burst into laughter. Mondale himself could not keep
from laughing. The mirth lasted so long that Reagan paused long
enough to get a drink of water, then add another joke.

The moderator laughed as well. Instead of forcing Reagan to answer
with at least some substance, he said only, through chuckles, "I'd like to
head for the fence and try to catch that one before it goes over, but I'll go
on to another question."

Many political commentators believe that moment sealed the election for Reagan and etched itself into political lore. Indeed, most people
recall very little of what else the two candidates said that night, but
Reagan's humorous response remains wildly popular even forty-four
years later.

We can debate until we all die whether Reagan was a great president, but no one can deny that he understood the power of a good joke.

It sets people at ease. It makes them want to listen to you. When someone is funny, we just assume they must also be a great person, especially when those jokes are well timed and not at the expense of others.

Peacemakers know how to use humor in this way. Reagan and many others are naturals. When they get up in front of a crowd or sense they need to use humor, they just do it. The question is: how do they do it, and what are they doing? Let's take a look.

HUMOR AS A POWERFUL TOOL FOR DISARMING PEOPLE

First, know that the notion of humor as a useful tool is not just something that sounds nice. Research has proven that some of the most effective leaders are those who know how to use humor effectively. Consider this from the *Harvard Business Review*:

> Research shows that leaders with *any* sense of humor are seen as 27% more motivating and admired than those who don't joke around. Their employees are 15% more engaged, and their teams are more than twice as likely to solve a creativity challenge—all of which can translate into improved performance. Studies even show that something as simple as adding a lighthearted line at the end of a sales pitch—like "My final offer is X and I'll throw in my pet frog"—can increase customers' willingness to pay by 18%. A bad dad joke can literally help you get paid.[2]

Part of the reason for this is that laughing causes our brains to release chemicals that reduce stress and help us feel calm and high all at the same time. When we do that with others, we feel a bond to them that is otherwise absent. They want to be with us, and, more importantly, they want to collaborate with us. When that occurs, successful conversation and problem solving is possible.

Humor can be especially helpful for relaxing the tension in tight situations. Finding ways to make people laugh when they might otherwise be worried you are out to condemn them immediately eases stress and opens channels of communication for better conversation. Consider this exchange between coworkers recently in a situation that could have potentially been high strung. It involved an administrator, an employee (we'll call Rob), and a boss. The administrator was supposed to have arranged a new space for the boss and the employee, but she had failed to do so for a number of reasons that were legitimately out of her hands. Still, it was entirely possible the boss would be angry about it, since there had already been many months of delays.

> Administrator: I'm so sorry we don't have the space ready yet. We tried and tried, but we just couldn't figure it out. So we've moved you over to some offices in the other wing that will just be temporary until we can get your space finalized over the next few months.
>
> Boss: As long as the offices are close enough together that I can throw things at Rob throughout the day, we should be fine.
>
> Rob (a few minutes later): I always appreciate your lightening things up with humor. I know she was super worried about your being upset.

Humor is a powerful tool. It puts people at ease. It opens doors. It builds relationships. The challenge is learning how and when to use it.

LEARN THE TYPES OF HUMOR PEOPLE APPRECIATE

One skill peacemakers understand is that different types of jokes work for different types of people. They know they need to understand both the type of humor that comes naturally to them and that of the people they are talking to.[3] This matters because the old idea that someone either has a good sense of humor or they do not is wrong. Instead, different people are funny in varying ways. When someone makes a joke and others do not laugh, that usually means that the listeners do not care for the *type* of humor, not that they don't care for humor at all.

We can analyze humor the way we analyze any topic—breaking it down into more and more nuanced and granular understandings. There are scholars who do just that, and they disagree over the best terms for how to describe different senses of humor. As with many topics in this book, we don't want to get lost in that jungle. Here are four categories that I have found easy to employ and one that is a little more tricky:

Aggressive Humor

This is the kind of humor often used by bullies. It generally involves insulting others or putting them down. Sometimes we see it when people are mocking someone else behind their backs. It comes up with certain stand-up comedians or in the context of events like a "roast," where two celebrities will try to mock one another. Others use it when talking about sports teams, usually in the name of "talking trash." In the right settings and in small doses, this humor can be entertaining and rewarding.

But while you may think it's funny when watching a roast or seeing someone do it to someone else on television, it generally doesn't work well in conversations with people close to us. I can offer one personal example from my own life. When I was younger, I found that I used this form of humor on a regular basis. I'm not sure why. When I met someone whom I truly respected and thought of as a close and dear friend, I often slipped into this humor with them. I would send them barbs and insults that, in my mind, I thought were just good-natured ribbing. I figured I would do it to them, and they would do it back to me. Only after a number of years and some sad experiences did I realize that I was often hurting the very people I valued the most. What I meant as playful expressions of esteem, they received as personal invectives that left them demoralized around me, not uplifted.

That was a painful realization. Ironically, the more I respected someone, the more likely I was to use aggressive humor against them. Not one of them ever said a word to me, but I began to perceive what I was doing. Only after I came to understand that my humor was hurting the very people I cherished the most did I realize that I needed to find a better way of communicating.

Analyze yourself and ask if you use this type of humor often. If so, it is probably best to check yourself. As I said, it may make sense in limited circumstances, usually those involving performances to an audience, but for purposes of civil conversation, the risk of harm is just too great. Instead of being seen as someone who can talk about hard topics, you may simply come across as a bully.

Relatable Humor

Tim Allen, Jerry Seinfeld, Jim Gaffigan, Nate Bargatze—these are some of the names that come to mind when we think of affiliative humor. They are comedians who use observations about everyday life that anyone can find funny. The great skill involved with this humor is the ability to take an otherwise mundane part of life that everyone can relate to and deliver a comment on it in a way that makes people laugh. The great challenge of it is that not everything is relatable to everyone, so findings those topics that are is a grand treasure hunt. Consider this monologue from Bargatze:

> I miss being young. Your twenties are great. You're down for whatever. Your friends call you. They're like, "Do you wanna go?"
>
> You're like, "I'll go." You don't even know where you're going. You're like, "I'll move, Dude. I'll set my apartment on fire. What do you want to do?"
>
> Your thirties come, and you're like, "Where are we going? How late are they open? Is it loud? . . . I am going to drive separate."
>
> Your forties, you're like, "I'm not going. I'm mad that you thought I would go."[4]

This joke is not an accident, or something he stumbled upon. It is carefully crafted to connect with anyone who is twenty-something-years-old and up. Anyone across almost any decade can relate to the joke in some way or another.

That kind of humor has the effect of bringing people together. It makes people feel giddy, joyful, and connected all at the same time. If this is your natural way of telling jokes, use it liberally. It can be a fantastic ice breaker and make otherwise distinct people feel part of the same group.

Self-Endearing Humor

People who excel at this sort of humor use personal stories from their everyday lives to make others laugh, but they do so in a way that often makes themselves the butt of the joke. The jokes are not self-demeaning, but they cast the speaker in a charming light. The story I shared in the opening chapter about my disastrous Nair incident is a good example. I often use that story when I speak to audiences around the world (although perhaps I won't be able to as much now that I've shared it here). It has a triple effect. It warms up audiences who are sometimes worried they are in for a boring night. It helps people feel attached to me and perhaps more willing to listen to what I have to say ("Nair guy must not be that bad of a guy"). And it defeats the sometimes-over-inflating effects of lofty introductions—too often, speakers get introduced with a long list of accomplishments and accolades that can make them seem inaccessible and unrelatable to their audiences. My Nair story helps me overcome that challenge.

Another example is one a family member of mine often shares. She is an excellent cook. It is one of many things she shines at. When she was a mom in the thick of raising her children, her family started a tradition of enjoying homemade pizza every Friday evening. At the end of a particularly hectic week, she made her excellent pizza as she usually does.

The family all sat around the table and got set to dig in. Almost immediately, the children and her husband noticed the pizza tasted horrible. This was not her normally fantastic work. But no one wanted to speak up, so they just choked it down.

After several minutes, the mom asked, "Does anyone else notice the pizza tastes weird?"

That opened the door. "Yes!" everyone screamed, almost in unison.

At that moment, the mom's eyes widened. "Wait," she said, putting out her hand. "Everyone stop eating!" She pushed away from the table and ran into the kitchen. Then, what she had done dawned on her: when she had been preparing the pizza, a task so routine that she often did it without thinking, she had sprayed the pizza pan with cooking spray. Except that instead of cooking spray, she had accidentally grabbed the bug killer Raid.

When she called poison control, the operator's only response was to burst into laughter. "You'll be fine," he said. "Just don't eat any more."

Using this type of humorous story can be quite effective. Search through your own life to see if you have any similar stories. They can be an excellent way to connect with people, both groups and individuals.

Self-Deprecating Humor

This humor is a cousin to Aggressive Humor, but the person you are attacking is usually yourself. It has its place. You can likely see how closely related it is to Self-Enhancing Humor. The difference is that this humor is even more aggressive, and it often casts the joke teller in an even worse light. As some psychologists have noted, it can be unhealthy. For example, if you find yourself using this form of humor because you are trying to stave off someone else attacking you, that may be a sign of an abusive (or at least unhealthy) relationship.

But where it can work is when someone uses it to deflect praise or to change the topic off themselves and onto more important subjects. One business leader I know is especially adept at using it. Consider this exchange I had with him:

> Me: My son [who was eighteen at the time] thinks you're the best leader he's ever worked with.
>
> Him: Eighteen-year-olds are easy to fool.

Tight, deflecting, self-deprecating, and charming. It has the effect of endearing listeners to the speaker while suggesting that he is actually not the great leader my son thought him to be. At the same time, it was not so self-effacing that it suggested an unhealthy sense of avoiding abuse.

This humor can be another useful arrow in your quiver. As with the other types, you need to analyze yourself carefully. Do you find yourself using it because you're afraid someone is going to attack you, and this is merely a preemptive defense mechanism? If so, it may be time to analyze the relationship more carefully. Are you using it in a way that unnecessarily demeans you or people in your group who associate with you? If so, it may be too deprecating and could even send a message that you are too insecure.

But outside of those instances, this can be an effective way to deflect praise and help people warm up to you.

Expressive Humor

Finally, there is a form of humor that has more to do with delivery than content. Its genius lies in *how* someone tells a joke, not necessarily the type of joke they tell. In that sense, it can apply to all the above categories.

This humor is tricky because it generally comes to people naturally, through their body language, tone of voice, and facial expressions. Think Eddie Murphy's laugh, Rodney Dangerfield's eyes, or Brian Regan's facial expressions. It is much harder to learn. While I don't think learning it is impossible, a better course of action is probably asking yourself if you have it. A good way to do that is to think back on your life and examine whether how you deliver certain messages makes people laugh.

I have found, for instance, that when I get up in front of a crowd, I often make them laugh without intending to. It often just happens in the way I say something. The humor is a mixture of my facial expressions, the way I deliver certain words, my huge stature and imposing voice, and the contrast between what I'm saying and the audience's expectations of what I'm going to say. Once I learned I had that effect on my audiences, I realized it was a tool I could use to great effect.

Ask yourself if you have that effect on people. If you do, don't be afraid to be you. The ability to make people smile, even while talking about the most difficult of subjects, is a rare one indeed.

LEARN WHICH HUMOR PEOPLE ENJOY

Understanding different types of humor is only the first step. The second is to figure out which people in your life appreciate which type of humor. This requires listening and watching the body language of those around us. As we do, we will come to understand what humor to use and in what circumstances. Does someone respond to self-deprecating humor but nothing else? Does someone appreciate aggressive humor, but you know using it will require you to insult other people around them? If so, you may be better off not trying to use humor at all. Does someone enjoy sharing little anecdotes about embarrassing things in their life? If so, enjoy that with them and share similar stories from your own experience.

It is important to realize that, generally, all of us are capable of each type of humor. Some forms will come more naturally to us than others, but we can all adjust depending on our audience. As I said, aggressive, barbing humor came naturally to me. I have had to learn to temper that and instead shift to using self-enhancing, affiliative, and expressive humor. That requires work. It is still my instinct to default to aggressive, but most of the people in my life do not appreciate that. It does more harm than good. In exchanges and conversations, I have to think harder and be far more intentional about the jokes I tell. When I put in that effort, the dividends are always worth it.

The result is that it is possible to use humor to make even the most difficult conversations a little less intimidating. I see this all the time in my own circles, especially when difficult conversations about hard topics come up. At conferences, when there are panel discussions about difficult topics—say, balancing the rights of LGBTQ+ citizens with those of religious believers of a more restrained sexuality—the best moderators are those who can bring humor into the room while not taking away from the seriousness of the topic. They do so in a way that signals they are aware of the seriousness of the topic but that we can all use a little more levity in our lives. Parents can do this when talking with children about hard topics. Coworkers can do it when dealing with a difficult topic about the office. Friends can do it when discussing even the most pressing questions of the day.

KNOW WHEN HUMOR IS APPROPRIATE

I have spent much of this chapter extolling the usefulness of humor. Knowing the value of it and its various forms is crucial.

Now allow me a word of caution. It begins with an anecdote about nothing less weighty than *Roe v. Wade*. We all know how contentious the issue of abortion can be. Over the past sixty years, there has been perhaps no more controversial topic in our national dialogue. It has largely driven the election of presidents. It has determined who becomes judges and justices. It has divided families. It has affected where people choose to live, leading some to move to states where there is easier access and others to states that make it illegal. It has led to entire constitutional movements and, some may argue, the left-wing homogeneity we now see in the legal academy.

We all know this, so we all know we must tread lightly when discussing it. At the oral argument for *Roe v. Wade*, the justices of the Supreme Court took to the bench to listen to advocacy from an attorney named Sarah Weddington, a twenty-six-year-old advocate attempting to persuade the court that the Constitution includes a right for a woman to receive an abortion if she chooses to obtain one. The justices peppered Weddington with questions for more than thirty minutes, grilling her on every aspect of her position.[5]

When she took her seat, she was replaced at the podium by a man named Jay Floyd. He was a seasoned lawyer and the assistant attorney general for the state of Texas. In his deep, gravelly voice and thick

Southern accent, he began oral arguments as any Supreme Court advocate does: "Mr. Chief Justice, may it please the court."

So far so good. He was here to address one of the weightiest issues
the court had or would ever consider. It didn't just impact a woman's
right to obtain an abortion. It implicated constitutionalism itself—what
methods our courts should use to interpret the Constitution. It affected
the power of the states versus the federal government. It even went to the
heart of democracy and what rights the people had retained and never
granted the legislature the power to regulate.

In light of all that, Floyd's next move was quixotic.

"It's an old joke," he said, "but when a man argues against two beau-
tiful ladies like this, they are going to have the last word."[6]

To this day, no one is quite sure what Floyd was hoping he would
achieve. Perhaps he wanted to lighten the tension in the room. Maybe he
was trying to ingratiate himself to the all-male justices. At minimum, he
may have just wanted a chuckle before diving into the weightier issues of
the case. It's likely he was hoping to attain everything I talked about in
the previous section.

Whatever his hopes, he was met with silence . . . awkward, painful silence that lasted over three seconds (an eternity in the context of
public speaking and especially in oral arguments in a courtroom). No
one chuckled. The joke was one that might have landed in a rural Texas
courtroom in the early 1970s. The justices of the United States Supreme
Court were not amused. Observers in the courtroom reported years later
that Chief Justice Warren E. Burger cast Floyd an icy glare.[7]

"I," Floyd said to break the quiet, ". . . uh . . . before I proceed to the
original issue in this case."

That was how he launched into one of the most consequential oral
arguments of all time.

The gaffe has become one of the primary teaching moments to lawyers about when and when not to use humor. It has led experts on legal
writing and case arguments to advise attorneys never to use planned
jokes in the courtroom and to leave all humor to the judges.[8]

For our purposes, it illustrates a related point. While humor can be an effective tool, you must know when it is appropriate. Humor is like social media; use it deliberately, at least in the context of discussions about hard topics. If you are getting ready to speak to a large crowd about an important topic, humor can be a great way to encourage the crowd to warm up to you. If you are in a small setting, a few well-placed jokes or funny stories can make everyone in the room enjoy your presence, so when a serious topic comes around, they will already think you're a wonderful person. But there are times for jokes and there are times to be serious. Funerals are almost never good for jokes, but they may be appropriate for humorous stories about the deceased.

You must read the room. But if you're in doubt, avoid the humor.

KNOW THYSELF; YOU MAY NOT BE
AS FUNNY AS YOU THINK YOU ARE

On a related note, self-awareness is a skill peacemakers use all the time. It is perhaps most important when trying to use humor. I would like to think that when Jay Floyd faced that wall of silence after his joke at oral argument, he realized that the setting was the wrong forum to make wisecracks. Hopefully he never tried it again.

But that was an extreme example, where the joke's failure was so obvious one would have to work not to notice it. In other areas of life, noticing that our humor is not working is not as easy. It requires introspection. It demands that we watch the body language and reactions of those around us. Are we laughing alone? Are other people smiling? Are they shifting uncomfortably? Are they looking at the floor or their phones?

Look for that body language. If you begin to see it in your interactions with others, then it is important to adjust your approach to humor. As we have learned, this doesn't mean you need to abandon humor altogether and wall yourself off in a cocoon of insecurity—that doesn't work either. It makes people around us sense our insecurity, which can then lead them to feel awkward any time they are around us.

More likely, it means you need to spend more time adjusting the humor you're using and tailoring it to the people around you. Figure out what makes them smile, then spend some time brightening up their day. You won't regret it. And along the way, you will open the doors for conversations about a host of topics you may have never thought possible.[9]

HABIT EIGHT: WHAT WE'VE LEARNED ABOUT USING HUMOR

In this chapter, we learned that peacemakers engage in the habit of using humor in their conversations. This means:

THEY RECOGNIZE THE VALUE OF HUMOR.

They know humor can be a powerful tool for putting people at ease and allowing more fruitful conversations.

THEY LEARN WHAT TYPES OF HUMOR PEOPLE APPRECIATE.

They know different people appreciate different humor. The five major types are aggressive, relatable, self-endearing, self-deprecating, and expressive. They learn which type people appreciate and adapt accordingly. They also learn which type comes naturally to them and which they must work to develop.

THEY LEARN WHEN HUMOR IS APPROPRIATE.

They know that many situations call for humor, and some don't, like funerals, arguments in formal settings such as a courtroom, when dealing with someone who is already upset, and so on. They learn to recognize those situations and refrain from humor when in those settings.

THEY READ OTHERS' BODY LANGUAGE.

They learn to recognize when their own humor is not working on someone. This means they watch to see if others are laughing, and if they are not, peacemakers adjust their humor to the type their listeners appreciate.

HABIT NINE
SEEK INNER PEACE

On February 3, 1943, just south of Greenland, a Nazi U-boat torpedo blasted a hole in the side of a troop carrier transporting more than nine hundred American soldiers. Panic ensued. Some men were immediately sucked into the ocean. Others dashed up to the main decks hoping to find a way to survive. They grappled with each other. Some, too much in a rush, failed to launch lifeboats properly. One man even appeared on the deck with a meat cleaver, swinging it at anyone who stood in his way.

Four men—all chaplains—remained calm. On the upper deck, they surveyed the situation. Then they set to work to save as many men as they could before the ship slipped into the frigid sea. They gave away their gloves, lifejackets, and gear. When younger soldiers could no longer think, they tried to guide them to safety.

Despite all the chaos swirling around them, they remained calm. Their inner peace allowed productive outward action. And even before that terrible night, each of the chaplains had reflected an interior confidence and calm that allowed them to interact peacefully with each other and the men they served, despite very real religious differences among all of them.[1]

Peacemakers take the time in their lives to engage in habits that cultivate inner peace, which then permeates outward into the rest of their lives. Because peacemakers come from nearly every background imaginable, not one of them has the market cornered on techniques to achieve inner peace. Theists often use prayer and religious practices. Others use meditation and mindfulness. Some rely on professional therapy. All seem to find ways to free themselves from the technological manipulation that controls far too many.

In this chapter, we will explore some of the practices stellar peacemakers use.

MEDITATION AND MINDFULNESS

Our bodies are designed to perceive and react to threats. Our brains have two amygdalae, designed to help us respond to emergencies. "When we perceive a threat, the amygdala sound an alarm, releasing a cascade of chemicals in the body. Stress hormones like adrenaline and cortisol flood our system, immediately preparing us for fight or flight."[2] This is an automatic response, one we cannot necessarily stop.

But we can control it. We can take steps to limit its effects. One of the best methods is trying to become more mindful. The term *mindfulness* has been around for some time. In short, it means staying in the present, allowing our brains to focus on the here and now, rather than drifting to other places and times.

Of course, there are times when mindfulness and tamping down our amygdalic response is not appropriate. If you're in the woods and a grizzly bear starts charging, by all means, let those chemicals flood your system and flee to safety. But in our daily lives, we can take steps to keep ourselves in the moment, to find internal peace even if the situation that surrounds us is one of turmoil.

One technique that can be helpful is meditation. This can come in many forms. This book is not the place to explain how to do it properly, but I recommend you search for books and other writings on meditative practices, including transcendental meditation. I have cited in the notes some helpful resources.[3]

Another habit that many peacemakers develop is intentional breathing. When our brains trigger our flight-or-fight instincts, which can happen when someone begins a conversation with an argumentative statement, our ability to remain calm on the inside is crucial. Breathing can help with this. One technique is to breathe in slowly while counting to four, hold that breathe for a count of four, and then release it while counting down from four.

That practice establishes a rhythm but also allows us to become more aware of our body and what it is doing. In that moment of awareness, we have more control of our emotions and can find inner peace. In my own life, I have found that I tend to experience a certain level of anxiety during almost any meeting, no matter if I'm talking to an audience of five thousand or am in a classroom with five students. Before I learned the value of breathing, I often handled that anxiety by turning to treats as soon as any interaction with another person was over. That is obviously not healthy. I needed another way.

I have found that breathing is one tool in my repertoire that helps. If I take but a few moments after an anxiety-producing conversation (which is most conversations for me) to stop and breathe, counting up, pausing, and counting down, I relax, and my internal sense of tranquility returns in a way it never does when I inhale a candy bar. This is because, as Dr. Alan Watkins has confirmed, breathing smoothly in rhythm has been proven to stop the production of both cortisol and adrenaline.[4] I can then tackle the next challenge the day will present to me.

SPIRITUAL PRACTICES

Many peacemakers find inner peace through spiritual practices. Because I am writing this book for everyone, regardless of whether they see themselves as spiritual or not and regardless of what religious beliefs they hold, I cannot emphasize just one faith tradition. I also recognize that this section may not resonate with those who do not value religion or are hostile to it.

But those who take their faith seriously—that is, those who are not affiliated with a religion just for cultural or worldly reasons—often find a powerful inner stillness that permeates throughout the rest of their lives. They find that through practices such as prayer, service, religious meetings, community worship, and the study of sacred texts. One reason for this is that it gives purpose, meaning, and focus to their lives.

If you are among those who take their religion seriously and would like to get more out of it on your path to becoming a peacemaker, one helpful practice is to begin the day with one of the above activities that will remind you of who you are and what your higher purpose is in this life. For some Catholics, that may mean beginning their day by attending Mass.[5] For others, it may mean starting their day with prayer and the study of scripture. Research has shown that prayer can have many of the same effects as meditation, and many studies have shown that prayer helps produce positive physiological and neurological results, along with increased calmness.[6] This is to say nothing of the faithful's belief that deity can and does intervene in their lives. For still others, beginning one's day with service to others may help them find the inner peace they need to be peacemakers throughout the day.

The teachings of many of the world's religions emphasize this. The primary idea is that, as people yield themselves to a higher power, they will find inner peace. In other words, we do not find peace by focusing on the self but by yielding the self. For Christians, this idea is reflected in the following:

> Men and women who turn their lives over to God will discover that He can make a lot more out of their lives than they can. He will deepen their joys, expand their vision, quicken their minds, strengthen their muscles, lift their spirits, multiply their blessings, increase their opportunities, comfort their souls, raise up friends, and pour out peace. Whoever will lose his life in the service of God will find eternal life.[7]

A similar idea was expressed here:

> Now, you may be thinking this sounds more like hard spiritual work than *rest*. But here is the grand truth: while the world insists that power, possessions, popularity, and pleasures of the flesh bring happiness, they do

not! . . . The truth is that it is much *more exhausting* to seek happiness where you can *never* find it![8]

For Christians, the notion is that peace comes to us as we give up all of our worldly desires, which can never be satisfied. We do this by yielding our desires to God's desires. His focus becomes our focus, and that single-mindedness is almost always the charitable, selfless service to others. To do this, however, Christians must engage in those habits that allow them to align their wills with God. And the practices of prayer, service, worship, and scripture study are among those. By making them a part of our day, we engage in practices of losing our desires for that which can temporarily satisfy but will always leave us wanting more.

For other religions, a similar principle applies. The daily practice of religious rites and activities can help us free ourselves from our bodily desires and the cravings of the self.[9] In Buddhism, this may come in the form of meditation, coupled with visualizing all beings as one. Or it may come in the routine of always wishing others the best, no matter who they are. Recognizing how interconnected we are with other humans and the world around us can free us from the turmoil that arises when we focus only on ourselves. As the Buddhist monk Thich Nhat Hanh explained, humans must "throw away . . . the notion of the self":

> There is the idea that I am this body, this body is me or, this body is mine and it belongs to me. We say these things based on the notion that "I am." But a better statement would be, "I inter-am." It's closer to the truth in the light of interconnectedness; we see there is no separate self that can exist by itself. You cannot exist without your parents, your ancestors, food, water, air, earth, and everything else in the cosmos. By looking deeply into the nature of reality, we can throw away the notion "I am."[10]

Meditation and visualizing positive outcomes for people other than ourselves is an important practice for many to achieve less concern about themselves, more compassion for others, and a sense of inner peace.

I could go on for hundreds more pages exploring the ways various religious practices help their adherents achieve inner peace. I give these few examples to illustrate the point that believers in many traditions find real value in engaging in religious practices. If you are among those who takes your religion seriously, dig deep into its traditions and practices on achieving contentment and peace, then put them to use in your life. You will find treasures upon treasures from doing so.

JOURNALING

Studies have consistently shown that journaling is good for our mental health. It can help reduce depression, anxiety, and stress, which in turn can improve immune function. It helps those who have psychiatric conditions recover faster.[11] And it also increases one's sense of gratitude. In short, it is a remarkable tool for helping us develop inner peace.

With all those benefits so readily apparent, the only reasonable question is: why wouldn't you journal? The answer is also readily apparent. Many of us feel we just don't have time. This is where habits come in. Perhaps the best way to make journaling a habit in our lives is to ensure we don't allow great expectations to be the enemy. In other words, we do not need to write a chapter in a book every day for journaling to be effective. Small entries, even a few bullet points, are fine.

Start small. Keep the journal where it is handy (I keep mine in my computer bag, which pretty much goes wherever I go). Write a few words each day to get into a routine, perhaps just about what you did or felt on a certain day. Your first entry could be as simple as "September 15. Feeling sad."

Those minor entries build on themselves. Over time, the journaling starts to propel itself as we feel and recognize its benefits. As it does, you will find yourself on the road to becoming a peacemaker, and you'll also have created a narrative of your life you and your posterity will cherish forever.

READING

Reading is a similar super habit for achieving inner peace. And by "reading," I don't mean scrolling social media or short, poorly written articles about some pop culture phenomenon. I'm talking about books. It helps develop intelligence and brain function (including memory as we age). Reading literary fiction can help us become more empathetic. It reduces stress and can help us relax.[12]

All of those benefits contribute to our inner calm and raise the same issues as with journaling. We know reading is valuable, so why don't we do it more? The key, once again, is establishing the habit. If we make it as easy as possible to read, we are more likely to engage in it. One way to do that is to ensure we have books that might interest us all over our home. I like to have books by my bed, my couch, my desk, and in every room. My hope is that if I put my phone down long enough, I'll pick up a book instead.

Listening to books can be effective as well, especially when doing activities like exercise, yard work, chores, or any other nonthinking mundane tasks.

Finally, the best tip is sometimes the hardest. Many of us naturally feel as though we must finish any book we pick up. The sooner we can quash that instinct, the better. There is something extremely satisfying about finishing a book, but if the result of trying to force ourselves through a tome before we're willing to pick up another is that we never read anything else ever again, it's best to set aside the book that isn't capturing our interest. As I explained way back in Habit One, there are more books than any of us could ever read even if all we did was read every second of every day for our entire lives. That means that if we pick up a book and it doesn't capture our interest, we can gleefully move on to the next one until we find a book we can't put down.

Life isn't school. No one will punish us for not finishing an assignment. We are reading to improve our minds and hearts and to develop that peace that we can hopefully share with others. If a book we have chosen doesn't help us achieve that within a reasonable number of pages, we can find one that does.

SCHEDULE MANAGEMENT

Cultivating the inner peace necessary to be a peacemaker requires something each of us has in very limited supply: time. No matter how much we may like to think otherwise, we are all running out of time. We may agree that journaling, reading, meditations, prayer, religious observances, or any combination of those activities are worthwhile, but finding time for them is difficult. Merely hoping we will find a window generally doesn't work. We tell ourselves we'll do it later in the morning, after dinner, or before bed, but more often than not, we are skipping it altogether.

Peacemakers deliberately carve out time for engaging in these practices. They recognize that the rest of their time is so much more valuable when they take care of themselves mentally and spiritually (for those who value spirituality). Perhaps the most important practice is setting aside a designated time each day to engage in these practices. For some, that may be first thing in the morning. Others may choose to do it over lunch or during the day. Still others try to allocate time immediately before bed. The precise time will be different for each of us, but the key is to set that time aside and treat it as sacrosanct.

Every aspect of the world will try to intervene. Emails and texts from bosses, coworkers, clients, or family will never stop. Our many obligations will always loom. The latest, most interesting news developments will ceaselessly beckon. But if we can wall ourselves away from those things for just long enough to engage in those practices that will help us move toward a sense of inner peace, we will have taken a huge step forward to becoming a peacemaker.

PROFESSIONAL HELP

For some of us, we experience troubles so severe we cannot navigate out of them on our own. If you find yourself in that situation, it may be time to search for professional help. Talking with a trained professional who understands and shares your values may be required. As we ponder this, we should ensure that we do not allow our pride to get in the way. There is nothing wrong with seeking guidance from those properly trained to give it.

HABIT NINE: WHAT WE'VE LEARNED ABOUT FINDING INNER PEACE

In this chapter, we learned that peacemakers engage in habits to find inner peace. This means:

THEY SEEK WAYS OF ACHIEVING MINDFULNESS.

Peacemakers use meditation, intentional breathing, and other forms of mindfulness to achieve inner peace.

THOSE SO INCLINED ENGAGE IN RELIGIOUS OR SPIRITUAL PRACTICES.

For those who take their religious identities seriously, religious practices such as prayer, the study of sacred texts, and worship can be powerful tools for building inner peace.

THEY JOURNAL.

Research has proven that journaling is helpful for nearly every measure of mental and emotional health. Peacemakers find a way to do it regularly, even if only in short spurts.

THEY MAKE READING A PRIORITY.

Like journaling, reading has many proven health benefits. Rather than waste their days on social media, peacemakers make time to read long-form writings.

THEY CARVE OUT UNINTERRUPTED TIME FOR DEVELOPING INNER PEACE.

Peacemakers protect the time necessary to do those practices that bring inner peace to them.

THEY SEEK PROFESSIONAL HELP WHEN THEY NEED IT.

Some trials are too great to conquer on our own. When necessary, peacemakers are humble enough to ask for help.

HABIT TEN
EMBRACE THE DISCOMFORT
OF NON-CLOSURE

A place of certainty is a comfortable place to be. It can also be deadly.

Some years ago, at the beginning of the warm season in Austin, our entire family was out in the yard doing spring chores. Pulling weeds, trimming bushes, mowing the lawn, cleaning up leaves, cutting vines, spraying for bugs—all tasks that come with owning a home in this part of Texas. My wife and I were focused on our duties, while the kids had theirs. Everyone was busy.

In this part of Texas, the summers can be so hot that at least half the single-family homes either have pools or are parts of neighborhoods with them. With extreme reluctance, we bought a home that came with a pool. I now refer to it as the "gift that keeps on taking." But my duties that day largely centered around getting it ready for the season.

Around midday, my wife and I crossed paths in the backyard outside the garage. Her arms were filled with two paper bags full of debris. "I'm gonna go to the store to grab some things," she said, heaving the bags into a rollable trash can.

"Hey! Why don't I go with you?" I said. "The kids are all doing what they're supposed to. They'll be fine without us. We could grab some lunch, make it a little day date."

Just then, the side door to the garage opened.

My then-ten-year-old son strutted out in a swimsuit, no shoes or shirt, a towel over one shoulder and a 30-foot construction-grade extension cord wrapped around the other.

I watched him for about five steps, then said, "What are you doing?"

"Don't worry, Dad," he said without looking at me. "I'll put it back."

"What. Are. You. Doing?" I said, raising my voice a bit.

"You know that floaty that has a slow leak and never stays blown up?" he said.

"Yeah?"

"I'm gonna blow it up. Then I'm gonna get on it in the pool with the extension cord plugged in and the air blower with me so that when it loses air, I can just blow it up while I'm out on the water."

My wife and I did not get to go on our day date. Instead, I spent some time teaching my son about electricity.

Before our lesson, he had been certain he understood electricity, and that certainty had made him comfortable and confident he was headed in the right direction.

But certainty is not always a good thing. And when we're talking about trying to solve all the world's most complex problems, it can often lead to nothing but fruitless and pointless arguments. The good news is that we don't need to solve all the world's problems. Once we recognize that, we will be comfortable no longer experiencing the painful need to win all arguments. More important, we will embrace the exciting proposition that there is always more to learn, new horizons to explore, novel discoveries and concepts to find, alternative ways of looking at our reality.

Think of every conversation you have as an opportunity for exploration. Once you reach a conclusion on something, settle into that uncomfortable reality that you may not have reached your final destination.

THE REALM OF REASONABLENESS AND BEING COMFORTABLE IN THE SPACE BETWEEN EXTREME CERTAINTIES

Human beings are not wired to acknowledge the gray areas of our lives. Instead, we have developed to engage in what neuroscientists call *dichotomous thinking*. We often hear this described as *all-or-nothing* or *black-and-white* thinking. Students of philosophy will recognize this idea as having similarities to Aristotle's teaching on the "golden mean," which is that virtues exist on a spectrum, with vices on either end and virtues resting in between.[1] For example, on one end of a spectrum we might find cowardice. On the other extreme is rashness. In between those two vices, we discover the virtue of courage. I don't want to get lost in Aristotelian philosophy. I flag him only to show that humanity has recognized our tendency towards dichotomous thinking for a long time.

We see this in our everyday lives, often in toxic ways: believing no one loves us, thinking that our only options are to binge on junk food or go on a strict diet, supposing we will either succeed wildly or fail miserably. We all experience this to some degree and at different times throughout our lives. Where it is most destructive at a societal level is when we allow ourselves to fall into it with our policy debates.

We experience this all the time, for every major issue.

The thinking by many scientists is that our brains developed to think this way as a survival mechanism. It relates to our earlier discussion of heuristics and the role they play in allowing us to navigate a complex work. If we constantly saw the nuance and complexity in every situation we encountered, we would be overwhelmed with information and complication. In short, we wouldn't be able to function. Given our limited cognitive ability, our brains simplify and categorize our world.

This thinking may make sense when we're trying to survive day to day. When the goal is just to get food on the table and make sure our kids are clothed (a grand achievement for most of us on some days), simplified dichotomous thinking saves us from having to allocate all sorts of mental resources to the complicated world around us. Such thinking likely also made sense for humanity back when being forced to reason quickly or die required it. If a large animal is chasing us, it doesn't make a whole lot of sense to stop and ponder that animal's moral luck in being born in a world in which human beings are encroaching on its territory. Your brain just needs to say: danger, run!

But in a more complex world, when thinking about the complicated issues of an intertwined advanced society, dichotomous thinking doesn't help us. It hurts us. Consider the complex problems in our world and where dichotomous thinking has left us. On so many of these issues, we are told we have only two options. You can be:

- pro-religion or pro-LGBTQ+ rights
- pro-abortion or pro-life
- for immigrants or against them
- pro-tax or pro-free markets
- pro-transgender rights or pro-woman
- in favor of full-blown critical race theory in schools or in support of white supremacy
- for black lives or against black lives
- pro-religion or purely secular
- pro-science or anti-science
- conservative or progressive
- pro-Israel or pro-Palestinian
- pro total gun control or in favor of no regulation whatsoever
- a believer of nurture or a believer of nature

The reality is that, on most of these issues, most of us do not fall cleanly on one end of the spectrum or the other. When pressed, or when we're alone truly thinking through a particular societal problem, we likely find that we lie somewhere between the extremes. But everything about our modern society, including our own natural tendency to engage in dichotomous thinking, pushes us toward the extremes.

Indeed, to even be a part of most modern groups, we are told we must reach an extreme conclusion and refuse to budge. If we do show any nuance in our position, we face excommunication from the group. Although we hate to admit it, the fear of that too often forces us to join one extreme camp or another.

As with most problems, becoming aware of it is the first step toward overcoming it. That is why I highlight dichotomous thinking here. If we know it is a tendency we all have, we can be on the lookout for it in our own lives, especially on the complex issues that so many of us struggle to discuss. Rather than allowing ourselves to fall into the trap of being pulled to extreme positions, we can instead look for those opportunities to feel comfortable in the space between them.

I call that space the Realm of Reasonableness.

Extreme	Realm of Reasonableness	Extreme

It matters for a couple of reasons. First, on our own positions, we want to make sure we lie somewhere in the Realm of Reasonableness. Lest there be any misunderstanding, I am not suggesting we must take moderate positions on all issues, or that right in the middle of the Realm of Reasonableness is the only proper place to be. There are some driving values that will and should move you toward one position on a particular issue. But you should engage in introspection to ensure your positions still lie in the Realm of Reasonableness. One way to know if they do is to ask whether taking action on your positions will yield absurd results.

To give an example, in my own field, scholars often engage in robust debates about how much protection the Constitution gives us against the formation of a state church. Occasionally, every few semesters, I will have students who argue there should be no restrictions whatsoever against the formation of a state church. They generally take that position because they think such a rule will work in their favor. When I point out to them that if we were to interpret the Constitution that way, it would mean Latter-day Saints could make their religion Utah's official state church, and atheists could make atheism the official religion of the Massachusetts commonwealth, they generally back off from their extreme position. Thinking through the consequences of your preferred policy positions and looking for any absurd outcomes that might result can keep you in the Realm of Reasonableness.

You should be aware that landing somewhere in that realm can often be uncomfortable. There is a tension there; it will sometimes feel as if you are being pulled apart by both extremes. Too many of us cannot handle that strain. It is far more comforting to move in to a place of firm conclusion and bask there among like-minded people. Comforting, but ultimately fruitless. Those who allow themselves to get pulled into the extremes will find it increasingly difficult to engage in helpful conversation with those around them. Staying in the Realm of Reasonableness comes from recognizing that there are always costs to every solution, ever-present arguments for why we might be wrong. Recognizing those will keep us from pushing for extreme positions that ignore costs and, in some instances, do more harm than good.

The second benefit of residing in the Realm of Reasonableness is that it can help us be more patient with those with whom we disagree. When we meet someone whose position is different from ours, one of our first internal questions should be to ask whether their position lies somewhere within the Realm of Reasonableness. If it does, we can acknowledge that. It means their position enjoys evidence and reason that is worthy of examination. You may reach an opposite conclusion, but at least you can see how they arrived where they are. It's also helpful to know if you're dealing with someone whose position is so extreme that it has no real evidentiary support beyond the person's own emotional convictions. When you meet someone like that, you may find peace in knowing that, at least on that particular issue, civil discourse is likely going to be impossible. That knowledge alone can save you from any number of fights when relatives visit.

Again, acknowledging that someone with whom you disagree holds a position that is at least reasonable, even if you find it wrong, can be uncomfortable. We want to make sense of our world. We want confirmation that how we view things is right. Knowing that someone else may have a reasonable position brings with it the possibility that our own position may be wrong. Because we are wired to try to simplify our existence into clear categories, that can be problematic for many of us. And acknowledging that both we and those with whom we disagree are both in the Realm of Reasonableness means admitting that we may not be as far off in our positions as we first thought. That's a scary thought if we've grown accustomed to seeing anyone who thinks differently from us as monsters or fools.

So how do peacemakers get themselves comfortable in the Realm of Reasonableness? Let's explore.

BASK IN DIFFERENCES

Some research shows that the more education someone obtains, the more likely they are not to engage in dichotomous thinking. But I want to emphasize an important point about this, hearkening back to Habit Two about real learning. Obtaining education is not the same as obtaining degrees. It is true those two things can and often do coincide, but the world is filled with people who have advanced degrees who have not engaged in obtaining any education beyond that which was required for the degree. This means they are often specialized in a particular area but have done nothing to engage in real learning in all the areas in which they did not specialize. Or it can mean they pursued their degrees merely to get the credentials or to confirm what they felt they already knew about the world. Either way, we must not equate education with diplomas. Perhaps nowhere more than in the halls of academia does the idea that "a little learning is a dang'rous thing" resonate more. Meanwhile, all over the globe, people are learning more and more about their world merely because they are curious and they are seeking to understand their existence more.

True education, not mere degrees, seems to be able to soften our tendency toward dichotomous thinking. It allows us to bask in new information and in new discovery. I consistently have conversations and dialogue with people with whom I disagree. If I were not able to do that, I couldn't function in my career, and neither could they. Regularly, I collaborate with people who don't see eye to eye with me on religion, politics, or constitutional interpretation. In fact, I would say that is far more the norm than an exception. It is especially true for me because my natural disposition often places me on an island by myself on a whole host of topics.

Some of my most enjoyable moments have been during the period after I've had a discussion with someone and we uncovered a disagreement. To me, those have not been moments of anger or argument. They have always led to my asking additional questions and challenging my own assumptions about the world. That, in turn, has forced me to read more and to engage in more study. When I do, I've always come away with a better understanding of the topic we were discussing.

Peacemakers bask in those moments. I hope we can all bask in them as well. All it requires is for us to be willing to consider others' perspectives and be open-minded regarding what we might discover. Clinging to firm, mostly uninformed conclusions will deprive us of that.

A STEP IN THE RIGHT DIRECTION IS A MARATHON

Recall how humanity creates knowledge. We do it by talking, exchanging information, presenting ideas, challenging those ideas, amassing evidence, debating the meaning of that evidence, searching for more information, presenting that information to others, reaching conclusions, allowing others to challenge those conclusions, and changing our minds as appropriate. Note how that happens. It is incremental. We amass knowledge little by little, line upon line, sliver of truth on sliver of truth.

For that to work, we must each recognize that we need not find grand conclusions in any one sitting. We need not solve every problem. We need only to make some progress. When we finish a conversation with someone about a difficult topic and have not found the perfect solution, that should only be a source of frustration for us if we learned nothing or if the dialogue ended in argument. But if we learned something new, if our way of thinking advanced, if we can now see the situation from a slightly different perspective, those are advances—ones we should cherish. It is okay that we are still undecided or haven't persuaded everyone to agree with us. We are making progress, and that is more than most people can say about many conversations.

WHEN CERTAINTY MATTERS

Please do not misunderstand me. None of what I have written is meant to suggest we should never be certain about some things. For all the praise I have given in this chapter, and really through this entire book, to uncertainty and humility, allow me to end on what I see as important truths.

The notion of embracing nonclosure can be a challenge because we all know there are some areas of life where we want to reach conclusions and never budge. Two decades ago, I read the following remarks from a prominent attorney:

> My recollection has been drawn to a comment made by a professional colleague some years ago. He said that as a young lawyer he inquired of a prominent judge in his community what it takes to be a successful courtroom advocate. This wise jurist responded with five words, words that in my judgment are profound in their own right and reach far beyond the courthouse . . . . He said, "The decided are always gentle."[2]

The decided are always gentle—we could probably spend days pondering that phrase. It has stuck with me ever since I first read it. To me, it means that there is a calmness and tranquility that comes to us once we have already made up our minds on a particular issue. We need not revisit it again and again every time we face it.

The obvious dilemma lies in determining the difference between those issues on which we should keep an open mind and those on which we should be "decided." I'm not sure any one of us can definitively know the answer for anyone else, but might I suggest at least one broad principle that can help guide you. It lies in how you treat others. Resolve to behave toward other people with a selfless desire to lift them up regardless of the consequences or who they are. If that is your standard, you will find many situations in which you can be gentle, because you will have already decided how to act.

Determining how that principle will play out in our lives is unique to each of us, but here are a few practical applications that will hopefully ground it in everyday reality. One of my favorite books is *A Christmas Carol* by Charles Dickens. The story has seen so much screen time and holiday commercialism that even bringing it up feels about as sophisticated as using *Star Wars* for profound life lessons. But we've already used *Batman* and *Groundhog Day*, so why not. You will recall that Ebenezer Scrooge has become a miserly, mean, grumpy old man who is rude to everyone around him despite his great wealth. One of the key lessons in the novel occurs when the Ghost of Christmas Past whisks him away to view himself as a younger man. He witnesses a party thrown by his former boss back when Scrooge was just starting on his own career path.

Scrooge observes his younger self talking with another coworker after the party about how wonderful his boss is. They heap praise upon him with an energy the elderly Scrooge could never hope to match.

The Ghost asks the older Scrooge, "He has spent but a few pounds of your mortal money: three or four perhaps. Is that so much that he deserves this praise?"

Scrooge, in perhaps his first moment of regret for how he has come to treat his own employee, the poor clerk Bob Cratchit, answers with the following:

> "It isn't that," . . . "It isn't that, Spirit. He has the power to render us happy or unhappy; to make our service light or burdensome; a pleasure or a toil. Say that his power lies in words and looks; in things so slight and insignificant that it is impossible to add and count 'em up: what then? The happiness he gives is quite as great as if it cost a fortune."

At that moment, Scrooge felt the Spirit's glance upon him and paused. That led to this exchange:

"What is the matter?" asked the Ghost.

"Nothing particular," said Scrooge.

"Something, I think?" the Ghost insisted.

"No," said Scrooge, "No. I should like to be able to say a word or two to my clerk just now. That's all."[3]

Scrooge realizes, for just a moment, that he holds the power to make someone else's day more enjoyable. That is no small matter.

For so many of the problems in this world, many of us are not in a position to make any true impact. But making someone else's day just a bit brighter is something we can do everywhere we go. To be decided, we can resolve to treat others with kindness and selflessness, regardless of the circumstances. This is especially true of those we interact with daily through stressful situations. As Scrooge realized, our "power lies in words and looks," the small mannerisms that make all the difference in the world to those around us. Saying thank you, offering praise, pausing to sincerely ask how someone is doing—we can be resolved to do those small acts everywhere we go.

In other settings, we can resolve to put our spouse or our children or our loved ones over our career. That has always been a decision for me that helped me become "decided." No matter what I was pursuing, regardless of the opportunities placed before me or the glimmer of the temptation, I decided long ago that my wife and my children would always come first. Such a commitment is easy to state and one most people give lip service to, but I knew that to do it, I would need to decide in advance my answers to some very practical questions. The results were commitments I made at the outset of my career and have never needed to revisit: except in rare emergencies (as determined by me and my wife), I would always be home for dinner, I would block off Monday evenings for family time, the weekends belonged to my spouse and children, and I would as much as possible not work more than forty hours per week so that I could spend that time with them. I recognize not everyone is in a place at all times in their lives to make these same commitments; some may not even see wisdom in them, but, for me, they have brought an enduring peace I could not have replicated in any other way.

Over the years, they have meant turning down lucrative jobs. They have included sacrificing money and prestige. They have meant declining invitations to happy hours and fancy gatherings from seemingly important people. They have meant giving up opportunities that I would have desperately wanted to pursue had I not already made those decisions. But I had already made the commitments. I was not going to revisit them. Each time an opportunity has arisen, I have not needed to face it with the turmoil of someone who has yet to commit. I've already known the answer and could move forward with serenity. In the time since, I have seen the fruits of those decisions in my relationships and that has increased the tranquility I feel.

You will likely have similar commitments in your life that relate to your loved ones. Decide now where your lines are, come what may, and enjoy the peace that follows.

There are many other settings where this principle of selflessness toward others can come into play. At work, we can decide to help others receive recognition and promotion instead of seeking it for ourselves. In all our interactions, we can decide well in advance that we will not speak ill of others behind their backs or insult them to their face. We can always choose not to physically harm someone. We can decide never to raise our voice in anger. (I know all the parents reading this are rolling their eyes at that one; but it's okay if some of these are aspirational).

These are old ideas, and their enduring nature should tell us something about their wisdom. Decide when you will allow a principle of selflessness to guide you in your behavior, and you will have found a broad swath of your day when you can be one of those decided people who are gentle.

Being a peacemaker does not mean avoiding taking positions based on your core values. If anything, it means knowing what your core values are, then reflecting them through an example of serenity and civility.

HABIT TEN: WHAT WE'VE LEARNED ABOUT EMBRACING THE DISCOMFORT OF NON-CLOSURE

In this chapter, we learned that peacemakers engage in the habit of embracing non-closure. This means:

THEY ARE COMFORTABLE WITH UNCERTAINTY.

Many of life's most complex problems are complex for a reason. Peacemakers recognize it is okay to be uncertain about many of the most pressing issues of the day.

THEY ENJOY DIFFERENCES OF OPINION.

Peacemakers are not afraid of finding that others disagree with them but instead look forward to a fruitful dialogue that can occur after a disagreement surfaces.

THEY RECOGNIZE THAT EVEN A SMALL STEP TOWARD RESOLVING A PROBLEM IS HUGE.

Peacemakers realize that for many problems, even a small step in finding a solution is important, and they know they cannot make those small steps in moments of hostility and argument.

THEY RECOGNIZE THERE ARE TIMES CERTAINTY MATTERS.

They all know that certainty matters. At times, they must be decided. For many of them, the realm in which they should be certain is in their dealings with other humans. They can commit to treating others with selfless love, come what may, while they strive to help solve many of society's toughest problems.

EPILOGUE

When Abraham Lincoln was still a practicing lawyer, he prepared notes for a lecture he was planning for other attorneys. In them, we find a particular piece of wisdom that has been oft-quoted in the hundred and seventy years since: "Discourage litigation," he wrote. "Persuade your neighbors to compromise whenever you can. Point out to them how the nominal winner is often a real loser—in fees, expenses, and waste of time."[1]

Lincoln was talking to lawyers about the adversarial litigation process, but his sentiments resonate in our day about so much more. In fighting over every issue that bursts on to the national scene, in allowing others to manipulate us into a constant state of battle, we are all losing. Even in those rare instances where a winner in a particular argument does emerge, the loss of time and good relations is so high, the winner is a victor in name only, and usually only in their own sight.

There are many issues on which we each know we cannot compromise. Our core values will not let us. But *how* we talk about those issues matters. How we treat others matters. If we want to change the world and preserve all that is good about it, we must start by not making everyone our enemy. Many of the world's seemingly intractable problems are not unsolvable.

What they require are peacemakers, those who can address them with civility, kindness, respect, thoughtfulness, pure knowledge, and flexibility. We are most likely to find workable solutions through dialogue and conversation led by people who know how to make those happen.

I hope the habits in this book will help you to become one of them.

ACKNOWLEDGMENTS

Every book is the product of a great team. Mine begins with my wife, who is one of the world's greatest peacemakers. As always, I am grateful for her generous spirit, brilliant mind, wise advice, and unfailing support. Close on her heels are my kids, who always make me laugh and who never let me forget what truly matters in life.

This book would not have been possible without the peacemakers who allowed me to pick their brains and rely on their experiences: David Rabban, Nadine Strossen, Samy Ayoub, Marian Edmonds-Allen, Ward Farnsworth, John Greil, John Inazu, Aaron Pierson, Nury Turkel, Doug Laycock, Paul Kerry, Clayton Dana-Bashian, Christopher Toll, and my own children.

My assistant, Sandra Garcia, who is a peacemaker in her own right and a confidant on so much, deserves as much praise as I can give her.

I owe my research assistants more than I can say. Morgan Wray, Meg McDonough, Colin Crawford, and Veda Tsai—you helped me find sources and ideas I wasn't sure any human could find. And your help continues. I'm grateful you never gave up. I'm thankful you've been by my side.

I am thankful for Susan Schulman, for her advice, wisdom, and integrity. She is one of the good ones.

As always, I'm grateful for the team at Shadow Mountain Publishing and for all their work in bringing a book like this to fruition. Most people don't realize how much goes into creating a book, but I am always mindful of it. Chris Schoebinger, Heidi Gordon, Lisa Mangum, Janna DeVore, Amy Parker, Garth Bruner, and Bre Anderl to name a few.

NOTES

INTRODUCTION

1. West Virginia State Board of Education v. Barnette, 319 U.S. 624, 641, 642 (1943).
2. Michael P. Wilmot and Deniz S. Ones, "Agreeableness and Its Consequences: A Quantitative Review of Meta-Analytic Findings," *Personality and Social Psychology Review* 26, no. 3 (February 2022): 242–80, https://doi.org/10.1177/10888683211073007.

HABIT ONE

1. Alexander Pope, *An Essay on Criticism,* 3rd ed. (London, 1713), 14.
2. Faye Marie Getz, "Black Death and the Silver Lining: Meaning, Continuity, and Revolutionary Change in Histories of Medieval Plague," *Journal of the History of Biology* 24, no. 2 (June 1991): 271–72, https://doi.org/10.1007/BF00209432.
3. Kira L. S. Newman, "Shutt Up: Bubonic Plague and Quarantine in Early Modern England," *Journal of Social History* 45, no. 3 (Spring 2012): 809–34, https://doi .org/10.1093/jsh/shr114.
4. Carmen Sanchez and David Dunning, "Overconfidence among Beginners: Is a Little Learning a Dangerous Thing?" *Journal of Personality and Social Psychology* 114, no. 1 (2018): 10, https://doi.org/10.1037/pspa0000102.
5. William Rehnquist, "Commencement Address of Chief Justice William H. Rehnquist," George Washington University Law School, May 28, 2000, https://www.supremecourt .gov/publicinfo/speeches/viewspeech/sp_05-28-00.
6. Nassim Nicholas Taleb, *The Black Swan: The Impact of the Highly Improbable,* 2nd ed. (New York: Random House, 2010), 1.
7. Justin Kruger and David Dunning, "Unskilled and Unaware of it: How Difficulties in Recognizing One's Own Incompetence Lead to Inflated Self-Assessments," *Journal of Personality and Social Psychology* 77, no. 6 (1999): 1121–34, https://doi.org/10.1037/0022 -3514.77.6.1121.
8. Thomas Schlösser, David Dunning, Kerri L. Johnson, and Justin Kruger, "How Unaware Are the Unskilled? Empirical Tests of the 'Signal Extraction' Counterexplanation for the Dunning–Kruger Effect in Self-Evaluation of Performance," *Journal of Economic Psychology* 39 (December 2013): 85–100, https://doi.org/10.1016/j.joep.2013.07.004.
9. Steven Sloman and Philip Fernbach, *The Knowledge Illusion: Why We Never Think Alone* (New York: Riverhead Books, 2017), 34.
10. Executive functioning has to do with the brain's ability to do things like plan ahead, show self-restraint, meet goals, follow multistep directions, change focus between tasks, store learned lessons in our long-term memories, and other similar tasks. For

an introduction to executive functioning disorders, a good starting source is "What Is Executive Function? And How Does It Relate to Child Development?" produced by the Center on the Developing Child at Harvard University (https://developingchild .harvard.edu/resources/what-is-executive-function-and-how-does-it-relate-to-child -development/#ef).

11. Jonah Koetke, Karina Schumann, Keith Welker, Peter T. Coleman, "Intellectual Humility Is Reliably Associated with Constructive Responses to Conflict," Department of Psychology, University of Pittsburgh, January 4, 2023.

12. Randolph N. Jonakait, "The Rise of the American Adversary System: America Before England," *Widener Law Review* 14, no. 2 (2009): 323–65; see also John H. Langbein, *The Origins of Adversary Criminal Trial*, Oxford Studies in Modern Legal History (New York: Oxford University Press, 2003).

13. Federal Rule of Civil Procedure 26.

14. Roland Fryer, "Roland Fryer Refuses to Lie to Black America," August 31, 2022, in *Freakonomics Radio*, produced by Alina Kulman, podcast, 35:43, https://freakonomics .com/podcast/roland-fryer-refuses-to-lie-to-black-america/.

HABIT TWO

1. Benjamin Henry Day, copyright claimant, *Lunar animals and other objects Discovered by Sir John Herschel in his observatory at the Cape of Good Hope and copied from sketches in the Edinburgh Journal of Science, 1835* [Entered according to Act of Congress, by Benj. H. Day in the Office of the Clerk of District Ct. of the United States for the Southern District of New York], photograph, Library of Congress, https://www.loc.gov /item/2003665049/.

2. Matthew Goodman, *The Sun and the Moon: The Remarkable True Account of Hoaxers, Showmen, Dueling Journalists, and Lunar Man-Bats in Nineteenth-Century New York* (New York: Basic Books, 2008), 180–82, 201–16.

3. Goodman, 221.

4. Edwin G. Burrows and Mike Wallace, *Gotham: A History of New York City to 1898* (New York: Oxford University Press, 1999), 524.

5. Isaac Newton to Robert Hooke, 1675, in David Brewster, *Memoirs of the Life, Writings, and Discoveries of Sir Isaac Newton*, vol. 1 (Edinburgh: 1855), 142. Digitized at *The Newton Project*, University of Oxford, Faculty of History, https://www.newtonproject.ox.ac.uk /view/texts/normalized/OTHE00101.

6. *The Metalogicon of John of Salisbury: A Twelfth-Century Defense of the Verbal and Logical Arts of the Trivium*, trans. Daniel D. McGarry (Los Angeles: University of California Press, 1955), 167.

7. William Stukeley, *Memoirs of Sir Isaac Newton's Life, 1752*, revised edition. Digitized at *The Newton Project*, https://www.newtonproject.ox.ac.uk/view/texts/diplomatic /OTHE00001.

8. Patricia Fara, *Science: A Four Thousand Year History* (New York: Oxford University Press, 2010), 165.

9. Fara, 164–65.

10. For a broad overview of Newton's work ethic and collaboration with others, see Richard Westfall, *Never at Rest: A Biography of Isaac Newton* (New York: Cambridge University Press, 1980).

11. Hooke to Newton, 1675, in Brewster, 1: 140.

12. Hooke to Newton, 1675, in Brewster, 1: 142.

13. Jonathan Rauch, *The Constitution of Knowledge: A Defense of Truth* (Washington, DC: The Brookings Institution, 2021), 93.

14. Rauch, 77.

15. Anna Lembke, *Dopamine Nation: Finding Balance in the Age of Indulgence* (New York: Dutton, 2021), 49.

16. See Lembke, 22–24.

17. Trevor Haynes, "Dopamine, Smartphones & You: A Battle for Your Time," *Science in the News* (blog), Harvard University Graduate School of Arts and Sciences, May 1, 2018, https://sitn.hms.harvard.edu/flash/2018/dopamine-smartphones-battle-time/.

18. Nir Eyal, *Hooked: How to Build Habit-Forming Products* (New York: Penguin Publishing Group, 2014) 2.

19. Eyal, 1.

20. Natasha Dow Schüll, *Addicted by Design: Machine Gambling in Las Vegas* (Princeton, NJ: Princeton University Press, 2012), 135.

21. Nicholas Koenig in Schüll, *Addicted by Design*, 109.

22. Schüll, 109; emphasis added.

23. Jean M. Twenge and Jonathan Haidt, "This Is Our Chance to Pull Teenagers Out of the Smartphone Trap," *New York Times*, July 31, 2021, https://www.nytimes.com/2021/07/31/opinion/smartphone-iphone-social-media-isolation.html.

24. Eyal, *Hooked*, 6.

25. Tobias Rose-Stockwell, *Outrage Machine: How Tech Amplifies Discontent, Disrupts Democracy—And What We Can Do about It* (New York: Legacy Lit, 2023), 33.

26. Rose-Stockwell, *Outrage Machine*, 33.

27. Steven T. Collis, *The Immortals: The WWII Story of Five Fearless Heroes, the Sinking of the Dorchester, and an Awe-Inspiring Rescue* (Salt Lake City, UT: Shadow Mountain, 2021), 3–5.

28. *Hitler's Table Talk, 1941–1944: His Private Conversations*, trans. Norman Cameron and R. H. Stevens, introduced and with a new preface by H. R. Trevor-Roper (New York: Enigma Books, 2000), 188.

29. See Garth S. Jowett and Victoria O'Donnell, *Propaganda and Persuasion*, 5th ed. (Los Angeles: SAGE Publications, 2012).

30. In Richard Engel, Kate Benyon-Tinker, and Kennett Werner, "Russian Documents Reveal Desire to Sow Racial Discord—and Violence—in the U.S.," NBC News, May 20, 2019, https://www.nbcnews.com/news/world/russian-documents-reveal-desire-sow-racial-discord-violence-u-s-n1008051.

31. Cailan O'Connor and James Owen Weatherall, *The Misinformation Age: How False Beliefs Spread* (New Haven, CT: Yale University Press, 2019), 170.

32. *Social Media Influence in the 2016 U.S. Election, Hearing before the Select Committee on Intelligence*, 115th Congress, November 1, 2017 (statement of Richard Burr, Chairman Select Committee on Intelligence), https://www.intelligence.senate.gov/hearings/open-hearing-social-media-influence-2016-us-elections#.

33. Clint Watts, "China, North Korea Pursue New Targets While Honing Cyber Capabilities," *Microsoft On the Issues*, blog, September 7, 2023, https://blogs.microsoft.com/on-the-issues/2023/09/07/digital-threats-cyberattacks-east-asia-china-north-korea/.

34. "Sophistication, Scope, and Scale: Digital Threats from East Asia Increase in Breadth and Effectiveness," *Microsoft Threat Intelligence*, Microsoft Threat Analysis Center (MTAC) report, September 2023, 6, https://query.prod.cms.rt.microsoft.com/cms/api/am/binary/RW1aFyW.

35. Watts, "China, North Korea Pursue New Targets."
36. Sander van der Linden, "Misinformation: Susceptibility, Spread, and Interventions to Immunize the Public," *Nature Medicine* 28, (2022): 460–61, https://doi.org/10.1038/s41591-022-01713-6.
37. Van der Linden, 461.
38. Van der Linden, 462.
39. Rose-Stockwell, *Outrage Machine*, 348.
40. Grace Raynor, "Dabo Swinney Draws Line between Black Lives Matter Messages and Politics," *The Athletic*, September 29, 2020.
41. David Hale, "Clemson Coach Dabo Swinney: 'On Board' with Black Lives Matter Messages, but Not Politics," ESPN.com, September 29, 2020, https://www.espn.com/college-football/story/_/id/30002252/clemson-coach-dabo-swinney-board-black-lives-matter-messages-not-political-organizations.
42. Jonathan Haidt, "Why the Past 10 Years of American Life Have Been Uniquely Stupid," *The Atlantic*, May 1, 2022, https://www.theatlantic.com/magazine/archive/2022/05/social-media-democracy-trust-babel/629369/.
43. William J. Brady et al., "Emotion Shapes the Diffusion of Moralized Content in Social Networks," *Proceedings of the National Academy of Sciences* 114, no. 28 (July 11, 2017): 7313–18, https://doi.org/10.1073/pnas.1618923114.
44. Abrams v. United States, 250 U.S. 616, 630 (1919).
45. United States v. Rumely, 345 U.S. 41, 56 (1953).
46. Learned Hand, United States v. Associated Press, 52 F. Supp. 362, 372 (1943).
47. See Rauch, *The Constitution of Knowledge*, 156–59.
48. "Ideological Placement of Each Source's Audience," Pew Research Center, Washington, DC (January 26, 2016), https://www.pewresearch.org/pj_14-10-21_mediapolarization-08-2/.
49. "Media Bias Ratings," AllSides.com, https://www.allsides.com/media-bias/ratings.
50. Vasili Arkhipov, "Presentation at the Conference on the Cuban Missile Crisis, October 14, 1997," 4, National Security Archive website, https://nsarchive.gwu.edu/document/29078-document-1-vice-admiral-vasili-arkhipov.
51. Arkhipov, 5.
52. Carmen Sanchez and David Dunning, "People Who Jump to Conclusions Show Other Kinds of Thinking Errors," *Scientific American*, October 15, 2021, https://www.scientificamerican.com/article/people-who-jump-to-conclusions-show-other-kinds-of-thinking-errors/.
53. See Petros Georghiades, "From the General to the Situated: Three Decades of Metacognition," *International Journal of Science Education* 26, no. 3 (February 2004): 365, https://doi.org/10.1080/0950069032000119401.
54. "meta," Merriam-Webster.com, 2024, https://www.merriam-webster.com/dictionary/meta.
55. For a better understanding of how Collins reconciles his beliefs in science and theology, see Francis S. Collins, *The Language of God: A Scientist Presents Evidence for Belief* (New York: Free Press, 2006).
56. Remedies law explores the various legal and equitable remedies available to someone who prevails in litigation. Scholars in the field study which remedies should be available, under what circumstances, to what degree, and for what reasons—all with a goal of ensuring the legal system continues to operate in a way that will best allow us to have a well-functioning society.
57. Douglas Laycock, "Religious Liberty as Liberty," *Journal of Contemporary Legal Issues* 7, no. 2 (1996): 353.

58. Laycock, 354–55.
59. Steven T. Collis, *Deep Conviction: True Stories of Ordinary Americans Fighting for the Freedom to Live Their Beliefs* (Salt Lake City, UT: Shadow Mountain, 2019), 174–89.
60. Henry J. Eyring, *Mormon Scientist: The Life and Faith of Henry Eyring* (Salt Lake City, UT: Deseret Book, 2007).
61. Eyring, 245–47.
62. Laycock, "Religious Liberty as Liberty," 355.

HABIT THREE

1. Ward Farnsworth, *The Socratic Method: A Practitioner's Handbook* (Boston, MA: Godine, 2021), 45.
2. Sloman and Fernbach, *The Knowledge Illusion*, 180–81.
3. Jonathan Haidt, *The Righteous Mind: Why Good People Are Divided by Politics and Religion* (New York: Vintage Books, 2013).
4. Home page, MoralFoundations.org, website run by YourMorals.org, https://moralfoundations.org/.
5. Haidt, *The Righteous Mind*, 179.
6. Jonathan Haidt, "The Moral Roots of Liberals and Conservatives," TED conference, March 2008, 8:23 to 8:52, https://www.ted.com/talks/jonathan_haidt_the_moral_roots_of_liberals_and_conservatives/transcript.
7. For examples, see Lawrence G. Sager and Christopher L. Eisgruber, *Religious Freedom and the Constitution* (Cambridge, MA: Harvard University Press, 2007); John Deigh, *The Sources of Moral Agency: Essays in Moral Psychology and Freudian Theory* (Boston, MA: Cambridge University Press, 1996); Douglas Laycock, "Formal, Substantive, and Disaggregated Neutrality toward Religion," *DePaul Law Review* 39, no. 4 (Summer 1990): 993–1018, https://via.library.depaul.edu/law-review/vol39. There are many, many others.
8. Sloman and Fernbach, *The Knowledge Illusion*, 192.
9. Peter C. Wason, "Reasoning about a Rule," *Quarterly Journal of Experimental Psychology* 20, no. 3 (1968): 273–78, http://dx.doi.org/10.1080/14640746808400161.
10. Rauch, *The Constitution of Knowledge*, 94.
11. For an in-depth look at trauma-informed care, see Center for Substance Abuse Treatment, *Trauma-Informed Care in Behavioral Health Services*, Treatment Improvement Protocol Series 57 (Rockville, MD: Substance Abuse and Mental Health Services Administration, 2014).
12. Judith E. Glaser, "Your Brain Is Hooked on Being Right," *Harvard Business Review*, February 28, 2013, https://hbr.org/2013/02/break-your-addiction-to-being.
13. "Racism: Getting to the Truth with Coleman Hughes," *The Rubin Report*, YouTube video, 3:10, October 12, 2018, https://www.youtube.com/watch?v=rdh8zPr_ZmI.
14. For example, compare Sahil Handa, "In Defense of Coleman Hughes," *National Review*, June 21, 2019, https://www.nationalreview.com/corner/coleman-hughes-slavery-reparations-defense/ (defending Hughes for speaking against Black orthodox views), with Nathan J. Robinson, "Why Reparations Should Be One of Today's Top Political Demands," *Current Affairs*, June 17, 2020, https://www.currentaffairs.org/2020/06/why-reparations-should-be-one-of-todays-top-political-demands (criticizing Hughes's position on reparations).
15. Coleman Hughes, "Debating Race and Incarceration with Vincent Lloyd," *Conversations with Coleman*, YouTube video, 0:06–1:04, May 5, 2023, https://www.youtube.com/watch?v=c8iuEprjv6I.

16. For example, the hesitation of the ACLU, a once-assiduous defender of free speech, to protect speech in the face of "structural and power inequalities in the community in which the speech will occur" reflects the broader societal shift to refusal to tolerate or listen to certain viewpoints. Dennis Chong, Jack Citrin, and Morris Levy, "The Realignment of Political Tolerance in the United States," *Perspectives on Politics* (2022): 1–22, https://doi.org/10.1017/S1537592722002079.

17. For a more in-depth discussion of the two theories and their overlap, read chapter 10, "Mapping the Postmodern," in Andreas Huyssen, *After the Great Divide: Modernism, Mass Culture, Postmodernism* (Bloomington, IN: Indiana University Press, 1986), 179–221.

18. See Elizabeth Deeds Ermath, "Postmodernism," *Routledge Encyclopedia of Philosophy Online*, Taylor and Francis (1998), https://doi.org/10.4324/9780415249126-N044-1.

19. Michel Foucault, "The Discourse on Language," in *The Archaeology of Knowledge and the Discourse on Language*, trans. A. M. Sheridan Smith (New York: Pantheon Books, 1972), 227–37.

20. Michel Foucault, "The Order of Discourse," in Robert Young, ed., *Untying the Text: A Post-Structuralist Reader* (Boston: Routledge & Kegan Paul, 1981), 48–78.

21. For an elaborated history of the Catholic Church's influence on geopolitics during the Middle Ages, see Hans Küng, *The Catholic Church: A Short History*, Modern Library Chronicles 5, trans. John Bowden (New York: Modern Library, 2001).

22. To learn more about the history of civility in Medieval times through the present, see Benet Davetian, *Civility: A Cultural History* (Toronto: University of Toronto Press, 2009) and Norbert Elias, *The Civilizing Process: Sociogenetic and Psychogenetic Investigations*, trans. Edmund Jephcott, rev. ed. (Malden, MA: Blackwell Publishing, 2000).

23. Sharika Thiranagama, Tobias Kelly, and Carlos Forment, "Introduction: Whose Civility?" *Anthropological Theory* 18, no. 2–3 (July 2018), 153.

24. Elizabeth DePoy and Laura N. Gitlin assert that critical theory is "a movement best understood by philosophers. Because critical theory is inspired by diverse schools of thought, including those informed by Marx, Hegel, Kant, Foucault, Derrida, and Kristeva, it is not a unitary approach." "Naturalistic Designs," in *Introduction to Research: Understanding and Applying Multiple Strategies*, 5th ed., (St. Louis, MO: Elsevier, 2016), 162.

25. See, for example, Keecee DeVenny, "How Language Is Weaponized to Oppress and Marginalize," Legal Defense Fund, July 12, 2023, https://www.naacpldf.org/white-supremacy-what-it-means-to-be-american/. DeVenny writes that "Today, politicians and others continue to manipulate language with the express goal of enshrining power. For example, 'woke'—a term originally used by Black people to signify being aware of the pervasive racial injustices that harm them—has become a villainized centerpiece for derailing anything from teaching students accurate history to human empathy."

    We hear in this way of thinking the echoes of Karl Marx. In the opening lines to *The Communist Manifesto*, he wrote the foundational premise to his worldview:

    The history of all hitherto existing society is the history of class struggles.

    Freeman and slave, patrician and plebian, lord and serf, guild-master and journeyman, in a word, oppressor and oppressed, stood in constant opposition to one another, carried on an uninterrupted, now hidden, now open fight, a fight that each time ended, either in revolutionary reconstitution of society at large, or in the common ruin of the contending classes.

26. Kimberlé Williams Crenshaw, a law professor at the UCLA School of Law and Columbia Law, is credited with coining the term Critical Race Theory. Professor Crenshaw describes

it as "a way of seeing, attending to, accounting for, tracing and analyzing the ways that race is produced, . . . the ways that racial inequality is facilitated, and the ways that our history has created these inequalities that can now be almost effortlessly reproduced unless we attend to the existence of these inequalities." In Jacey Fortin, "Critical Race Theory: A Brief History," *New York Times*, November 8, 2021, https://www.nytimes.com/article/what-is-critical-race-theory.html.

27. Mari Matsuda, an early critical race theorist and law professor at the University of Hawaii, describes the theory as a "method that takes the lived experience of racism seriously, using history and social reality to explain how racism operates in American law and culture, toward the ending of eliminating the harmful effects of racism and bringing about a just and healthy world for all." In Fortin, "Critical Race Theory."

28. Take one example: Paulo Freire advanced "critical consciousness," an educational concept grounded in critical theory, to liberate people from systemic inequality. Critical consciousness pushes for education to help people become aware of and to consistently resist oppressive ways of being in order to target inequity. If education does not do this, it perpetuates systemic inequality, he says. See Alexis Jemal, "Critical Consciousness: A Critique and Critical Analysis of the Literature," *The Urban Review* 49, no. 4 (May 2017): 602–26, https://doi.org/10.1007/s11256-017-0411-3.

29. In Richard D. Brown and Richard L. Bushman, "The Politics of Civility: From George Washington to Donald Trump," Yale University Press, October 9, 2017, https://yalebooks.yale.edu/2017/10/09/the-politics-of-civility-from-george-washington-to-donald-trump/.

30. Martin Luther King famously said, "a riot is the language of the unheard." Martin Luther King, "The Other America," speech delivered at Grosse Pointe High School, March 14, 1968, Gross Pointe Historical Society, http://www.gphistorical.org/mlk/mlkspeech/index.htm.

31. Consider this: "But civility is not always restraining and conservative. In the mid-1960s, the American civil rights movement promoted civility as a direct challenge to racism. . . . Martin Luther King and other members of the Southern Christian Leadership Conference used 'civil disobedience' in order to expose and undermine the racial supremacism embedded in daily life and supported by the policies of the US state. By engaging in self-limiting forms of civil protest, one of the key aims of the Selma march was to demonstrate the African-American community's distinctive and specific capacity for civility—rooted in Christianity rather than the dominant liberal notions of individual rights and the rule of law. African-American forms of civility deployed across the South were a form of political protest that sought to call the US state back to its own claims of civilization and to hold white citizens accountable. This type of non-violent civility tried to use the moral power of restraint and respect in order to bring about radical change across political and civil society." (Thiranagama, "Introduction: Whose Civility?")

32. Martin Luther King, Jr., "I've Been to the Mountaintop," in *A Call to Conscience: The Landmark Speeches of Dr. Martin Luther King, Jr.*, ed. Clayborne Carson and Kris Shepard (New York: Warner Books, 2001), 213.

33. Laura Hillenbrand, *Unbroken: A World War II Story of Survival, Resilience, and Redemption* (New York: Random House, 2014), 354–55.

34. See Hillenbrand, 375–91.

35. Mathew 6:14 (King James Version).

36. Mohammed Abu-Nimer and Ilham Nasser, "Forgiveness in the Arab and Islamic Contexts," *The Journal of Religious Ethics* 41, no, 3 (2013): 474–494.

37. Chien-Te Lin, "With or Without Repentance: A Buddhist Take on Forgiveness," *Ethical Perspectives* 28, no. 3 (2021): 263–85, https://philarchive.org/archive/LINWOW.
38. Seneca, *On Clemency*, I.14–16; I.19.9.
39. Man Yee Ho et al., "International REACH Forgiveness Intervention: A Multi-Site Randomized Controlled Trial," OSF Preprints, March 3, 2023, https://doi.org/10.31219 /osf.io/8qzgw.
40. Erica J. Boothby, Gus Cooney, Gillian M. Sandstrom, and Margarete S. Clark, "The Liking Gap in Conversations: Do People Like Us More Than We Think?" *Psychological Science* 29, no. 11 (2018): 1742, 1743, https://doi.org/10.1177/0956797618783714.

HABIT FOUR

1. Proverbs 15:1 (King James Version).
2. Piotr Bystranowski et al., "Anchoring Effect in Legal Decision-Making: A Meta-Analysis," 45 *Law and Human Behavior* 45, no. 1 (2021): 1–23, https://doi.org/10.1037 /lhb0000438.
3. EJ Gonzales-Polledo and Silvia Posocco, "Forensic Apophenia: Sensing the Bioinformation Archive," *Anthropological Quarterly* 95, no. 1 (2022): 97–124, https://doi.org/10.1353 /anq.2022.0002.
4. Michael I. Norton, Daniel Mochon, Dan Ariely, "The 'IKEA Effect': When Labor Leads to Love," *Journal of Consumer Psychology* 22, no. 3 (July 2012): 453–60, https://doi .org/10.1016/j.jcps.2011.08.002.
5. Lee Ross, David Greene, and Pamela House, "The 'False Consensus Effect': An Egocentric Bias in Social Perception and Attribution Processes," *Journal of Experimental Social Psychology* 13, no. 3 (May 1997): 279–301, https://doi.org/10.1016/0022-1031(77)90049-X.
6. Andrew Jay McClurg, "Logical Fallacies and the Supreme Court: A Critical Analysis of Justice Rehnquist's Decisions in Criminal Procedure Cases," *University of Colorado Law Review* 59 (1988): 741–844, https://papers.ssrn.com/sol3/papers.cfm?abstract _id=1633960.
7. Scott Millis et al., "Assessing Physicians' Interpersonal Skills: Do Patients and Physicians See Eye to Eye?" *American Journal of Physical Medicine & Rehabilitation* 81, no. 12 (2002): 946–51, https://doi.org/10.1097/01.PHM.0000034917.06066.29.
8. Baruch Fischhoff and Ruth Beyth, "'I Knew It Would Happen': Remembered Probabilities of Once-Future Things," *Organizational Behavior and Human Performance* 13, no. 1 (February 1975): 1–16, https://doi.org/10.1016/0030-5073(75)90002-1.
9. Carlo Caponecchia, "It Won't Happen to Me: An Investigation of Optimism Bias in Occupational Health and Safety," *Journal of Applied Social Psychology* 40, no. 3 (March 2010): 601–17, https://doi.org/10.1111/j.1559-1816.2010.00589.x.
10. Neil Metz and Chintamani Jog, "High Stakes, Experts, and Recency Bias: Evidence from a Sports Gambling Contest," *Applied Economics Letters* 30, no. 18 (2023): 2525–29, https://doi.org/10.1080/13504851.2022.2099517.
11. Daniel Kahneman, *Thinking, Fast and Slow* (New York: Farrar, Straus and Giroux, 2011), 28.
12. J. Prescott Johnson, "The Idea of Human Dignity in Classical and Christian Thought," *Journal of Thought* 6, no. 1 (1971): 23–38, http://www.jstor.org/stable/42588230.
13. Cicero, from *De Officiis*, I, 30, in Michael Rosen, *Dignity: Its History and Meaning* (Cambridge, MA: Harvard University Press, 2012), 11–13.
14. Giovanni Pico della Mirandola, *Oration on the Dignity of Man: A New Translation and*

Commentary, ed. Francesco Borghesi, Michael Papio, and Massimo Riva (Boston, MA: Cambridge University Press, 2012).

15. Oliver Sensen, *Kant on Human Dignity* (Berlin: De Gruyter Verlag, 2011), 2; cf. 28, 32, 174, 176, https://doi.org/10.1515/9783110267167.

16. Kenneth S. Abraham and Edward White, "The Puzzle of the Dignitary Torts," *Cornell Law Review* 104, no. 2 (2019); 325–26. Note that the term *republicanism* as used here does not refer to the modern-day Republican Party, but to those people interested in establishing republican forms of government, which include the idea that the people are the sovereign and government enjoys only that power given to it by the people.

HABIT FIVE

1. John Stuart Mill, *On Liberty, Utilitarianism, and Other Essays*, ed. Mark Philip and Frederick Rosen (New York: Oxford University Press, 2005), 37.

2. Milton Friedman, *There's No Such Thing as a Free Lunch* (LaSalle, IL: Open Court Publishing Company, 1975).

3. Sam Harper et al., "The Effect of Mandatory Seat Belt Laws on Seat Belt Use by Socioeconomic Position," *Journal of Policy Analysis and Management* 33, no. 1 (2014): 141–61, https://doi.org/10.1002/pam.21735,

4. See, for example, Greg Lukianoff and Jonathan Haidt, *The Coddling of the American Mind: How Good Intentions and Bad Ideas Are Setting up a Generation for Failure* (New York: Penguine Press, 2018); Philip Rieff, *The Triumph of the Therapeutic: Uses of Faith After Freud* (Wilmington, DE: Intercollegiate Studies Institute, 2007); Charles Taylor, *Sources of the Self: The Making of the Modern Identity* (Cambridge, MA: Harvard University Press, 1992); Charles Taylor, *A Secular Age* (Cambridge, MA: Belknap Press, 2018); Carl R. Trueman, *The Rise and Triumph of the Modern Self: Cultural Amnesia, Expressive Individualism, and the Road to Sexual Revolution* (Wheaton, IL: Crossway, 2020).

5. Anne Lembke, *Dopamine Nation: Finding Balance in the Age of Addiction* (New York: Dutton, 2021), 36.

6. Ashley V. Whillans et al, "Buying Time Promotes Happiness," *Proceedings of the National Academy of Sciences* 114, no. 32 (August 8, 2017): 8523–27, https://doi.org/10.1073/pnas.1706541114; Niraj Choksi, "Want to Be Happy? Buy More Takeout and Hire a Maid, Study Suggests," *New York Times,* July 27, 2017, https://www.nytimes.com/2017/07/27/science/study-happy-save-money-time.html.

7. Parental Rights in Education Act (HB 1557) (2022).

8. "Word of the Year 2022," Merriam-Webster Online, November 26, 2023, https://www.merriam-webster.com/wordplay/word-of-the-year-2022.

9. Robin Stern, *The Gaslight Effect: How to Spot and Survive the Hidden Manipulation Others Use to Control Your Life* (New York: Harmony Books, 2007).

10. Jennifer Sweeton, "Bringing Gaslighting to Light, Part II," *Psychology Today,* May 5, 2016, https://www.psychologytoday.com/za/blog/workings-well-being/201605/bringing-gaslighting-light-part-ii.

11. 548 U.S. 617 (2018); For an in-depth exploration of that case, see Steven T. Collis, *Deep Conviction* (Salt Lake City: Shadow Mountain, 2019).

12. Kim Parker and Kiley Hurst, "Growing Share of Americans Say They Want More Spending on Police in Their Area," Pew Research Center, Washington, DC (Oct. 26, 2021), https://www.pewresearch.org/short-reads/2021/10/26/growing-share-of-americans-say-they-want-more-spending-on-police-in-their-area/.

13. Rashawn Ray, "What Does 'Defund the Police' Mean and Does It Have Merit?" Brookings Institute, Washington, DC (June 19, 2020), https://www.brookings.edu/articles/what-does-defund-the-police-mean-and-does-it-have-merit/.

14. Jessica M. Eaglin, "To 'Defund' the Police," *Stanford Law Review* 73 (2021): 120–40.

15. Fryer Jr, Roland G. "An Empirical Analysis of Racial Differences in Police Use of Force." *Journal of Political Economy*, 127 (2019) No. 3, 1210–1261.

16. Mariame Kaba, "Yes, We Mean Literally Abolish the Police," *New York Times*, June 12, 2020, https://perma.cc/8D6M-K23U.

17. Eaglin, "To 'Defund' the Police."

18. Elizabeth Weill-Greenberg, *Chicago Lawmakers Push to Build Team of Emergency Responders Who Aren't Police*, The Appeal, website, September 28, 2020, https://perma.cc/4VH5-6ZU6.

HABIT SIX

1. Derek Webb, "The Original Meaning of Civility: Democratic Deliberation at the Philadelphia Constitutional Convention," *South Carolina Law Review* 64, no. 1 (2012): 195, https://scholarcommons.sc.edu/sclr/vol64/iss1/6.

2. Webb, 196.

3. Webb, 195–6.

4. West Virginia State Board of Education v. Barnette, 319 U.S. 624, 642–43 (1943).

5. *Barnette*, 319 U.S. at 636.

6. *Barnette*, 319 U.S. at 638.

7. *Barnette*, 319 U.S. at 643 (Hugo Black, concurring).

8. Nadine Strossen, *Hate: Why We Should Resist It with Free Speech, Not Censorship* (New York: Oxford University Press, 2018).

9. Kristen Waggoner and Nadine Strossen, "Web Designer's Free Speech Supreme Court Victory Is a Win for All), Bloomberg Law, July 10, 2023, https://news.bloomberglaw.com/us-law-week/web-designers-free-speech-supreme-court-victory-is-a-win-for-all.

10. Jay J. Van Bavel and Dominic J. Packer, *The Power of Us: Harnessing Our Shared Identities to Improve Performance, Increase Cooperation, and Promote Social Harmony* (New York: Little, Brown Spark, 2021).

11. Dominic Packer and Jay Van Bavel, "The Myth of Tribalism," *The Atlantic*, January 3, 2022, https://www.theatlantic.com/ideas/archive/2022/01/tribalism-myth-group-solidarity-prejudice-conflict/621008/

12. Jacqueline Novogratz and Anne Welsh McNulty, "The Most Critical Ingredient in Leadership," *Stanford Social Innovation Review*, July 6, 2022, https://ssir.org/articles/entry/the_most_critical_ingredient_in_leadership#.

HABIT SEVEN

1. Note here that, arguably, what the founders actually did was *postpone* warfare. The Civil War has often been described as the last great war of the American Revolution. The founders could not resolve the issue of slavery during their debates, so they found a way to form a country while recognizing that issue would still need to be resolved.

2. Derek Webb, "The Original Meaning of Civility: Democratic Deliberation at the Philadelphia Convention," *South Carolina Law Review* 64, no. 1 (2012): 192, https://scholarcommons.sc.edu/sclr/vol64/iss1/6.

NOTES

3. Bernard Williams, "Moral Luck" in *Moral Luck: Philosophical Papers 1973–1980* (Cambridge: Cambridge University Press, 1981), 20–39.

4. See, for example, Sam Harris, *Free Will* (New York: Free Press, 2012), 5 (arguing that human action is determined by genetics and life experience, and consequently that "free will *is* an illusion"); Robert M. Sapolsky, *Determined: A Science of Life without Free Will* (New York: Penguin Press, 2023).

5. See, for example, Charles Gagnon, "For a Scientific Vision of the World: Determinism or Free Will," *Proletarian Unity* 5, no. 2 (April–May–June 1981): 29, 30 (arguing that because "history cannot be seen primarily as the result of the conscious actions of this or that class," a society ought to "put an end to capitalist exploitation and all the forms of oppression that it perpetuates").

6. See, for example, Brian Rosebury, "Moral Responsibility and 'Moral Luck,'" *The Philosophical Review* 104, no. 4 (1995): 499, 505–24, https://doi.org/10.2307/2185815 (arguing that moral luck does not exist).

7. Michael J. Zimmerman, "Luck and Moral Responsibility," *Ethics* 97, no. 2 (January 1987): 374–86, https://doi.org/10.1086/292845 (noting that the concept of moral luck is dangerous to society because it injures individuals' sense of moral responsibility).

8. *Batman Begins*, directed by Christopher Nolan, 2005.

HABIT EIGHT

1. "October 21, 1984 Debate Transcript: The Second Reagan-Mondale Presidential Debate," The Commission on Presidential Debates website, https://www.debates.org/voter-education/debate-transcripts/october-21-1984-debate-transcript/.

2. Jennifer Aaker and Naomi Bagdonas, "How to Be Funny at Work," *Harvard Business Review*, February 5, 2021, https://hbr.org/2021/02/how-to-be-funny-at-work. See also Wayne H. Decker, "Managerial Humor and Subordinate Satisfaction," *Social Behavior and Personality: an International Journal* 15, no. 2 (1987): 225–32, https://doi.org/10.2224/sbp.1987.15.2.225; Karen O'Quin and Joel Aronoff, "Humor as a Technique of Social Influence," *Social Psychology Quarterly* 44, no. 4 (December 1982): 349–57, https://doi.org/10.2307/3033903.

3. Rod A. Martin et al., "Individual Differences in Uses of Humor and Their Relation to Psychological Well-Being: Development of the Humor Styles Questionnaire," *Journal of Research in Personality* 37, no. 1 (February 2003): 48–75, https://doi.org/10.1016/S0092-6566(02)00534-2.

4. Nate Bargatze, *Hello World* Amazon Prime Original, January 30, 2023, at 28:09.

5. Oral arguments, 0:00–34:00, *Roe v. Wade*, 410 U.S. 113 (1973) (No. 70-18), https://www.oyez.org/cases/1971/70-18.

6. Oral arguments, at 34:10–34:27.

7. David J. Garrow, *Liberty and Sexuality: The Right to Privacy and the Making of* Roe v. Wade (Berkeley: University of California Press, 1998).

8. Antonin Scalia and Bryan A. Garner, *Making Your Case: The Art of Persuading Judges* (St. Paul, MN: West Group, 2008); David C. Frederick, *The Art of Oral Advocacy* (St. Paul, MN: West Group, 2003).

9. For some different ways of thinking about humor and to get a sense of what your own humor style is, see Jennifer Aaker and Naomi Bagdonas, *Humor, Seriously: Why Humor Is a Secret Weapon in Business and Life* (New York: Currency, 2021).

HABIT NINE

1. Steve Collis, *The Immortals: The World War II Story of Five Fearless Heroes, the Sinking of the* Dorchester, *and an Awe-Inspiring Rescue* (Salt Lake City, UT: Shadow Mountain, 2021).

2. Diane Musho Hamilton, "Calming Your Brain during Conflict," *Harvard Business Review,* December 22, 2015, https://hbr.org/2015/12/calming-your-brain-during-conflict.

3. Daniel Goleman and Richard J. Davidson, *The Science of Meditation: How to Change Your Brain, Mind and Body* (New York: Penguin Life, 2018); Sharon Salzberg, *Real Happiness: A 28-Day Program to Realize the Power of Meditation* (New York: Workman Publishing, 2019); Jon Kabat-Zinn, *Mindfulness for Beginners: Reclaiming the Present Moment and Your Life* (Boulder, CO: Sounds True, 2012); Daniel Goleman and Richard Davidson, *Altered Traits: Science Reveals How Meditation Changes Your Mind, Brain, and Body* (New York: Avery, 2017).

4. Alan Watkins, *Coherence: The Science of Exceptional Leadership and Performance* (London: Kogan Page, 2021).

5. Louise Merrie, "The Everyday Grace of Weekday Mass," *Catholic Exchange,* January 4, 2023, https://catholicexchange.com/the-everyday-grace-of-weekday-mass/.

6. For a review of the literature, see Laura Upenieks, "Unpacking the Relationship Between Prayer and Anxiety: A Consideration of Prayer Types and Expectations in the United States," *Journal of Religion and Health* 62, no. 3 (2023): 1810–30, https://doi.org/10.1007/s10943-022-01708-0.

7. Ezra Taft Benson, "Jesus Christ—Gifts and Expectations," *Ensign,* December 1988, 4.

8. Russel M. Nelson, "Overcome the World and Find Rest," *Liahona,* November 2022, 97.

9. Jay L. Garfield, *Losing Ourselves: Learning to Live without a Self* (Princeton, NJ: Princeton University Press, 2022).

10. Thich Nhat Hanh, *Beyond the Self: Teachings on the Middle Way* (Berkeley, CA: Parallax Press, 2010), 37.

11. Eric Stice et al., "Randomized Trial of a Brief Depression Prevention Program: An Elusive Search for a Psychosocial Placebo Control Condition," *Behaviour Research and Therapy* 45, no. 5 (May 2007): 863–76, https://doi.org/10.1016/j.brat.2006.08.008 (on depression and journaling); Parisa Hasanzadeh, Masoud Fallahi Khoshknab, and Kian Norozi, "Impacts of Journaling on Anxiety and Stress in Multiple Sclerosis Patients," *Complementary Medicine Journal* 2, no. 2 (September 2012): 183–193; Karen A. Baikie and Kay Wilhelm, "Emotional and Physical Health Benefits of Expressive Writing," *Advances in Psychiatric Treatment* 11, no. 5 (2005): 338–46, https://doi.org/10.1192/apt.11.5.338 (on journaling and immune function); Benjamin Villaggi et al, "Self-Management Strategies in Recovery from Mood and Anxiety Disorders," *Global Qualitative Nursing Research* 2 (2015): https://doi.org/10.1177/2333393615606092 (on journaling and recovery).

12. Stuart J. Ritchie, Timothy C. Bates, and Robert Plomin, "Does Learning to Read Improve Intelligence? A Longitudinal Multivariate Analysis in Identical Twins from Age 7 to 16," *Child Development* 86, no. 1 (2015): 23–36, https://doi.org/10.1111/cdev.12272 (on reading and developing intelligence); Elizabeth A.L. Stine-Morrow et al., "The Effects of Sustained Literacy Engagement on Cognition and Sentence Processing Among Older Adults," *Frontiers in Psychology* 13 (2022): 923795, https://doi.org/10.3389/fpsyg.2022.923795 (on reading and brain function as we age); David Comer Kidd and Emanuele Castano, "Reading Literary Fiction Improves Theory of Mind," *Science* 342, no. 6156 (October 2013): 377–80, https://doi.org/10.1126/science.1239918 (on reading

and empathy); Denise Rizzolo et al., "Stress Management Strategies for Students: The Immediate Effects of Yoga, Humor, and Reading on Stress," *Journal of College Teaching & Learning* 6, no. 8 (December 2009): 79–88, https://doi.org/10.19030/tlc.v6i8.1117 (on reading and stress reduction).

HABIT TEN

1. Aristotle, *Nicomachean Ethics*, trans. W. D. Ross, book 1, The Internet Classics Archive, MIT, http://classics.mit.edu/Aristotle/nicomachaen.1.i.html.
2. Lance B. Wickman, "The Decided Are Always Gentle," *Clark Memorandum*, Spring 2003, 4.
3. In Charles Dickens, *A Christmas Carol and Other Christmas Books*, ed. Robert Douglas-Fairhurst (New York: Oxford University Press, 2006), 37.

EPILOGUE

1. "Fragment: Notes for a Law Lecture," in *Collected Works of Abraham Lincoln*, vol. 2, ed. Roy P. Basler (New Brunswick, NJ: Rutgers University Press, 1953), 81.

INDEX

INDEX

Ignorance, acknowledging, 11–15
Immigration, 124–25
Imposter syndrome, 120
Inner peace, seeking, 204–5; through
meditation and mindfulness, 205–6;
through spiritual practices, 206–9;
through journaling, 209; through reading,
210; through professional help, 211–12;
through schedule management, 211
Insecurity, 93–94, 120–21
Intellectual humility, 8–15, 22–25. *See also*
change, being open to
Internet: and acquiring knowledge in real
time, 67. *See also* smartphones; social
media

Jackson, Robert H., 3–4
Jehovah's Witnesses, Pledge cases of, 2–4,
172–77
John of Salisbury, 29–30
Jolie, Angelina, 115–16
Journaling, 72–73, 209
Judges, 80–81
Judgment, 15

Kahneman, Daniel, 128
Kant, Immanuel, 134
Khodorkovsky, Mikhail, 45
Kindness, treating people with, 96–98,
222–23
King, Martin Luther, 114, 234nn30–31
Knowledge: lack of, 8–15; and expertise,
22–25; understanding generation of, 29–
36; acquiring, in real time, 67; and being
open to change, 175–77; understanding
generation of, 220. *See also* learning,
seeking real; understanding
Kruger, Justin, 13

Language, manipulation of, 233n25
Laycock, Douglas, 74–76, 78, 182
Leadership, 180, 192
Learning, seeking real, 26–29; and
understanding knowledge generation,
29–36; and recognizing forces facing
you, 36–47; and acknowledging
susceptibility to misinformation, 48–49;

and breaking free from manipulation,
49–51; and catchphrases and heuristics,
51–57; and news that isn't news, 57–58;
and diversifying news sources, 61–67;
and being slow to come to conclusions,
67–73; and acquiring knowledge in real
time, 67; and spiritual learning, 73–78;
and being open to change, 175–77; by
spending time with people, 182. *See also*
knowledge; understanding
Legal system, adversarial framing in, 16–17
Leisure time, 50–51, 58
Lembke, Anna, 37, 147–48
LGBTQ+ issues, 150–51, 154–55, 156–57
Lincoln, Abraham, 226
Locke, Richard Adams, 28
Logical fallacies, 127
Love, selfless, for others, 138–40
Loyalty, as moral psychology, 86
Luck, moral, 184–86, 188–89
Lukianoff, Greg, 6
Lunch, free, 145–46

Madison, James, 171
Marketplace of ideas, 59–60, 66, 179
Martin, Trayvon, 54
Marx, Karl, 233n25
Mason, George, 170
*Masterpiece Cakeshop v. Colorado Civil Rights
Commission* (2018), 154–55, 156–57
Mathematicians, and smartphone use,
39–44, 58–59
Matsuda, Mari, 234n27
McNulty, Anne Welsh, 180
Media, 62–66, 143–44. *See also* news
Medical field, gender pay gap in, 19–22
Meditation, 205–6, 208–9
Metacognition / metacognitive training,
71–73
Middle Ages, 108–9, 113–14
Mill, John Stuart, 144
Mindfulness, 205–6
Mirandola, Giovanni Pico della, 133–34
Misinformation, 35–36, 46–51, 57–58, 63
Misperception, 93–94, 119–21

INDEX